READING FUNDAMENTALS

FOR

PRESCHOOL AND PRIMARY CHILDREN

Robert L. Hillerich

Bowling Green State University

CHARLES E. MERRILL PUBLISHING COMPANY
A Bell & Howell Company
Columbus   Toronto   London   Sydney

Dedicated to Dottie.

The Charles E. Merrill
Comprehensive Reading Program
Arthur W. Heilman, Consulting Editor

Published by
Charles E. Merrill Publishing Company
A Bell & Howell Company
Columbus, Ohio 43216

This book was set in Times Roman and Olive Antique Medium.
The production editor was Jan Hall.
The cover was designed by Will Chenoweth.

ISBN: 0–675–08543–8

Library of Congress Catalog Card Number: 76–46128

4 5 6 7 8 9 — 85 84 83 82 81 80

Photos on pages 76 and 96 by LaVisa Wilson;
on all other pages by University of Maryland photographer Richard Farkas
Printed in the United States of America

Acknowledgments

Much of the thinking contained herein could not have matured were it not for the constant stimulation of my graduate students. A special word of thanks, however, is due William Spaulding for his repeated challenges about the theoretical basis of beginning reading and to Lil Stevens for her assistance over the years as we turned theory into practice with young children.

The research and modification of the early diagnostic techniques were made possible through the generous cooperation of curriculum directors Jim Montgomery (Arlington Heights, Illinois), Mary Roche (Marquardt, Illinois), and Jo Telford (Schaumburg, Illinois). To them and to kindergarten and first-grade teachers in those districts, thanks again.

R.L.H.

Contents

Introduction   **1**

1   What Is Reading?   **4**

Decoding Emphasis Programs   6
"Linguistic" Programs   7
Meaning Emphasis Programs   9
The Foundation for an Approach to Beginning Reading   9
Comprehension   14
Summary   15

2   What Is Readiness?   **18**

Traditional Concerns   19
Testing for Reading Readiness   25
When Should Formal Skills Instruction Begin?   26
Summary   31

3   Prereading: Language Understandings and Skills   **36**

Basic Skills and Methods   37
Early Identification   44
Summary   50

4   Prereading: Foundation Skills in Decoding   **54**

Overview of Skills   55
Using Oral Context   55
Discriminating Letter Forms   56
Identifying Beginning Sounds   61
Associating Consonant Letters and Sounds   65

Using Oral Context and Initial Consonant Sound Associations
  to Read a Printed Word   69
Left-to-Right Orientation   69
Recognizing High-Frequency Words   70
Summary   72

5 Reading: In the Beginning   76

The First Book Materials   77
Introducing New Words   78
Extending Consonant Sound Association Skills   79
Inflectional Endings   83
Word Recognition with Beginning Readers   83
Word Recognition with Older Children   83
Practice Materials   88
Avoiding Questionable Practices   90
The Role of Oral Reading   90
Reading to Children   91
Summary   92

6 Vowels: What Can Be Taught?   96

What are Vowels?   97
Reading versus Spelling   98
How True Are Vowel Generalizations?   99
The Nature of Vowel Symbol-Sound Correspondence in English   101
The Effectiveness of Teaching Vowel Rules to Children   121
What Should Be Taught about Vowels?   123
Summary   125

7 Comprehension Skills: From the Beginning   132

Levels of Comprehension   133
Teacher Questioning Techniques   134
The Comprehension Skills   136
Literary Appreciation   145
Study Skills: The Beginnings   146
Summary   151

8 Dictionary Skills: Moving to Maturity in Reading   154

Dictionary Readiness   155
Basic Dictionary Skills   156

Teaching the Locational Skills   157
Using a Dictionary for Meaning   159
Using a Dictionary for Spelling   160
Using a Dictionary for Pronunciation   160
Structural Analysis: Syllabication and Affixation   162
Summary   164

9 Using Reading Skills: The Independent Reading Program   166

The World of Children's Books   167
The Selection of Library Books   168
Scope of Materials   171
Elements of a Good Independent Reading Program   178
Summary   187

10 Individual Differences: Recognizing and Adjusting to Them 190

Range of Differences   191
Grouping for Instruction   192
Identifying Differences in Reading Levels   194
Pacing   196
Diagnosing Skill Needs   197
Teaching Children from Different Language Backgrounds   201
Teaching Children from Black Dialect   203
Specific versus Built-In Adjustments to Individual Differences   207
Summary   208

Name Index   211

Subject Index   213

Introduction

This book presents a sequence of prereading and reading skills deemed essential for individuals at the prereading and early reading levels. Beginning with the elements of language development, it moves through basic decoding and comprehension skills.

Specifically, Chapter 1 lays the philosophical foundation for an approach to beginning reading. Discussion of the process of reading, as well as major strengths and weaknesses reflected in divergent philosophies, leads to a proposed approach utilizing strengths.

Chapter 2 presents evidence for discarding many traditions of "reading readiness" and encourages recognition of the background already possessed by typical four and five year olds. Chapter 3 begins an instructional sequence of oral language development appropriate for preschool children—or for older pupils who have not developed those skills. It includes a diagnostic procedure to determine if children entering nursery school or kindergarten have adequate language skill to begin reading instruction.

For youngsters who demonstrate appropriate oral language development, the sequence of decoding skills is presented in chapters 4–6. These skills begin with the use of oral context and simple consonant letter-sound associations (Chapter 4), continue through consonant clusters, inflectional endings, and word recognition in Chapter 5, and conclude with some new research evidence to support a differing view of vowel generalizations in Chapter 6.

Chapter 7 deals with the comprehension skills, what they are, and how they are developed. Dictionary skills are presented in Chapter 8 as the bridge from basic decoding to maturity in reading, as the student moves into material that includes words outside his listening/speaking vocabulary.

Both the end and means of reading instruction are represented in Chapter 9. Ideas for implementing the independent reading program are offered as opportunities for using skills—for the enjoyable application and practice of the skills developed in order to further increase those skills.

While techniques throughout the book imply a diagnostic approach to instruction, Chapter 10 deals specifically with concerns for atypical learners and with methods for identifying their needs and working effectively with them.

While this book could be used as a cookbook, hopefully it will not be. The skills and methods are the warp and woof of a philosophy of reading and are supported by research evidence to encourage a deeper understanding of the reading process and of the most effective means of helping children to master that process.

Age or grade designations usually are not applied to these skills and understandings because they may be mastered by a bright, well-prepared four year old or they may still be needed by a twelve year old—or adult, for that matter—who has not had the experiences or instruction required.

This fact that individuals differ prescribes that the book deal with the *what, how,* and *why* of instruction rather than with *when.* Much has been debated about *when* instruction should begin, but the fact remains that *when* is most often a function of *how.* It has been demonstrated, for example, that most four year olds in a group learned skills traditionally reserved for seven year olds, but the former were taught as four year olds.

The content of reading instruction—*what* should be taught—is seen as a sequence of skills and understandings needed by anyone at the beginning level of skill development. In some instances, the sequence is rigid. For example, no child can be taught to read if he does not yet comprehend the oral language. In other instances, the sequence is loose. Work on word recognition, word identification, and comprehension skills is simultaneous and interchangeable.

Methods—the *how* of instruction—are based on research dealing both with the relative effectiveness of techniques and with how children learn. Those methods dealing with the specific skills to be mastered are precisely outlined in terms of research. There are other aspects of reading, however—matters of understanding that grow out of manipulation of language—that are suggested as open, unstructured experiences. The most important aspects of method cannot be determined through any book. To insure children's success, the teacher must enjoy working with children and language, must insure the success of each child at each step of the process, and must help children discover that reading and the manipulation of language can be fun!

Because I am convinced that good teachers are more than followers of a cookbook, much of this book is devoted to an explanation of the *why* of instruction. Unless we as teachers constantly evaluate *why,* we get into a rut and continue doing what we have always done and only because we have always done it.

The *why*'s expounded in this text are of two types: Sometimes they are the research foundation on which a given method is based; at other times, they are the logical or philosophical foundation underlying a given skill or understanding. The author has attempted to identify those methods and techniques supported by research and to distinguish them from his own biases based on experience.

The contents are limited to reading and reading-related activities. This is not to imply that the many other preschool and primary activities are not important: Music, rhythms, crafts, and other affective and psychomotor activities are a part of the individual's total development. On the other hand, there is no need to think in terms of a false dichotomy of either/or; the aforementioned activities can be continued along with the content of this book. And certainly, the primacy of literacy, both in and out of school, needs no justification.

1

What Is Reading?

Reading has been defined in a variety of ways as everything from getting meaning from print to bringing meaning to print. Some authors even ignore meaning entirely at the beginning levels and define reading as merely decoding or converting the printed form of language to the spoken form.

Harris presented a succinct definition of reading as "the meaningful interpretation of written or printed verbal symbols" (Harris, p. 3).

Bond and Tinker offered a more elaborated definition, expressing the same general philosophy:

> Reading involves the recognition of printed or written symbols which serve as stimuli for the recall of meanings built up through the reader's past experience. New meanings are derived through manipulation of concepts already in his possession. The organization of these meanings is governed by the clearly defined purposes of the reader. In short, the reading process involves both the acquisition of the meanings intended by the writer and the reader's own contributions in the form of interpretation, evaluation, and reflection about these meanings. (Bond and Tinker, p. 22)

Spache was undoubtedly safer when he devoted an entire chapter to "ways of defining the reading process." These included reading as skill development, as a visual act, as a perceptual act, and as a thinking process. Reading is all of these things—and more.

Many authors of texts on the teaching of reading avoid defining the reading process, and perhaps rightly so. Reading is a multifaceted operation that defies simple definition. It is a sophisticated process whereby the reader brings past experiences to the printed page, recognizes most words instantaneously, decodes a few, skips a few, and in the process approximates the meaning intended by the author.

As noted by F. Smith, the printed page has an abundance of redundancy. The mature reader processes the print in a manner that takes advantage of only as many of the superfluous clues as are needed to reduce uncertainty and to approximate the meaning intended by the author. On the other hand, the beginning reader—and especially the nonreader— doesn't have a repertoire of skills that he can use. He certainly doesn't have any words in a recognition vocabulary; that is, there are no words that he can recognize instantaneously when he sees them in print. And so the question is, where does one start with an individual who is not yet reading?

There are many different philosophies insofar as suggesting the starting point in reading. On the one hand are the extreme decoding or synthetic phonic approaches to beginning reading. On the other are the meaning emphasis or analytic phonic approaches. Somewhere in between is the preferred approach to beginning reading: one that utilizes the strengths of both extremes and avoids the weaknesses inherent in each. Justification for this position can be found not only in this book, but in a comparison of reading programs revised in the 1970s with their earlier versions which shows definite movement away from the extreme and toward a blurring of their distinctive philosophies.

It is not our purpose to present analyses of specific programs for beginning reading, but only to review divergent philosophies as a foundation for presenting the skills and methods deemed essential for success in beginning reading. The reader who seeks detailed information about specific approaches to beginning reading is referred to Aukerman, who offers a thorough review of one hundred approaches. While one might disagree with some of his evaluations, his factual descriptions are excellent.

Basal reading programs in recent years have become more alike as meaning emphasis programs incorporated more phonics earlier. Nevertheless, some distinctions can be made in philosophy. Many writers have classified programs as synthetic versus analytic, as early phonics emphasis versus delayed phonics emphasis, as programs that introduce phonics before words versus those that introduce words before phonics. The classifications used here are not so concerned with *how early* phonics is introduced but rather with the more important point: Is the emphasis on decoding only (sounding out letter by letter, for example) or is it on meaning with phonics used as one tool in the reading process?

Decoding Emphasis Programs

Programs at this extreme provide for teaching reading as a matter of teaching how to convert the printed word to the spoken word. As such, these programs usually teach youngsters to respond to a given letter with the sound for which that letter stands. Unfortunately, some even refer to "the sound the letter says," as if letters speak to the reader.

These programs may vary in terms of their format, but essentially they are attempting to teach children, through a stimulus-response kind of approach, the sound that each of the letters represents. Such an approach is often called "synthetic" phonics because readers are to synthesize the individual sounds into a word. When they come, for example, to the word *boat,* they are encouraged to sound it out: "buh, oh, tuh." Such noises do not result in the word *boat.*

Some extreme phonics programs merely drill on isolated letters until the child, upon seeing a given letter, responds with a given sound. Others require the verbalization of rules or use artifacts such as color, diacritical marks over the letters, or even entirely new symbols for the different letter sounds.

At the initial stage, using the mechanical device as a clue, the child is to respond with the appropriate sound for each of the letters. Because of the emphasis on converting print to sound in such programs, there is no teaching (unless the gap is filled in by a wise teacher) of the use of context. Reading is converting letters to sounds.

From the standpoint of research, it would be most difficult to prove any one program is significantly better or worse than any other. The general tendency from the research is to reveal that the extreme decoding emphasis programs often result in higher reading achievement at the end of first grade (Bliesmer and Yarborough; Chall). Part of the reason for this finding, however, is the fact that reading achievement scores at the first-grade level rely heavily on word recognition; if the youngster can sound out the word, that is, say the word, that child can most likely respond successfully on the first-grade reading achievement tests. What is seldom noted is the long-range effect of an extreme emphasis on phonics, where the youngster makes noises or says words without using context or without reading for understanding.

One of the few longer-range studies (Morgan and Lightfoot) was a natural study, not planned in advance. The authors compared third-grade reading achievement in four schools, two that used a rule-oriented phonics program and two that used a standard basal reading program. They found a significant difference in favor of the basal program in both reading vocabulary (significant at .05—chances are less than 5 percent that the results occurred by accident) and reading comprehension (significant at .001).

Sparks and Fay compared two schools in the same community with similar type of students and staff; one used a meaning emphasis basal series while the other used that same series along with a synthetic phonics program. Pupils were followed and tested from first grade through fourth. The investigators found that at the end of the first grade, the children enrolled in the school with the extra program in phonics had higher scores in reading achievement as well as in other subtests. At the end of second grade, differences were not clear-cut: on some tubtests the phonics emphasis children were ahead; on others, the meaning emphasis pupils scored higher. By the end of fourth grade, there was no significant difference in the achievement of the groups, despite the use of two reading programs by the phonics group.

Sparks and Fay also found that by the end of the fourth grade, the "fast learners" in the single basal program were superior to those in the phonics program. The point is that once children reach higher levels, where comprehension becomes a more important factor in the testing of reading achievement, the extra phonics is of little value. An extreme phonics emphasis tends to become a handicap because the reader has developed the habit of processing all the letters in print and is too often satisfied with saying the words rather than getting the meaning.

The artificial isolation of the sounds in words, as advocated by Lippincott, Open Court, Distar, and others, also creates a problem that would not normally exist. The child taught to read letter by letter is then faced with the problem of blending these isolated sounds back together into a meaningful word. For example, this author recalls a student who had been drilled in this kind of phonics. He sounded out "nuh" "eh" "suh" "tuh" *five times* before he recognized that he was trying to say *nest*.

"Linguistic" Programs

As one linguist stated, "Once again it must be emphasized that there can be no such method as a linguistic method of teaching reading" (Wardhaugh, p. 14). Linguists have methods, but these are methods of studying the language. Reading programs obviously include the language and may draw on the findings of linguists in terms of what is taught about the language.

In his summary of research on "linguistic" approaches, Wardhaugh further stated: "In conclusion, it is suggested that what we know as the linguistic method is neither very good linguistics nor very good method . . ." (Smith, N., p. 265).

The so-called linguistic programs certainly are not either extreme decoding or meaning emphasis programs. The fact that they do not isolate individual letter sounds distinguishes them from the synthetic phonics programs. Instead of teaching children to read by the phonic approaches of sounding out letter by letter, linguistic approaches use patterns: they attempt to teach inductively the generalizations that are often taught deductively in the phonics emphasis programs. For example, instead of teaching a rule that the letter *a* between two consonants stands for its "short sound," linguistic programs provide pattern experience with stories about "Nan can fan Dan" or "A fat cat sat on a mat" with the intent of having the children, through this experience, generalize that when they see the letter *a,* or especially the phonogram *an,* they can use their understanding of that phonogram to unlock a strange word.

This "linguistic" approach rests on a very tenuous foundation. In fact, on the basis of two theses and a considerable review of existing research, the author would claim that the whole basis for a linguistic program seems unfounded if, from such experience, one expects children to apply this pattern approach to unlock a strange word.

This rather strong statement is based on evidence from investigations by Murray and Lyttek, both of whom tested a total of 194 children individually with 16 phonograms to discover which of the phonograms each child could recognize. Then each child was given a word recognition test consisting of a randomized list of 151 words generated from these 16 phonograms. If the basis of linguistic programs is sound, one would expect children to recognize most of the words generated from recognized phonograms and not to recognize many of the words generated from unknown phonograms. Both investigators took care to insure that initial consonant sound associations were established, so that lack of ability in this area was not the problem.

Results of these two studies revealed only one observable pattern: Children tended to recognize the more commonly used words and tended not to recognize less commonly used words, regardless of whether or not they recognized the phonogram from which the words were generated. In fact, the study by Lyttek also compared children who were using a linguistic program with children who were in a standard meaning emphasis program. Despite the fact that children in the linguistic program were tested two months later than those in the basal and had been taught to use patterns, she found a slightly greater tendency for those in the standard basal series to recognize words generated from known phonograms as compared to children who were in the linguistic program.

Knafle also presented evidence to this point. In a study of 636 children who were in a linguistic reading program (kindergarten through third grade), she found that errors in word identification tended to be made with a correct first letter, for example, an error for *fog* would be *fan* or *fat,* not *log* or *dog.*

The philosophy of linguistic programs is more closely related to extreme phonics programs than it is to meaning emphasis programs, except for the fact that consonant sounds are not isolated. These programs differ from meaning emphasis programs because they make no attempt to encourage the use of context; children are encouraged exclusively to decode the word.

This emphasis is in keeping with the very clear statement of Fries who indicated that he saw three levels of reading: The first level is one of "transfer," where the individual who is learning to read makes a conscious effort to convert symbol to sound; the second stage is the point at which the reader can do this converting automatically; it is only at the third and final stage that the individual is able to use this basic skill in order to get information or enjoyment from the printed page.

Meaning Emphasis Programs

Most standard basal reading programs would be considered meaning emphasis programs. These programs are sometimes called "analytic phonic" programs. The child is taught to recognize a certain number of words at sight; then, on the basis of this recognition vocabulary, he is taught to analyze the words in order to develop phonic generalizations based on knowledge of the particular words known. For example, a child who knows the words *man, mop,* and *mitt* can then be shown and helped to understand that these three words are alike in that all three begin with the same letter and all three begin with the same sound. Therefore, children are to remember that the letter *m* stands for the sound they hear at the beginning of *man, mop,* and *mitt.*

From the beginning, stories are discussed that have content and meaning for the children. The intent is to make reading a pleasure and an information- or enjoyment-getting process. Children are taught to use picture context and printed context as clues to help them recognize or unlock a strange word.

The weakness of this analytic approach, implied in the preceding discussion of phonics emphasis programs, is that children do not get as quick a start in reading. Research indicates that at the first-grade level especially, they do not achieve as high on reading tests. On the other hand, they usually make greater gains later on, and comprehension tends to outstrip word recognition. The strength of the meaning emphasis program lies in its long-term results: Children are learning to read for understanding; they are using context and, therefore, are developing comprehension from the very beginning stage. They do not look upon reading as merely saying the words. A danger lies in the tendency of many meaning emphasis programs to teach reading as learning words, with phonics as somewhat of an afterthought.

The Foundation for an Approach to Beginning Reading

We are convinced, both from the research and from working with children, that the approach to beginning reading need not be an either/or situation. We need not capitalize on the strengths of a phonics emphasis while suffering with its weaknesses, nor do we need to try to capitalize on a meaning emphasis while suffering with its weaknesses. We can have the best of both worlds.

Improved reading instruction must rest on both logic and research. That research cannot be the global comparison of programs to see which is better, such as was attempted in "The Cooperative Research Program in First-Grade Reading Instruction" (Bond and Dykstra). In this massive study, reading programs were compared in various combinations in twenty-seven centers around the country. Some of the studies were extended through second grade and a few through third grade. The results, collected and blessed by computer statistics, should have surprised no one: In terms of the reading achievement of children, there was more difference between teachers in the same program than there was between programs.

This finding is often interpreted to mean "the teacher makes all the difference." While few will disagree that good teachers are essential, the finding is also a good indication that such broad comparisons are not researchable. There are entirely too many uncontrolled variables: Anyone who has visited elementary classrooms can recall teachers who had an adopted meaning emphasis reading series in the class, but who taught that program as if it were a synthetic phonics program; and, of course, the reverse is just as true.

To make a significant contribution to our knowledge of reading instruction, research studies must be more limited, with tighter control of the variables. Then, with a series of "smaller answers," practitioners might put the pieces together to arrive at better instructional procedures. Such is the hope of this author, and such was the policy in the development of the teaching procedures suggested in this book.

In addition to discarding "the teacher makes all the difference" belief as an excuse to minimize our efforts to improve teaching methods and materials, we must also rid ourselves of another item of conventional wisdom that exists in education today. This is the often heard statement "Children learn to read in many different ways." To many people, this is a license to confuse children. If certain children are not successful initially in a given program, it becomes an excuse to change them to a different program with a completely different philosophy and different *modus operandi*. To do this to children at the beginning stage of reading only confuses them. For example, suppose the youngsters have started out in a program that, by implication at least, is guiding them to the conclusion that to unlock a strange word they should make a noise for each of the symbols. Those children who are not successful are pulled out of the program in which they started and are now put into a program that instructs them that to unlock a strange word they are to remember patterns, or, in other instances, to remember the words the teacher has taught them. To do this changes the rules on them in midstream, and in some cases at a point when the light was just about to go on and they were about to understand this thing called "reading."

On the other hand, one cannot quarrel with the statement, "Children learn to read in many different ways," if it is interpreted only to mean that no one can prove one program is completely better than another through the research; that is, if the statement is interpreted as meaning "I have seen children learn to read in Program X, Program Y, and Program Z." This is true: Most children will learn to read in almost any program in existence. However, this fact is no excuse for saying one program is as good as any other. As professionals concerned with the teaching of reading to children, it is our responsibility continually to try to improve upon our methods and to follow the research on specific techniques and approaches that will enable us to do a better job. At present, one of the most certain facts is that consistency in philosophy, or in what we tell the child to do, is going to be most helpful at the early stages of reading development.

Still another tack is often justified by the statement "Children learn to read in many different ways." Some educators interpret it as meaning that some children are visual learners while others are auditory learners; therefore, they justify different approaches, depending upon the preferred modality. This particular point was researched by Bateman who divided four classes of first-grade children into groups based on their identification as auditory learners or visual learners. She then randomly assigned half the auditory learners to an auditory emphasis in beginning reading and the other half to a visual emphasis. She did the same with the visual learners: half were assigned to an auditory emphasis and half to a visual emphasis. When the children were tested for reading achievement at the end of first grade, Bateman reported that those who were taught by an auditory emphasis scored higher in reading achievement, regardless of whether they were classified as auditory or visual learners.

Bateman's conclusion has been verified by others (Benenson; Waugh) and seems to fit rather well with the findings that in an extreme phonics program—which does involve an auditory emphasis—children score higher in reading achievement at the end of first grade.

Another consideration in any decision about an approach to beginning reading is the concern we ought to have that children get started efficiently and economically in reading, but that they get started in a way that does not become a handicap at more mature levels of reading. For example, if reading is interpreted as making noises for symbols, children easily become handicapped, plodding readers who do not understand what they read. To seek an answer to the efficient, nonhandicapping approach, let's consider elements used by adults in the process of reading.

The Reading Process

No literate adult would have any difficulty in reading the following sentence:

W- m-st t--ch -ll ch-ldr-n t- r--d w-ll.

In reading the foregoing sentence, you may not know exactly what you did. On the other hand, probably no one—after noting that the dashes stood for vowels—looked at the first word and decided that the letter *e* was the only letter that would make sense, then, came to the word *m-st*, went through the process of *mist, mast, most, must,* and gave up helplessly. Many readers may not have noted consciously that dashes substituted for vowels.

Most likely the reader identified the word *children,* possibly associated *teach,* and from there went on to build context, which indicated that the last word had to be *well,* not *will* or *wall.* In other words, as adults we still use the consonant sound associations that we've established automatically through our experience with print, and we still use context to anticipate words that would make sense. We certainly do not process words letter by letter in our reading.

The importance of this use of consonants can be demonstrated further by a repeat of the sentence presented above, using only the vowels instead of the consonants:

-e -u-- -ea-- a-- --i---e- -o -ea- -e--.

Obviously, no one could read the sentence presented with only the vowels. There are at least three good reasons why the consonants in the first sentence provided more reliable information than did the vowels.

First of all, consonants tend to be more limited in their sound representations; that is, if the reader sees the letter *m* at the beginning of a word, he can be relatively certain that word is going to begin with the same sound as that heard at the beginning of *must*. In dealing with vowels, if the reader sees the letter *a* at the beginning of a word, all he can be certain of is that the letter's name is *a*.

The second difference that makes the consonants more helpful is that in English, there are roughly two consonant sounds for every vowel sound represented on a page of text. Therefore, the reader has twice as many clues from the consonants.

Finally, consonants are the letters that have the ascenders and the descenders, while the vowels tend to be very neatly all the same size. Hence, it's the consonants that provide the quick recognition clues sometimes referred to as configuration. For example, notice the greater difficulty in reading when the type is all caps:

-LL CH-LDR-N M-ST B- T--GHT T- R--D W-LL.

This use of context and the development and use of consonant letter-and-sound associations becomes an important basis for beginning reading. For example, at the listening level, most four year olds are accustomed to anticipating words that make sense when someone speaks to them in their native language. One would certainly get a reaction, in talking to a four year old, to a statement such as "Sky the dog little airplane."

When being read to, many preschool children will supply a missing word if the adult stops before reading the final word in a sentence. We can help four or five year olds to become consciously aware of what they are doing: They are using the sense of other words that are spoken to them to anticipate a word that would make sense, or to supply a word that might be missing in a sentence that is spoken.

If we make children aware of their ability to use spoken context and if we also teach them the sound associations for consonant letters, they can begin reading printed words at that very point. For example, consider yourself as a nonreader. If you were provided orally with the words printed in English in the following sentence and if you had been taught that ⊕ stands for the sound you hear at the beginning of *wagon* and *wind*, you should be able to read the strange printed word that has been underlined in the following sentence:

It was a hot day so we decided to go for a
swim in the ⊕ ✳ ◁. _____

In the foregoing case, you were able to read a strange word using only the context and the first consonant letter. You didn't really care what sounds the other letters represented because you knew what the word had to be. This is an important point to teach children from the very beginning: They need not—in fact, should not—use every possible phonic understanding they have in order to unlock strange words; they should use the meaning and only as many of the letter sounds as they need in order to read that printed word.

Obviously, this is a primitive stage of reading, but it is a beginning. To carry the same point further, if ⊕ represented the sound you hear at the beginning of *path* and *pan,* then the printed word in the same context might be *pond* or *pool.* Then the reader would have to use the final consonant to determine which word was correct. In any event, the reader still doesn't care what sound the vowel letter stands for in that particular word. In fact, there are very few instances where the vowel letter becomes crucial if the reader is using context. And it's very seldom—except in some artificial school situations—that one doesn't have context. Even a grocery list is context of a sort: The reader does not expect to find *cloud, house,* or *airplane* on a grocery list.

Given context, there are very few examples where the vowel sound representation is essential. A few of the limited possibilities are "We wanted to go fishing, but we couldn't find the b--t" (*boat, bait*) or "Mother sent me to the store to get some s--p" (*soup, soap*).

The World of Phonics

The preceding explanation lays the foundation for what this author sees as the best of both worlds, capitalizing on the strengths of both the phonics and meaning emphasis programs, that is, developing consonant letter/sound associations, but using these only to the extent necessary along with context. Such an approach develops the habit of reading for understanding from the very beginning. Furthermore, the beginning reader is not taught to be a context guesser nor a letter by letter "sounder outer" of words. That beginning reader uses context and phonics together in order to get meaning from the printed page.

To carry this thought one step further, however, we must recognize the limited role of phonics in the process of reading. Phonics enables beginning readers to approximate the sound of a word that they know the meaning of when they hear that word; phonics is only helpful if the word is already in the reader's listening-speaking vocabulary. Further than this, phonics is of no help. For example, the child who has been taught both sounds represented by *th* (/th̲/ as in *the* and /th/ as in *thumb*) may, upon seeing the word *the,* recall only the sound heard at the beginning of *thumb.* That youngster would attempt to say /thə/ and recognize there's no such word. However, that child would be so close to the actual pronunciation /th̲ə/ that he would know what the word was.

If a word is outside the reader's listening-speaking vocabulary, then phonics is of no value at all. The italicized word in the following sentence may be strange to you:

> He decided to *parget* the brick wall in his kitchen.

If you've never heard the word *parget,* no amount of phonics is going to help you decide what that word means—and meaning should be the primary concern of the reader. The only alternatives are to use the context, which in this case is very weak, or to use a dictionary.

Perhaps if you came across this word in your reading, it may have been in stronger context; the sentence may have continued:

> . . . because he didn't like the rough surface.

Using this additional context, you may be satisfied with the very general meaning you get for *parget;* that is, it has to do with eliminating or smoothing the rough surface of the brick wall. Then you may just continue reading, unless it is important to you to know exactly what the meaning is, in which case you are still faced with the necessity for using a dictionary. Sometimes, of course, you may have very strong context; for example the sentence might have continued:

> . . . and decided that plaster would be better.

In this case, you have a synonym for *parget* and you are completely satisfied in terms of meaning. If, however, you are asked to read that portion to a group, your concern also includes the pronunciation of the word. Does phonics help the reader to pronounce a strange word? As stated previously, it will enable only approximation of the word. If the reader has never heard the word before, there is no way of knowing whether the attempted pronunciation is correct or not.

One might attempt to apply all kinds of rules that beginning readers are often taught, all to no avail. For example, let's apply the rules to *parget*. First of all, structural analysis leads us to note there are two consonants between two vowels. According to the often taught rule, if there are two consonants between two vowels, and the consonants are neither a digraph nor a consonant cluster (already a tough decision for a beginner!), the reader is to syllabicate between the two consonants. Doing so results in the two syllables *par* and *get*.

In each of the two syllables there is a single vowel between two consonants, leading to the next rule: When there is a single vowel between two consonants, that vowel has its "short" sound, unless it is followed by *r,* in which case it has a sound that is neither "long" nor "short." The latter part of the rule merely tells the reader what the sound is *not*. The first portion of the rule, according to Clymer, holds true 57 percent of the time; Hillerich's examination of 2,650 primary words revealed it to be true 56.5 percent of the time. In either event, one would have to be quite a gambler to rely publicly on such rules.

Other questions still remain before the word can be pronounced: Does the *g* represent its "hard" or "soft" sound; does the *et* have the regular English pronunciation or the French /ā/ ending; and, finally, how do we accent the word, like *TARget* or like *forGET*? It is truly doubtful that anyone, using only knowledge of the rules we foist on children, would want to pronounce *parget* in public.

Comprehension

Of course, if the teacher of reading looks upon learning to read as a matter of learning words or learning to make noises in response to printed letters, then a discussion of comprehension has no meaning whatsoever. However, if one looks upon reading as a process whereby the reader is gaining information and reacting to information on a printed page, then the area of comprehension is the heart of reading.

Comprehension skill should start before the beginning of "reading." Reading comprehension skill is thinking skill applied in the reading act. Therefore, preliminary to any actual reading, the prospective reader can begin to develop—and should be developing—thinking skills in the oral language: the ability to draw conclusions, to make judgments, to predict outcomes, and so on. This means that long before any formal skill related to reading is introduced, young children can be responding orally in terms of these thinking skills. They should be responding to stories read to them and to ideas told to them. They should be responding in terms of their own telling of experiences and thoughts. Practically all of the skills called "reading comprehension skills" can be taught at the listening-speaking level before children ever begin to read. If children cannot perform these thinking skills at the oral level, they can hardly be expected to perform them in reading. Furthermore, the more experience children have with these skills at the oral level, the more proficient they will be when applying them in a reading situation.

Even more basic to beginning reading is the assumption that individuals already speak and understand the language in which they are expected to learn to read. At best, those who don't speak the language can do no more than learn to parrot noises for printed words; they certainly cannot be expected to learn to read with any meaning. This point applies not only to one who comes from a different language background, but also to the child who was born into the standard English-speaking family but who, for one reason or another, has not been able to communicate in the native language.

SUMMARY

This chapter has presented a basic foundation and a philosophy of beginning reading. Learning to read is neither a matter of learning to make noises for print nor is it merely a matter of remembering words. It is a skill that involves the use of context and consonant letter/sound associations in a meaningful process aimed at getting information or enjoyment from an author's printed ideas. This technique, as developed in Chapter 4, capitalizes on the strengths of an early phonics emphasis by teaching the beginning reader some of the most effective phonic generalizations at the earliest stages of learning. It also capitalizes on the meaning emphasis in that the child is using context to read for understanding from the very beginning. It avoids the most common pitfalls of these two approaches because the child does not sound out letter by letter or rely only on remembering words over a period of time. The child learns basic skills that can be used from the very beginning in unlocking a strange word. Implied in this approach is, of course, a degree of experience and some oral control of the language to be read.

References

Aukerman, Robert. *Approaches to Beginning Reading*. New York: John Wiley & Sons, 1971.

Bateman, Barbara. "The Efficacy of an Auditory and a Visual Method of First Grade Reading Instruction with Auditory and Visual Learners." In *Perception and Reading*, p. 105–12. Newark: International Reading Association, 1967.

Benenson, Thea. "The Relationship between Visual Memory for Designs and Early Reading Achievement." Ph.D. dissertation, Columbia, 1972. (Eric Document Reproduction Service No. 065 854.)

Bliesmer, Emory, and Yarborough, Betty. "A Comparison of Ten Different Beginning Reading Programs in First Grade." *Phi Delta Kappan* 46(1965):500–503.

Bond, Guy, and Dykstra, Robert. "The Cooperative Research Program in First-Grade Reading Instruction." *Reading Research Quarterly* II(1967):5–142.

Bond, Guy, and Tinker, Miles. *Reading Difficulties: Their Diagnosis and Correction*. New York: Appleton-Century-Crofts, 1973.

Chall, Jeanne. *Learning to Read: The Great Debate*. New York: McGraw-Hill Book Co., 1967.

Clymer, Theodore. "The Utility of Phonic Generalizations in the Primary Grades." *The Reading Teacher* 16(1963):252–58.

Fries, Charles C. *Linguistics and Reading*. 1962. Reprint. New York: Holt, Rinehart and Winston, 1963.

Harris, Albert. *How to Increase Reading Ability*. New York: David McKay Co., 1970.

Hillerich, Robert L. *Grapheme/Phoneme Correspondence for Vowels*. Mimeographed. Glenview, Ill.: Glenview Schools, 1966.

Knafle, June D. "Word Perception: Cues Aiding Structure Detection." *Reading Research Quarterly* VIII(1973):502–23.

Lyttek, Elaine. "A Comparative Study of Second Graders Taught By a Linguistic and Basal Reading Approach and Their Ability to Use Phonograms as Cues to Unlocking New Words." Masters thesis, National College, 1974.

Morgan, Elmer F., and Lightfoot, Morton. "A Statistical Evaluation of Two Programs of Reading Instruction." *Journal of Educational Research* (1963):99–101.

Murray, Corallie. "An Inquiry into the Use of Phonograms in Decoding by First and Second Grade Children." Masters thesis, National College, 1974.

Smith, Frank. *Understanding Reading*. New York: Holt, Rinehart & Winston, 1971.

Smith, Nila B. *Current Issues in Reading*. Newark: International Reading Association, 1969.

Spache, George. *Reading in the Elementary School*. Boston: Allyn Bacon, 1964.

Sparks, Paul, and Fay, Leo. "An Evaluation of Two Methods of Teaching Reading." *Elementary School Journal* 57(1957):386–90.

Wardhaugh, Ronald. *Reading: A Linguistic Perspective.* New York: Harcourt Brace Jovanovich, 1969.

Waugh, Ruth. "Modality Preference as a Function of Reading Achievement" (ED 054-921). Washington, D.C.: U.S. Office of Education, 1971.

2

What Is Readiness?

Reading readiness has been defined as everything from having a tea party to fussing with phonics. Most often it has consisted of generalized social and language activities.

While some would argue that "readiness" cannot be taught, others contend that it is not educationally sound merely to sit around and wait for it to happen. Probably the best general definition of readiness was that of Carpenter who said that "readiness is somewhere between wanting to and having to." We might amend this statement to include "and being able to."

Certainly reading readiness is not a subject to be taught from 9:00 to 9:30 between socialization and nap, nor is it a stage of development that occurs at a specified age. Readiness is a continuously developing process: It begins at conception and continues at ever higher cognitive levels until death, as each experience and strengthening of skill makes the individual ready for the next step.

Such a view recognizes reading readiness as a continuous developmental process, beginning with abilities to perceive visually and auditorily and extending to abilities to function receptively and expressively in language. At whatever point more formal or intensive instruction intervenes in the natural informal development of the learner, that intervention must begin by identifying the level of the learner's development and must result in placing that learner into appropriate experiences on the continuum.

Traditional Concerns

Too often traditional concepts of reading readiness deprive the child, even in kindergarten, of the experiences for which he is ready. Too often discussions of reading readiness present unsubstantiated beliefs that delay the kind of instruction from which many children would benefit. The following points, often considered as important reasons for delaying reading instruction in the kindergarten need analysis on the basis of existing evidence:

1. Mental Age. Many still believe that a child must attain a given mental age—usually six or six and a half—before being ready for reading instruction.
2. Visual Maturity. Some contend that at age five, children's eyes are not adequately developed physically for reading instruction.
3. Language Development. Most often this point is interpreted as a need for additional vocabulary development prior to reading instruction.
4. Experiences. Children must have a variety of experiences in order to have established referents for the items about which they will read.

5. Motivation. The child must want to read before instruction in reading can begin successfully.

6. Social Development. At age five, children need to develop socially before being introduced into any formal activity such as reading.

7. Visual Discrimination. The child has traditionally been taught to see gross differences in shapes and geometric forms. The child really needs to notice fine differences that distinguish one letter from another.

8. Auditory Discrimination. This has traditionally been interpreted to mean that a child must be taught to hear differences in sounds before being exposed to reading instruction.

Let's examine each of the foregoing in terms of the evidence that exists.

Mental Age

The claim that a given mental age is necessary for beginning reading is based on a report by Morphett and Washburne from a study they did in 1928 in Winnetka, Illinois. While one might question details of the study, such as the definition of "satisfactory progress" as being the completion of thirteen progress steps and a knowledge of thirty-seven sight words by February of the first grade, the important point is that certainly methods, materials, teacher preparation, and children are different today from what they were in 1928 in Winnetka. Equally important, as Gates stated in an early criticism of that study, readiness does not relate to mental age per se, but is a function of method.

Finally, we need only to look at the research correlating mental age or IQ with reading achievement at the beginning levels to recognize that there is far from a one-to-one correspondence. Studies (Durkin, 1962; Anderson) have shown a low correlation at the beginning level, a correlation typically ranging about .44 or 10 percent better than chance. In fact, while Durkin found the correlation between the *Stanford-Binet IQ* and reading achievement to be about .40, she found no apparent relationship between the *Kuhlman Anderson* and reading.

From another aspect, Durkin (1964) found that the lower a child's IQ, the greater the advantage of an early start in reading. This point is well worth remembering in education: Rather than avoid instruction with the child who is less advantaged, give him even greater support through instruction.

Visual Maturity

We have yet to find evidence that exposure to print *at any age* can be harmful to a child's eyes. In contrast, there is evidence from a variety of sources that indicates that exposure to print is *not* harmful. Specifically in terms of the visual development of five-year-old children, Eames, a medical doctor at the Harvard Psycho-Educational Clinic, stated:

Children five years of age were found to have *more* accommodative power than at any subsequent age. The poorest *near* visual acuity found among the pupils studied was quite sufficient for reading the usual texts. (Eames, p. 432)

Going even further, Shaw, a medical doctor at Boston's Beth Israel Hospital Eye Clinic, reported that most normal children can focus and accommodate visually by twelve months of age. After that, he says they are seeing efficiently enough to be taught to read.

Flom indicated that acuity at one year of age is at about 75 percent of adult level, and by age two, is approximately at adult level. According to Young, there is no evidence that reading leads to myopia.

Language Development

There is always a need for further language development. However, are there certain developmental activities in language that must be accomplished with all four or five year olds prior to instruction in reading skills? Consideration of this point must be expanded beyond the mere concern for vocabulary development to include the expressive use of language, auditory discrimination, the production of sounds, and the use of language patterns.

Expressive language, of course, begins at birth. We know, for example, that even congenitally deaf infants vocalize during the early months. Normal children reach a peak in vocalization at about eight to ten months of age. During that time of cooing and babbling, infants produce most—if not all—of the sounds in the languages of the world. Gradually, with reinforcement of certain sounds and lack of reinforcement of others, infants continue to develop only the sounds within their native language.

By age two, children typically have a vocabulary of about 200 words and are speaking in at least two-word sentences. From the age of thirty to forty-two months, the youngster experiences a rapid growth in vocabulary, culminating this period with an expressive vocabulary of about 1,000 words (Menyuk, 1971).

According to Templin, various studies have estimated the average listening vocabulary by age six to be from 13,000 to 23,000 words, with a range as high as 48,000 words. While such vocabularies are more than adequate for beginning reading instruction, Schram reported that children who viewed television during the preschool years were about one year more advanced in vocabulary development than those who did not view television. This finding would suggest that children today are ready about a year sooner if vocabulary development is the criterion for instruction.

The acquisition of syntax—the organization of words into sentences—is apparent in two year olds, who have already abstracted certain rules that are applied in the use of one- and two-word sentences (McNeil). This skill develops rapidly from about age three. By age five, it is clear from a variety of studies (Hunt; Loban; O'Donnell; Strickland) that the typical five-year-old English-speaking child produces all the sentence patterns of the language. Loban indicated that one could not distinguish the kindergartner, from the sixth grader in terms of basic sentence patterns used. In fact, Menyuk stated that all children by age three were using the basic structure rules with the exception of a few complex transformational structures such as passive voice and reflexive pronouns, and 50 percent of the three year olds were using those.

An important point in this development of syntax is that the type of error the preschool child makes moves from its beginning in omissions to substitutions, alterations, and finally to redundancy as he experiments with the basic principles of English syntax. This sequence occurs as a result of normal preschool language experiences. In studies attempting to develop better control of syntax in young children, Menyuk reported that this acquisition seemed to be more than mere imitation. For example, one group of children was trained by having the teacher expand each child's original statement and then having the child repeat the expanded statement; the other group had intensive verbal stimulation without imitation. Results indicated that increased verbal stimulation was better than an equal amount of time devoted to practice with expanded statements.

The importance of a rich language environment has also been verified in other studies. Stein reported that four year olds reproduced only half as many actions from a simple nonverbal film as did seven year olds. However, when an adult verbally labelled the actions in the process of the silent film, the four year olds reproduced as many of the actions as the seven year olds. This importance of verbal mediation has also been reported by Corsini.

In terms of the patterns of language development, however, a less traditional point ought to be made here. While typical four and five year olds may have mastered the basic patterns of the oral language, they may not be familiar with the patterns of the printed language if they have not been read to at home. A transcript of spoken language will indicate very quickly that the oral mode represents a rambling, back-and-forth, fragmentary, self-interrupting kind of pattern. In contrast, the printed or literary language is a linear, direct kind of communication. Hence, the child who has not been read to must be provided that experience in order to become familiar with literary patterns as well as with the oral patterns.

Finally, consideration must be given to oral language development in terms of phonology if a reading program is going to have youngsters working with beginning consonants in words. According to Templin, all of the single consonant sounds in English except z were produced correctly in initial position by 75 percent of four year olds. Since the production of sounds is more difficult than their auditory discrimination, one should expect no difficulty on the part of most four or five year olds in the discrimination of those single consonant sounds in initial position.

Experiences

Concerns for providing experiences prior to any instruction in reading skills were based on the desire to be certain children had referents for the things about which they would read. While this is an important consideration, the reality is that there are very few children today who don't have adequate experiences to make the content of early reading materials meaningful to them. Obviously, those who don't have pertinent experiences will require them. For most children, about all we can say is "What's new in the early levels of any reading program?"

Motivation

No one can argue with the importance of motivation; children should want to read by the time they are going to be taught how to read. However, this point seems somewhat overstated if one looks at reality. Often we are probably doing more to unmotivate children with the delaying tactics practiced in many kindergartens and first grades. One needs only to ask a young child about to enter kindergarten why he is going to school. The response usually is "to learn to read."

The social pressure, the prestige of being able to read, and the typical preschooler's fascination with the idea of words in print all indicate that the child *is* motivated to read if only we will take advantage of that motivation. In our culture, even the adult thinks nothing of joking about his inability in math with statements such as "I'm so poor in math, I can't even balance my checkbook." However, where does one find the adult who, even if it were true, would admit "I'm so poor in reading that I can hardly read the newspaper"?

To continue the preexisting motivation, of course, means to provide experiences that incorporate success. There is no better motivation for achievement than success each step of the way.

Social Development

Obviously there is a need for social development at any age. This does not imply that time must be taken to see that children grow socially before they are prepared to develop reading skills. There is no evidence that children can develop socially only in a play situation. In fact, most of the social experiences of the preschool child have been in play situations. Nor is there evidence to suggest that a skill-oriented game will not provide as much social skill development as playing in the sandbox.

Visual Discrimination

Traditionally, activities in visual discrimination have been considered the formal part of reading readiness. The task was to teach children to see differences in pictures and geometric forms. Children were asked to look at a row of rabbits, one of which had only one ear, and to mark the one that was different. Such an activity has nothing to do with reading and is really an insult to the intelligence of a five year old who can already distinguish his own black cocker spaniel from that of a neighbor when the two dogs are playing down the street.

The ability to read has nothing to do with seeing the difference between one-eared and two-eared rabbits. Who ever reads pages of rabbits? Learning to read does have to do with noticing the fine difference between *m* and *n,* and between *b* and *d.* In other words, what has been called "visual discrimination" practice ought to be converted to an effecteive readiness program to provide practice in letter form discrimination. The letters *b* and *d,* for example, are really the same symbol, and the child does need attention called to their idiosyncrasies if he is going to be successful in reading. When the young child looked at his dog, whether the dog was looking to the east or to the west, it was still the same dog; when the child looks at the printed letter, if it is turned one direction, it is *b,* but later we turn that letter around and insist that it is now a different letter. This is the kind of distinction a youngster needs to make in order to be successful in reading.

Auditory Discrimination

Traditionally, auditory discrimination activities have followed the same pattern of instruction in gross differences as visual discrimination activities, trying to teach children to recognize differences that have nothing to do with reading, trying to teach them to hear the difference between the roar of a jet and the rumble of a truck, between the slamming of a door and the ringing of a bell. Such activities are sheer nonsense for any three year old who can speak his language, unless the point of such activities is merely to teach those children what is meant by "same" and "different."

It is not necessary to teach children who have learned to speak their native language to hear such gross differences in sounds. These children can already hear a difference of one phoneme in words. For example, the English-speaking child can hear the difference between *hat* and *pat,* a difference of one phoneme.

Evidence on this point was very clear to the author in 1965, during a summer spent evaluating Head Start centers in the Midwest, from central city to rural Appalachian areas. Because of his interest in beginning reading and auditory discrimination, he made it a practice in every center to ask various children, "What is your name?" If a child replied "Johnnie," the author would say, "Oh, Tonnie?" After a response of "No, Johnnie," he would follow with "Oh, Bonnie?" "Oh, Connie?" and so on, until some of the youngsters were completely disgusted with him.

Not one child accepted the change in name. Those "disadvantaged" four and five year olds were discriminating the difference of one phoneme in a word. On the other hand, it should be obvious that if the children had been asked, "What did I do to your name?" or "Did I change the beginning sound?" they would have been unable to understand or to verbalize an explanation about beginning sounds; in fact, they would not understand what was meant by "beginning sound." The point is that, barring physical impairment, the English-speaking child already discriminates the difference of one phoneme in a word.

It should be clear that any child who speaks his native language must hear differences of sounds in words or he would not have learned to speak the language. How would a child know, without the ability to hear the difference of single phonemes in words, whether a speaker is asking for "a bite from your bread" or "a mite from your head"? When asked, the typical four year old will bring the *rock,* as opposed to the *lock,* when both items are lying together on a table.

All this is not to say that the four year old could reply accurately if one asked whether two words began with the same sound or different sounds, anymore than the Head Start children would have been able to verbalize what the author was doing in changing the beginning sounds of their names. This point, the difficulty of helping children to understand what is meant by the beginning of a spoken word, will be discussed specifically in Chapter 4.

In summary, evidence suggests that typical statements about reading readiness are irrelevant delaying tactics that ought to be abandoned. They have traditionally been identified as some sort of official starting point for formal education, usually in the kindergarten, whereas reading readiness is actually a continuum that begins long before the start of formal education. By nursery school or kindergarten age, most children are well beyond the elements most often considered in the preceding list. In other words, instead of talking about reading readiness, for some children we ought to talk about the prereading foundation in language (presented in Chapter 3) and for many children by age four or five, the prereading decoding skills (presented in Chapter 4).

Testing for Reading Readiness

We see readiness as a continuum in terms of development in language. In contrast, those who view readiness as a *point* in development—and its teaching as a fixed block of content—are inclined to use readiness tests to measure whether or not a child has achieved the appropriate level, that is, whether or not the child is "ready." On the basis of returns from 795 public schools, Morrison reported that reading readiness tests were ranked as the number one criterion for readiness by administrators.

The typical reading readiness test is made up of a battery of items that have been found to correlate with future reading success. Those correlations, based on a compilation of twenty-six studies, average .49 for boys and .57 for girls (Hillerich, 1966b). The range in twenty-six studies was from .36 to .79, indicating an average predictive value about 15 percent better than chance.

Such odds certainly should raise questions about the use of a readiness test to assign children for instruction. Kingston, for example, correlated the reading readiness test scores of 269 children with their third- and fourth-grade reading achievement and concluded that prediction for individual pupils was not feasible.

Probably the best statement on the matter was made by Silberberg, Iversen, and Silberberg when they correlated reading readiness test scores with reading achievement: "A great saving in testing time could well stem from using only the letters and numbers subtests or, perhaps, by not testing readiness at all. In either case, the sacrifice in information would be minimal."

Since the late 1950s, as a result of the work of Durrell at Boston, educators have recognized that a simple test of letter names is as good a predictor of future reading success as any commercial readiness test. Correlations have been reported of .55 (Olson), .67 (McHugh), .63 (Lowell), .65 (Johnson).

The important point, however, is not to predict future reading success or failure but to diagnose youngsters' needs in order to assure future reading success. The danger with predictions is that they become self-fulfilling prophecies. Children are identified as "not ready" and are assigned to generalized kinds of activities while those identified as "ready" are taught to read. When achievement in reading is tested, which group is likely to read better? How much does this policy help to continue even the modest correlation we now find between reading readiness scores and reading achievement scores?

This point of the instructional determination of success or failure has never been better demonstrated than in the study by Fry. His study was designed to discover whether or not reading readiness was necessary. Subjects for the study were eight sections of entering first graders who were randomly assigned to "readiness" or "nonreadiness" groups. The former were assigned to readiness experiences while the latter began immediately with preprimers of the basal program. When reading achievement was tested, the investigator found that the nonreadiness groups scored significantly higher in reading.

Behind these results are some interesting points. The children's "reading achievement" was tested with a word recognition test (words in isolation) in December of the first grade. At that time, many of the "readiness" children were still "reading pictures"; they had not been exposed to print. It's little wonder that those who had an opportunity to see words in print recognized more words on the recognition test than did those who had never had such an opportunity! As Fry clearly pointed out, "Hopefully, it won't come as too much of a surprise to many educators that children learn to read if they are taught to read" (p. 5).

Results of Fry's study were verified in a second study by Fry and Emmer that extended a full year and used standardized reading tests. Such studies demonstrate that if instruction is not provided, children are not likely to learn to read. Still another way to look at this position is in terms of the time spent for instruction. An evaluation of Sesame Street indicated that children who watched most gained most; those who watched least gained least (Ball and Bogatz).

Dunn reported a study of the effectiveness of teaching letter names, sounds, and twenty-two high-frequency words to children aged two to five. She then correlated achievement with four factors: age, verbal IQ, socioeconomic level, and time spent in follow-up activities. Time spent was the most significant contributor to gain in learning among these children. Incidentally, here again, age and IQ levels were not significantly related to gain.

In their summary of evidence on factors contributing to achievement, Wiley and Harnischfeger clearly indicate the importance of time as the factor in achievement, whether this be measured in terms of length of school day, school year, or amount of schooling.

When Should Formal Skills Instruction Begin?

Even though great strides have been taken since the early 1960s, many kindergarten and nursery schools are still involved in a generalized kind of readiness program for all children. While specific language development (see Chapter 3) is still necessary for some children at age five—or even six or seven—most children by age five are ready for more formal skills instruction in reading.

Even in 1964 when less evidence was available, Morrison reported the lag in practice as compared with the thinking of reading specialists. While 73 percent of

795 responding school districts did not allow kindergartners to go beyond traditional reading readiness, 58 percent of the specialists surveyed felt that "formal reading instruction extending beyond readiness should be provided in the kindergarten" (p. 3).

As pointed out by Almy and Heilman, the 1960s represented a period of polarization on the question of early skills instruction. Professional articles ranged from "Harm Might Result" (Sheldon) to "They Should Have the Opportunity" (Durkin), and included the challenge "Dare We Evaluate Paradise?" (Hillerich).

A cursory examination of the research supporting and disclaiming the early introduction of reading skills might suggest that the evidence is mixed. A closer look, however, may offer clarification of direction. First of all, we have been able to find fewer studies discounting the importance of formal skills instruction in kindergarten or prekindergarten as compared with the number of those that find the early teaching of formal skills effective. Perhaps one reason for this condition is that those who are opposed to earlier teaching of formal skills are not about to attempt this teaching with children.

Studies suggesting that formal teaching is not effective also seem somewhat limited in their extent. For example, Ploghoft reported a study of the effectiveness of using a readiness workbook in kindergarten; however, the study included only one teacher with two sections of kindergarten. One section used workbooks and one did not. The kind of workbook was not mentioned, and the effectiveness of the program was measured only with a reading readiness test, which indicated no significant difference in readiness scores between the two groups.

Blakely and Shadle reported the same kind of study, comparing a workbook with an informal program in kindergarten. Again, only one teacher was involved with two sections of children, and the authors reported the teacher's bias toward the informal approach. Effectiveness was again measured only with a readiness test. Results indicated that girls benefitted equally in either program, but boys benefitted more from the informal as opposed to the workbook approach.

Weeks compared 158 kindergarten children in terms of the effectiveness of an informal as opposed to a workbook approach. He found the workbook approach was less effective as measured by a reading readiness test. The author also reported no anxiety was demonstrated by children who used a workbook approach.

An important point to make about all three of these studies, in contrast to studies that have found formal skills instruction more effective than the informal, is that the preceding studies used as their "formal" programs materials such as *We Read Pictures;* that is, materials in workbook form that merely dealt with generalized kinds of language activity as opposed to specific reading skills. As pointed out previously (Hillerich, 1966a), this seems to be one of the clearest explanations for the difference between research studies that report no significant difference between formal and informal approaches and those studies that do report differences in favor of children who are taught the formal skills in kindergarten or earlier. Studies reporting the latter finding, with or without a workbook, are usually dealing with specific reading skills as opposed to merely the reading of pictures.

In contrast to the foregoing studies that tended to be limited in time, numbers of children, and the use of a readiness test as the criterion for success, there are a number of studies that demonstrate the effectiveness of teaching formal skills in kindergarten.

Probably the largest is a study by Brzeinski who randomly assigned 122 kindergarten classes to experimental or control groups. The experimental groups were taught prereading skills of using oral context and consonant letter-sound associations to read printed words, while control groups participated in a regular informal kindergarten program. Table 1 shows how the kindergarten groups were randomly assigned to a total of four treatment groups in first grade, with group A serving as the control.

Table 1. *Kindergarten and First-Grade Treatments*

Kindergarten	First Grade
Regular Informal	A. Regular (Variety of Programs) B. Prereading Skills
Prereading Skills	C. Regular (Variety of Programs) D. Follow-Up of Prereading Skills

Results, measured by a reading achievement test at the end of first grade, indicated a significant difference between each of the groups. Highest was group D, which had been taught the prereading skills in kindergarten and had a follow-up program that took advantage of that instruction; next highest was group C, which had developed the skills in kindergarten regardless of the reading program in first grade. Lowest of all was group A, which never received the specific skills in the format taught in kindergarten. In other words, the study clearly indicated that the formal teaching of the prereading skills in kindergarten was most effective, even if not followed-up in first grade. While Brzeinski's study continued through sixth grade with findings still in favor of group D, results along the way were contaminated with other factors.

Wise reported a study with 1,600 kindergarten children, half of whom were in an informal kindergarten program and half of whom were taught the specific prereading skills of using oral context and consonant letter-sound association. He found that reading achievement at the end of grade one was significantly higher for those taught formal skills, regardless of geographic location in the city (socioeconomic level), mental ability, and chronological age.

Schoephoerster, Barnhart, and Loomer reported a study of forty-five sections of kindergarten. Twenty-two sections used workbooks for the specific prereading skills, while the others were taught the same skills without the use of workbooks. Children in both workbook and nonworkbook groups were ranked by mental ability into above average, average, and below average classifications. On a test of the specific prereading skills at the end of the kindergarten year, Schoephoerster reported the average of the low mental ability group using workbooks to be almost as high as the average of the average ability group that did not use workbooks. Put another way, in comparing the two groups of above average mental ability children, 85.9 percent mastered the skills without using workbooks as compared with 95.8 percent of those who used workbooks. In fact, 84.2 percent of the average ability children who used workbooks mastered the skills—almost as many as in the above average ability, group without workbooks.

Kelly and Chen reported the results of going beyond prereading skills to teach reading in kindergarten. This study included 221 children and reported their reading achievement to be significantly higher than for those not taught reading in kindergarten, regardless of IQ or readiness level. These authors did find that children who were not taught reading had more favorable attitudes toward school, suggesting that the reading instruction was too structured.

Sutton reported results of teaching reading to selected children from a total of 134 kindergarten children. As should be expected, children who were taught to read scored higher in reading than those not taught.

Hillerich reported a study involving twenty-two sections of kindergartners. In this study, teacher and program variables were relatively controlled by using the previous year's children as controls and their reading achievement at the end of first grade as the criterion against which to measure the experimental group of the following year.

This study set out to identify whether (1) kindergarten children could master the prereading skills requiring use of oral context and consonant letter-sound association to read printed words, (2) this could be done more effectively with or without use of a workbook in kindergarten, (3) the skills would be retained over the summer, and (4) teaching of such skills in kindergarten would result in higher reading achievement at the end of first grade.

In answer to the first consideration, it was reported that 70 percent of the kindergarten children mastered the skills at the end of the kindergarten year. Mastery was measured with an achievement test for the skills taught.

Half of the sections developed the skills with the aid of a workbook; the others were taught the same skills, but without the use of workbooks. The effectiveness of the workbook was clearly indicated in that 88 percent of the children using the workbook mastered the skills compared with only 50 percent of those who did not use workbooks.

The prereading skills achievement tests were repeated at the beginning of first grade before instruction or review took place to measure the degree of forgetting over the summer. The average loss was 2.6 points on the fifty-eight-item test. While statistically significant, this loss was not deemed of practical significance.

Reading skill was measured at the end of first grade. There was a significant difference in favor of children who had been taught the prereading skills in kindergarten, despite their slightly lower academic aptitude when compared with the control group.

A replication of this study the following year, with all children using the workbook, indicated that 83 percent of the kindergartners mastered the skills in kindergarten. A check on retention over the summer, this time using a survey form of the test, indicated a loss of 1.1 points.

Wolf reported a study of the effectiveness of teaching the specific prereading skills to four-year-old prekindergarten children. This study involved five sections: One control group of fifteen children and four experimental groups totaling forty-eight.

The investigator reported that twenty of the forty-eight experimental group children mastered the skills, while only one of the control group did so. As an interesting sidelight of this study, mastery of the skills was correlated with the chronological age of the prekindergarten children and resulted in a correlation of only .34 or a forecasting efficiency about 7 percent better than chance.

Durkin (1974–75) followed thirty-seven children who were introduced to instruction in school at age four. She found no significant correlation between their chronological ages and reading achievement. These children scored higher in reading achievement than the contrast group until they reached grade three. The investigator saw failure of later teachers to adjust to the children's levels as the prime reason they failed to continue their lead in reading.

Durkin makes two noteworthy points in her conclusions:

> No school should introduce reading instruction into its kindergarten unless that instruction can be of a kind that will add both enjoyment and self-esteem to the fifth year of a child's life. (p. 60)

> Earlier starts in reading are meaningless if schools are unwilling to alter what is taught in the years that follow kindergarten. (p. 60)

The foregoing findings clearly suggest the effectiveness of teaching prereading skills, if not reading itself, before the first grade. On the other hand, this author would hasten to point out that, while 80 percent of the children in his own study benefitted from the earlier introduction of specific skills, 20 percent of the children did not master those skills. This word of caution should be obvious: All children are not ready for any given activity at any given time. The teacher's method is of utmost importance if skills are to be taught to young children; most of the teaching ought to take place through verbal activity, physical movement, and games. A workbook may then be used to summarize the skill point of the activities.

There are educators who would group children and teach skills to some while not to others. We still lack the evidence and instruments to make these kinds of groupings with any degree of confidence. Hence, an exposure program in kindergarten or nursery school seems far more appropriate: All children have the opportunity to play the games and to participate in putting marks on workbook pictures; while many, if not most, will develop the skill intended, others are still participating and enjoying that participation with their peers. Those who do not master the skills must be retaught those skills at a later time.

We—while admittedly without solid research evidence for or against the point— firmly believe that those children who have been pleasantly exposed to the skills, even though they haven't mastered them in kindergarten, are in a better position to master those same skills at a later time than they would be if they had never been exposed to them. This, of course, is in line with a point made elsewhere: The child who needs the most help ought to receive it as early as possible; that child ought not be shunted aside to wait for that help.

SUMMARY

This chapter has reviewed the evidence relating to reading readiness, first in terms of the elements traditionally considered a part of reading readiness, then in terms of the effectiveness of teaching formal prereading skills before the first grade. The conclusion seems to be clear that many children are ready for specific skills instruction in the years before first grade. This does not mean that we should expect all children to master the skills anymore than we should expect the opposite—that no children should learn the skills. To take the former view is just as inconsiderate of individual differences as has been the traditional view that, as if by magic, sometime in October of first grade children suddenly became "ready" for formal reading instruction. The important first step at any level is that of diagnostic teaching, discovering where the child is in his development and beginning there.

While definite research evidence is still lacking in terms of whether the specific skills can best be taught to select groups or to all on an exposure basis, this author has seen the effectiveness of the latter in terms of skill development and enjoyment. There is no contradiction implied in the teaching of formal skills in an informal atmosphere. Certainly young children are not ready to be told repeatedly that they are wrong! (Even older students might do better if this point were considered.)

References

Almy, Millie. *The Early Childhood Educator at Work.* New York: McGraw Hill Book Co., 1975.

Anderson, Dorothy M. "A Study to Determine if Children Need a Mental Age of Six Years and Six Months to Learn to Identify Strange Printed Word Forms When They Are Taught to Use Oral Context and the Initial Sound of the Word." Ed.D. dissertation, Colorado State College, 1960.

Ball, Samuel, and Bogatz, Gerry Ann. *A Summary of the Major Findings in "The First Year of Sesame Street: An Evaluation."* Princeton: Educational Testing Service, 1970.

Blakely, W. Paul, and Shadle, Erma M. "A Study of Two Readiness-for-Reading Programs in Kindergarten." *Elementary English* 38(1961):502–5.

Brzeinski, Joseph E. "Beginning Reading in Denver." *The Reading Teacher* 18(1964): 16–21.

Carpenter, Ethelouise. "Readiness Is Being." *Childhood Education* 38(1961):114–16.

Corsini, David A. "Kindergarten Children's Use of Spatial-Positional, Verbal, and Nonverbal Cues for Memory." *Journal of Educational Psychology* 63(1972):353–57.

Dunn, Barbara J. "The Effectiveness of Teaching Selected Reading Skills to Children Two through Five Years of Age by Television." Paper presented at the Council of Exceptional Children. Chicago, April 23, 1970.

Durkin, Dolores. "A Fifth-Year Report on the Achievement of Early Readers." *Elementary School Journal* 65(1964):76–80.

———. "An Earlier Start in Reading." *Elementary School Journal* 63(1962):147–51.

———. "Should the Very Young Be Taught to Read? They Should Have the Opportunity." *National Education Association Journal* 52(1963):20–24.

———. "A Six Year Study of Children Who Learned to Read in School at the Age of Four." *Reading Research Quarterly* 10(1974–75):9–61.

Eames, Thomas. "Physical Factors in Reading." *The Reading Teacher* 15(1962):427–32.

Flom, Merton C. "Early Experience in the Development of Visual Coordination." In *Early Experience and Visual Information Processing in Perceptual and Reading Disorders,* edited by Francis A. Young and Donald B. Lindsley. Washington: National Academy of Science, 1970.

Fry, Edward. "Are Reading Readiness Materials Necessary in the First Grade?" Paper presented at American Educational Research Association Annual Meeting. February 1965.

Fry, Edward, and Emmer, Sara. "The Effect of the Use of Reading Readiness Materials in the First Grade." Paper presented at the American Educational Research Association Annual Meeting, 4 February 1971, New York.

Gates, Arthur I. "The Necessary Mental Age for Beginning Reading." *Elementary School Journal* 37(1937):497–508.

Harris, Albert J., and Sipay, Edward R. *How to Increase Reading Ability,* Chapter Two. New York: David McKay Co., 1975.

Heilman, Arthur W. *Principles and Practices of Teaching Reading,* Chapter Four. Columbus: Charles E. Merrill Publishing Co., 1972.

Hillerich, Robert L. "Dare We Evaluate Paradise?" In *New Directions in Kindergarten Programs.* Cambridge: Lesley College, 1963.

————. "An Interpretation of Research in Reading Readiness." *Elementary English* 43(1966a):359–64, 372.

————. "Predictive Value of Letter Name Test, Preliminary Study." Glenview: Public Schools Bulletin, June, 1966b.

————. "Pre-Reading Skills in Kindergarten: A Second Report." *Elementary School Journal* 65(1965):312–17.

Hunt, Kellogg W. *Grammatical Structures Written at Three Grade Levels.* Champaign: National Council of Teachers of English, 1965.

Johnson, Ronald. "The Effect of Training in Letter Names on Success in Beginning Reading for Children of Differing Abilities." Paper presented at American Educational Research Association Annual Meeting. March 1970.

Kelley, Marjorie K., and Chen, Martin K. "An Experimental Study of Formal Reading Instruction at the Kindergarten Level." *Journal of Educational Research* 60(1967): 224–29.

Kingston, Albert J., Jr. "The Relationship of First-Grade Readiness to Third- and Fourth-Grade Achievement." *Journal of Educational Research* 56(1962):61-67.

Loban, Walter D. *The Language of Elementary School Children.* Champaign: National Council of Teachers of English, 1963.

Lowell, Robert. "Reading Readiness Factors as Predictors of Success in First Grade Reading." *Journal of Learning Disabilities* 4(1971):563–67.

McHugh, Walter J. "Indices of Success in First Grade Reading." Paper presented at American Educational Research Association Annual Meeting. February 1962, Chicago.

McNeil, David. *The Acquisition of Language.* New York: Harper & Row, Publishers, 1970.

Menyuk, Paula. *The Acquisition and Development of Language.* New York: Prentice-Hall, 1971.

Morphett, Mabel V., and Washburne, Carleton. "When Should Children Begin to Read?" *Elementary School Journal* 31(1931):496–503.

Morrison, Coleman. "A Comparison Between Reported and Recommended Practices Related to Selected Aspects of Kindergarten and Beginning Reading Programs," Paper presented at American Educational Research Association Annual Meeting, February, 1964.

O'Donnell, Roy C.; Griffin, William J.; and Norris, Raymond C. *Syntax of Kindergarten and Elementary School Children: A Transformational Analysis.* Champaign: National Council of Teachers of English, 1967.

Olson, Arthur V., Jr. "Growth in Word Perception as it Relates to Success in Beginning Reading." Ed.D. dissertation, Boston University, 1957.

Ploghoft, Milton H. "Do Reading Readiness Workbooks Promote Readiness?" *Elementary English* 36(1959):424–26.

Schoephoerster, Hugh; Barnhart, Richard; and Loomer, Walter M. "The Teaching of Prereading Skills in Kindergarten." *The Reading Teacher* 19(1966):352–57.

Schramm, Wilbur; Lyle, Jack; and Parker, Edwin B. *Television in the Lives of Our Children.* Palo Alto: Stanford University Press, 1961.

Shaw, Jules H. "Vision and Seeing Skills of Preschool Children." *The Reading Teacher* 18(1964):33–36.

Sheldon, William. "Should the Very Young Be Taught to Read? Harm Might Result." *National Education Association Journal* 52(1963):20–22.

Silberberg, Norman; Iversen, Iver; and Silberberg, Margaret. "The Predictive Efficiency of the Gates Reading Readiness Tests." *Elementary School Journal* 68(1968):213–18.

Stein, Aletha H. "Mass Media and Young Children's Development." In *Early Childhood Education,* edited by Ira J. Gordon, p. 182. Chicago: National Society for the Study of Education, 1972.

Strickland, Ruth. *The Language of Elementary School Children: Its Relationship to the Language of Reading Textbooks and the Quantity of Reading of Selected Children.* Bloomington: Indiana University Press, 1962.

Sutton, Marjorie Hunt. "First Grade Children Who Learned to Read in Kindergarten." *The Reading Teacher* 18(1965):192–96.

Templin, Mildred. *Certain Language Skills in Children: Their Development and Interrelationships.* Minneapolis: University of Minnesota Press, 1957.

Weeks, Ernest E. "The Effect of Specific Pre-Reading Materials on Children's Performances in the Murphy-Durrell Diagnostic Reading Readiness Test." Ph.D. dissertation, University of Connecticut, 1964.

Wiley, David, and Harnischfeger, Annegret. "Explosion of a Myth: Quantity of Schooling and Exposure to Instruction, Major Educational Vehicles." *Educational Researcher,* 3(1974):7–12.

Wise, James. "The Effects of Two Kindergarten Programs upon Reading Achievement in Grade One." Ed.D. dissertation, University of Nebraska, 1965.

Wolf, Lois. "Reading Readiness: An Experimental Study of the Effects of Specific Reading Skills Instruction on Sixty-Three Four Year Olds in Winnetka, Illinois." Masters thesis, National College of Education, 1972.

Young, Francis. "Development of Optical Characteristics for Seeing." In *Early Experience and Visual Information Processing in Perceptual and Reading Disorders,* edited by Francis A. Young and Donald B. Lindsley. Washington: National Academy of Science, 1970.

3

Prereading: Language Understandings and Skills

As indicated in Chapter 1, the act of reading involves the ability to think in the language being read, and requires the ability to manipulate sounds of words in the language. It also requires the ability to understand the spoken language and to use the spoken language. Chapter 2 discussed the process called readiness and pointed out the great amount of language expertise possessed by the typical preschool child by age four or five. It is the purpose of this chapter to analyze the oral language needs of the preschool child and to discuss ways of developing specific aspects of language mastery in the child who needs these kinds of skills.

This chapter will deal, item by item, with those skills and understandings that are most often developed in the home in the preschool years. If they are not developed when the child enters a more formal school situation, they are the point at which the teacher must start, regardless of the child's age. While the specifics are given in an approximate sequence, there is no solid evidence to indicate that this is the necessary or only sequence in development; most often each of these items is developed at various stages of sophistication while other elements are being initiated or further developed.

Basic Skills and Methods

For those who seek a hierarchy of the language skills, we might argue that a receptive activity is easier than that same kind of activity used expressively. Hence the following listing (in hierarchical order) suggests one kind of reasonable progression of the language skills.

Receptive Skills	Expressive Skills
Auditory Discrimination	
Basic Vocabulary	
Listening Comprehension	Basic Vocabulary
Ability to Use Oral Context	Oral Language Development
Ability to Follow Oral Directions	
Recalling Sequence of Events	Arranging in Sequence

Let's examine each of the language skills (in order of testing) in terms of what each consists of and how they can be further developed.

Auditory Discrimination

Authorities are in agreement that auditory discrimination is essential in learning to read. We would go even further and say that auditory discrimination is absolutely essential if one is to understand the spoken language. After all, how would a child know if someone were asking for *silk* or *milk* unless that child could discriminate the difference of one phoneme in those two words? While much has been made of auditory discrimination and its lack among children who are not successful in reading, there is a serious question as to whether it is an inability to discriminate auditorially or an inability to follow directions on tests that leads a child to score poorly on an auditory discrimination test. More will be said about this in connection with early identification later in this chapter.

At this point, it should be obvious that children learn their native language only by listening and imitating. They are not born with language competence, and no one sits down to drill them, sound by sound, on the sounds in their language. They listen and imitate, and at age two they may not imitate very accurately. By age three, as indicated in Chapter 2, they are beginning to do a fairly good job; and by age four typical children have not only pretty well mastered the ability to discriminate but demonstrate this mastery by the ability to reproduce and to communicate back the appropriate sounds of language.

A parent or teacher who has some doubt about a child's ability to discriminate can test that child's ability by using a few toy props. For example, place a rock and a lock on the table. Ask the child to bring (by name) one of the items. Put a letter and a nail on the table and ask the child to bring mail or nail. The youngster who consistently brings the item requested obviously can hear the difference of one phoneme in a word.

This same principle can be applied to checking ending sounds or vowel sounds. Take care that the words are discernible, for example, *ladder/latter* or *pedal/petal* are pairs that are not distinguished in the speech of many people. Among the more difficult sounds to discriminate are the simple vowel sounds, such as in *pit, pet, pat, put, putt, pot.* Even here, with certain dialect exceptions, one is hard pressed to find an English-speaking four year old who can't bring the *pin* or the *pen,* depending upon which is requested. In other words, children actively speaking their native language have already demonstrated their ability to hear differences in sounds in words. When there is a doubt, activities such as the following can be used for further practice in auditory discrimination:

1. Provide the child with lots of oral language experience, talking about anything and everything, as well as taking walks, trips, and so on, so that the child has more to talk about and listen to.
2. Read nursery rhymes to the youngster and talk about them.
3. Collect pictures and miscall the names of some of them. For example, hold up a picture of a ball and ask the child, "Is this a call?" "Is it a tall?"
4. Play a game of funny questions: "Do you eat Jell-O or yellow?" "Do you sleep

in a red or a bed?" Often four year olds will begin to participate by making up funny questions themselves.

5. Collect pictures that represent minimal pairs, that is, words that differ by only one phoneme, whether that be the initial consonant, vowel, or final phoneme. Then put a pair of pictures on a table and ask the child for one of the two; for example, from the pair *wing* and *ring,* ask for the wing.

6. Read a story such as "Henny Penny." Then have the child make other combination words that differ by only the beginning sound, following the pattern of Henny Penny and Ducky Lucky. The child can also make these alliterative names from common objects around the house: pickle nickle, cake lake, bare chair, and so on.

7. At a slightly more advanced level, have youngsters collect all the pictures they can find whose names have the same beginning sound. They might even paste these on a scrapbook page. For example, cut out a picture of *moon* or *monkey* and paste it at the top of the page. Have the children then name other pictures and compare the beginning sounds to decide which ones begin with the sound heard at the beginning of *moon* or *monkey.*

8. Have youngsters engage in a "treasure hunt." This is the same kind of activity suggested in number 7, but they will collect all the little toys or objects they can find whose names begin with the same sound.

It is important not to confuse immature speech with problems of auditory discrimination. For example, this author has tested for auditory discrimination a considerable number of four and five year olds who exhibited immature speech. Yet, those youngsters who would call both *wing* and *ring* "wing" could very clearly distinguish which was being asked for. In other words, immature speech is usually an expressive problem; it doesn't indicate a receptive problem.

Listening Comprehension

Children who, from their very earliest experiences, are involved in an active interchange with peers and adults usually develop quite adequately in the area of listening comprehension. On the other hand, the youngster who has been deprived of active participation in language will need considerable experience to develop the ability to comprehend in the oral language.

The experience of some children may have been limited to conversational, or informal, oral language. Those children, if they've never been read to, may also have some difficulty in comprehending the more organized, linear language of print. The general solution is to provide these youngsters with experiences in listening actively and in reacting to what is heard. Some experiences that can be conducted at home or at school with the child who needs additional help would be the following:

1. Read to the child and discuss the story *for fun.* In reading to a youngster, the discussion should never become a quiz to find out if he understood everything;

rather it should be a discussion to encourage active participation, using questions beginning "Would you have . . . ?" "Why do you think . . . ?" "Do you think . . . ?"

2. Give the youngster nonsense questions to listen and to react to: "Do chairs eat?" "Do dogs fly?"

3. Make up some "Who am I?" or "What am I?" riddles for the child to answer. "I am planted in the ground. I have a long trunk and wear leaves in the summer. What am I?" "I have four legs and I'm furry. I bark at you when you come home. Who am I?"

4. At a more advanced level, read a three- or four-sentence story and ask the child what it was about. Then reread it, changing a major situation or event. Have the child tell what was different.

5. Have the child listen to a story and then draw a picture of his interpretation of the story.

In a school situation, the kindergarten or nursery school teacher cannot always spend sufficient time with each individual child. In such situations, parents or older students can be used to read to individuals or small groups and to discuss the stories with them. Story records can also be used, and the child may draw a picture in reaction to a short story. The tape recorder is also a good device to use for children to listen to a short story and then make a picture of their interpretation of that story.

Recalling Sequence of Events

The ability to recall the sequence of events is a more sophisticated skill in the area of language comprehension. Experiences in this area can begin at a very basic level: children are more likely to recall a sequence of events that actually happened to them than they are to be able to recall a sequence from a story read to them. Hence, the first items suggested here are items that deal with children's direct experiences.

1. Help children become aware of natural sequences in daily activities: They eat breakfast before they eat lunch, and lunch before dinner; they turn on the water faucet, and then the water comes out.

2. When the child goes for a short trip, even to the grocery store, discuss the sequence of events with him: "What did we do first?" "What did we do next?" The point here is not to recall every detail that took place, but to report the recalled items in the proper sequence.

3. In a group situation, involve youngsters in sequencing by taking slides or pictures of the group on a field trip or engaged in some activity that has a sequence to it. Have children place three or four pictures in the proper sequence.

4. Read a short story or nursery rhyme to the children. Then have them recall what happened first, what happened next, etc.

5. Sequence sets of pictures are available commercially and are often used in nursery schools and kindergartens. When these are used, the sets should be

limited to four to six cards. To get beyond this number is to make the mechanics more difficult than the skill you are trying to develop.

6. Create homemade sets of sequence pictures from old picture books or magazines. Always accept any justifiable sequencing of the pictures.

Oral Language Development—General

The child who cannot function satisfactorily at the oral level is not likely to be able to function in beginning reading. The lack of oral language development by its very nature also implies the kinds of activities that the youngster needs: Experiences in talking and any experiences that will stimulate talking are going to contribute to oral language development. Of course, there are at least two necessary elements to this activity. First of all, the child must have something to talk about; secondly, that child must have someone who is willing and able to listen. Following are some examples of experiences that can stimulate a child to use oral language:

1. Take the child for a short walk for a specific purpose: "To see how many sounds we can hear," ". . . colors we can see," ". . . shapes we can see."

2. In the home, have a party where cookies are served and a small group of children engage in a few games, group singing, or impromptu dramatizations.

3. Use the old kindergarten prop—a "feely box." This is a carton with hand holes at opposite ends that are covered with cloth so no one can see into the box. An object is placed in the box, and a child sticks his hands into the ends to feel and to describe the object. The idea is to determine from the sense of touch what the object is. The running narrative by the child helps develop oral language. Prompting with questions sometimes helps, but—as much as possible—the child should do the talking.

4. Keep the children talking during sharing time in nursery school or kindergarten. It is important that children be in small groups so that more of them get chances to talk. Volunteers are handy here as additional ears while the youngsters talk.

5. Either at home or at school, use a grab bag of pictures. Children may reach in, pull out a picture, and tell a story about their picture. For reluctant or reticent youngsters, the adult can participate or "go first" in this game.

6. Use pictures of common objects. Have children tell how the object is used, what it's made of, and what they think about it.

7. At a more advanced level, have youngsters listen while a short story is read aloud. Then the reader can suggest a changed event in the story and ask the children what they think would have happened if . . . For example, in the story of Goldilocks, what might have happened if the bears had been home when Goldilocks first arrived?

Incidentally, this idea of reading a complete story and then having youngsters predict outcomes based on the change of an event in the story seems a better technique than reading part of the story and having the child suggest the ending. In the latter approach, when children hear the ending as printed in the story, they may get the feeling that they came up with the "wrong answer," whereas changing an event leaves the possibilities open: No right or wrong answer is implied.

Oral Language Development—Basic Vocabulary

While general oral language development is a top priority in that youngsters must be able to use the normal patterns of their language, they must also have a certain basic vocabulary of common words that they can understand and use. The most effective way of developing vocabulary related to common objects is to provide direct, personal experiences with those objects. Sometimes vocabulary weakness may be identified within a particular category, such as animals, articles of clothing, or foods. In such cases, the children can have direct experiences in a variety of ways within the category. In instances where direct experience is not possible, a variety of pictures to see and talk about is the next best alternative.

At a slightly more sophisticated level in terms of vocabulary development, several youngsters can be brought together to play an add-on game, where an object such as a ball is held in view. One child will use the name of the object in a sentence: "This is a ball." The next child will add another word to say something about the ball: "This is a blue ball." The next child will continue with another word: "This is a big blue ball."

In the process of vocabulary development, youngsters can also be given some experiences in generalizing through categorizing. While developing this ability, the young child tends to generalize in terms of a specific and applies the specific to a category. For example, the two year old may refer to all dogs by the name of his dog, or to all small animals as dogs.

Begin the idea of categorizing at a basic level while children are sorting and naming pictures. For example, give them three or four pictures, one of which is not in the same category; for example, a picture of a cow, a dog, a sweater, and a cat. Ask which picture does not belong with the others and why it does not belong.

Common materials can be used for further practice in sorting: blocks of various sizes and colors, bottle caps, buttons, pictures, seeds, leaves, marbles, rocks, stamps, and so on. They can be sorted into piles by size, color, texture, use, or whatever. The learning experience to be achieved here—but not necessarily verbalized—is that sorting is a matter of making certain rules and then following them. For example, one might have six items, and those items might be grouped by color into two piles of three items each. By changing the rules and deciding to group by size, the child may reclassify those same items into different groups.

Another aspect of vocabulary development deals with the everyday structure words of the language, most often the prepositions. Youngsters from very early in life are directed to sit *in*, get *on*, go *around*, wait *beside*, and so on. Yet, some five year olds don't have a clear understanding of the relationships indicated by the various relationship words. The implication for instruction is again obvious: Give youngsters an opportunity to manipulate objects in terms of *in, on, under, beside,* and in terms of *little, big, top, bottom, front, back.*

In the nursery school or kindergarten, this kind of experience can also be provided with toys. For example, use a large toy train, where children can put blocks *in, in front of, in back of,* or *beside.* Even a bulletin board picture of a train or a truck can be used, and children can put other pictures in relationship.

Movement is an important part of a young child's life. These relationship words can also be learned through enjoyable play by using a large furniture box or refrigerator box that the youngsters can get *in, go around,* get *behind,* get *on.* The expressive language element can even be added by having children take a position and announcing where they are: "I am *in* the box," "I am *on* the box."

The Ability to Follow Oral Directions

This aspect of listening comprehension should begin with simple one-step oral directions. They can be involved with body movement, such as "touch your head," "touch your toes," "sit on the floor."

Many of the language activities can be interrelated. Directions, for example, can involve expressive as well as receptive language. The child may follow a direction and then give a direction back to the parent or teacher. The child may also be referred to objects in the room and given directions to get a certain object. Playing the game "Simon says" is always a good activity for practicing the ability to follow oral directions.

These activities can be expanded to two- and three-step directions. In other words, begin with the simple direction, "Please bring me that book from the table." Follow with "Please get that book on the table, put it on the shelf, and sit in this chair." Children may also play grocery store and follow directions to get one, two, or three items from the store. Depending upon the child's age and his level of skill development, activities involving following directions can be expanded to include directions to color, fold, cut, and so on.

The Ability to Use Oral Context

Most four year olds, if they have learned to speak their native language, are already intuitively using oral context. It is not uncommon for a four year old to supply a missing word if he is being read to and the person doing the reading omits a word or fails to complete a sentence. However, most children can profit from more practice in using oral context. From a reading viewpoint, most children need to be made consciously aware of this intuitive ability they have of using the sense of other words to decide on a missing word. This task can be clarified initially by talking with the child along the following lines:

> I'm going to say something, but I won't finish it. You finish what I start to say. Tell me what word would make sense to finish what I say. For example, I might say it is so hot, I want a drink of cold _____ . What do you think I was going to say? (If the child hesitates too long, help to clarify what you mean.) Could it be milk, I want a drink of cold milk? What else might it be? Yes, it could be water, tea, soda, or anything we drink, couldn't it? (Hillerich, 1974, page 9)

Then continue by suggesting another sentence. Keep the context broad so that many different words would make sense. As children begin to catch on to the idea, invite them to make up incomplete sentences for which you or others can supply the missing words.

Another activity would be to show children an action picture. You describe it, but allow the children to supply the key word: "This boy was running and now he _____ ."

Such activities can gradually become more sophisticated as categories become more limited. Then begin to narrow the context to items such as "My brother wrote a letter with his _____ ," "We wanted to go on a picnic and decided to take _____ for lunch," "We went to the zoo and had fun watching the _____ "

Actually, none of these language activities is completely discreet in dealing with only one skill. In fact, the adult working with the child should deliberately attempt to interrelate the skills. As an example, in helping youngsters to become aware of their ability to use oral context, riddles such as "Who am I?" or "What am I?" can be developed. From this experience, youngsters can begin to make up riddles, thereby developing their oral language skill as well as their ability to use oral context to determine what is being talked about.

Early Identification

In recent years, one of the educational slogans at the nursery and kindergarten level has been "early identification." Some educators have become seriously concerned about the kinds of the activities engaged in under this banner. Too often early identification has been little more than early labelling of children. This early labelling can result in early assignment of some children to failure.

To be more explicit, what too often happens in early identification programs is that a battery of tests is put together consisting of various activities that correlate with reading success or failure. These activities may be anything from the ability to copy geometric forms to the ability to walk a balance beam. Investigators then test kindergarten children with these activities, classify the children according to the results of the testing, and then give a reading achievement test at the end of first grade to verify the self-fulfilling prophecy that they established: Children who scored low on the items that correlated with reading success were indeed the ones who were not successful in reading. And so the investigators congratulate themselves on having successfully predicted reading failure.

As reported in Chapter 2, Fry demonstrated how well this classification for failure can work. Children do "learn to read if they are taught to read" (p. 5), and they will not learn to read if we deprive them of the opportunity to learn.

It is not the task of educators, any more than it is the task of parents, to *predict* reading failure; the task is to *prevent* that failure. This prevention entails not merely testing with items that correlate with reading success or failure; it entails testing diagnostically to discover what the youngster needs or doesn't need in order to be successful, and it must include follow-up of that diagnostic testing with instruction in the areas of weakness.

Probably the first point to be clarified in regard to the preceding comments is the business of "correlation." Merely because two items correlate well with one another does not necessarily mean that one causes the other. For example, it should be obvious that there is a high correlation between the height of elementary school children and their reading achievement: Sixth graders are taller than kindergarten children and they also read better. This correlation certainly does not mean that if you make a child taller, he will be a better reader. Correlation merely indicates the two factors fluctuate together, either directly or inversely.

Factors Often Considered in Early Identification

DeHirsch and others compiled an excellent summary of factors related to reading failure. While their study was a correlational one and involved only fifty-three children, they administered a total of thirty-seven tests to these children and correlated the results with reading, spelling, and writing achievement at the end of second grade. In their report, they summarized evidence on the various factors often considered in early identification. Most helpful is the direction their summary ought to give educators in terms of recognizing that reading failure is not something to blame on the child. It's time for us as educators to look at ourselves and what we're doing or not doing in order to explain why a youngster is not successful in reading.

In reviewing various factors within the child or related to the child, Jansky and deHirsch pointed out that these are usually not important factors. For example, chronological age is not related significantly to reading achievement, even in terms of correlation. Further evidence on this point was presented in Chapter 2.

Jansky and deHirsch also pointed out that, according to the evidence, socioeconomic status was not a significant factor in reading success or failure. Whether other research verifies this claim or not, the point is an important one to make in terms of our attitudes. Too often low socioeconomic status has been used as an excuse for not teaching. Furthermore, back to the diagnostic point, socioeconomic status is not an item of information that the educator is likely to be able to change, so it has no implication for instruction.

These same investigators also reported that while a few children do have serious neurological deficits, such deficits were not the cause of most children's reading disability. This position is in agreement with the summary by Bond and Tinker. Related to neurological development is the question of laterality, which ought to be dismissed as a concern in the area of reading (Hillerich, 1964).

While emotional problems may be a factor among some children, this has been a most difficult area to investigate; and much more research is needed. The general evidence suggests that research has not identified which came first, the emotional problem or the reading problem. Obviously, one can aggravate the other. It might be suggested that success in reading through appropriate instruction in the skills will certainly not intensify a preexisting emotional problem. On the other hand, lack of success in reading is most likely to aggravate the emotional problem. To put it another way, the existence of emotional problems may indicate the need for additional help with those problems, but it does not suggest that appropriate instruction be avoided.

As discussed in Chapter 2, reading readiness tests have been a way of life with kindergarten teachers for many years. Unfortunately, while they are a tradition, their use for individual children has very little justification. As Jansky and deHirsch pointed out, the results of such tests should never be used to classify an individual child. Karlin found that the predictive value of a reading readiness test was about 4 percent better than chance.

Teacher judgment was reported by Jansky and deHirsch to be a reliable indicator or predictor of reading success or failure. This author would certainly verify that point from experience in working with kindergarten teachers. Whenever the kindergarten teacher, in a summary report, used the word *immature,* this was a red flag that reliably indicated a child who was likely to have difficulty in reading later on.

Most of the commonly discussed items above have little or no relationship to future reading success or failure. Teacher judgment is an exception. On the other hand, all of these items—including teacher judgment—are of little value in diagnosing what instruction is required to avoid having difficulty in the future—the task is not to *predict* but to *identify* diagnostically where the youngster needs help so that help can be provided.

Of the thirty-seven tests administered in the deHirsch studies, most correlated significantly with reading success or failure. However, the fact that they correlated significantly needs to be examined. Statistical "significance" merely means that given the same procedures and the same type population, the investigator is most likely to get the same results. It does not mean that the correlation is necessarily dependable in terms of the accuracy of prediction. For example, the test that correlated most highly with reading success was a test of the child's knowledge of letter names. This correlation was only .55, which means—in terms of predictive value— that it was only about 16 percent better than chance.

The predictive value of a test of letter names has been known for many years. As the major contributor on this point, Durrell found that knowledge of letter names was the best single predictor of reading success. On the other hand, the reader is reminded once more that correlation does not imply cause-effect. The case of letter names and their teaching is discussed in Chapter 4.

The five best predictors from the deHirsch study, in addition to letter names, included picture names, word matching, items from the *Bender Motor Gestalt Test,* and sentence memory items. Considering these individually, one might identify the ability to name pictures and sentence memory as two subtests that do have diagnostic value. Going back to comments in the early part of this chapter, mastery of the language in terms of general vocabulary and in terms of language development are essential if one is to be successful in learning to read.

Word matching, which has to do with the visual discrimination of words, may relate to reading success if one considers that the child doesn't notice fine differences in observed items. On the other hand, lack of this particular ability might be questioned even in the case of a four year old. More specific needs along this line are discussed in Chapter 4.

The copying of geometric shapes, such as those included in the *Bender Gestalt,* has been an element in most reading readiness tests since they were developed. The fact that this ability correlates with reading achievement has been known for a long time. On the other hand, there is absolutely no evidence that the ability to copy geometric forms is necessary in order to be able to learn to read. In fact, when one gets into this area of visual motor development, there is considerable evidence that training in visual motor skills does not contribute to reading success (Cohen; Hammill, 1972; Jensen and King).

Since we are concerned in this book only with the relationship of these items to reading success, we might stop at this point. However, Hammill (1974) went a step further: He indicated in his summary of the research in this area that training in visual motor activities does not even develop visual motor skill.

A Diagnostic Approach to Early Identification

As educators we ought to be anxious to move into the area of determining needs and avoiding reading failure. In order to do this, we need to take a diagnostic approach to early identification. We need to discover what essential background, experiences, and skills children have and which they don't have, and to provide the ones they need so they can be successful in future reading activities. Hence, we need to consider what the necessary elements are for success in reading.

The act of reading involves the ability to function in the language, that is, to think in the language. This means children must have a certain meaningful vocabulary and control over the syntax of the language. This, in turn, presumes auditory discrimination ability, that is, the ability to hear differences in the sounds in words. In addition, it should be obvious that the act of reading involves printed symbols, so visual discrimination of letters and words is necessary. In order for youngsters to be successful, certain physical conditions are also important: They need to have adequate vision, auditory acuity, and a general physical health that will enable them to devote their energies to the learning task.

These prerequisites must exist in the child who is going to be introduced to basic reading skills; for those who lack them, the prerequisites themselves must be supplied. A lack or a deficit in these areas is not a signal to avoid instruction and to wait; it is a signal to provide even more intensified efforts at instruction, so that child will be given the background he lacks.

Specifically, a diagnostic approach to early identification should include a battery of tests to identify children's development in terms of the preceding language and physical health items. This battery ought to incorporate items such as the following:

1. Auditory Discrimination. As indicated early in this chapter, it is most doubtful that any child who speaks his native language has a problem in this area. Those who disagree with this point often base their position on experiences with the *Wepman Auditory Discrimination Test* (1958). That test was criticized by Flower as being more a test of auditory memory than one of auditory discrimination. In fact, comparisons of results on the *Wepman* and *PDQ* (Hillerich, 1974)—the latter using picture pairs—indicated that five year olds made as many as ten times the number of errors *on the same sound contrasts* when using the *Wepman*.

   The child being tested should be shown pairs of pictures and told that the examiner will name two pictures and ask him to point to one. If the child consistently points to the designated picture, that child obviously can hear the difference between minimal pairs. The testing should range through the speech categories and should include sounds in initial position, such as *wing/ring;* final position, *Ruth/roof;* and vowel sounds, such as *pin/pen.*

2. Listening Comprehension. Read a short paragraph or story to the child and then ask what the story was about.

3. Vocabulary. Present pictures of common items that a kindergarten youngster is expected to recognize and have the child name the pictures.

4. Relationship Words. The basic words that the child ought to demonstrate understanding of are words such as *in, under, on, beside, little, big, top, bottom, front, back.* Test these words with manipulative objects by having the child put the block *in* the box, and so on.

5. Sequence. This can be tested in two ways. In one method, have the child recall the order in which events happened in a story read to him; secondly, have the child arrange in order three or four pictures to tell a story.

6. Oral Language Development. Have the child tell a story about a set of pictures arranged in sequence. This story should be recorded on tape and then analyzed for length of T-units. This particular measure of language development was found by Hunt to be the best single measure of mastery of language.

   A T-unit (minimal terminal unit) is an independent clause with all of its modifiers and subordinate clauses. Essentially, it is the same as a sentence, except if one used words per sentence as a measure, five year olds would speak in 150-word sentences because they tend to string sentence after sentence together with *and.*

   To measure words per T-unit, the teacher need only count the total number of words used and divide by the number of T-units. Garbles and repetitions are not counted in the word count.

7. Following Oral Directions. To test this ability, give the child one-, two-, and three-step directions orally, as suggested earlier in this chapter.

8. Using Oral Context. To test this ability, give the child oral sentences with a word missing, as demonstrated earlier in this chapter.

Finally, in testing visual and auditory acuity, the former should always include a test at near point, since this is the reading distance. Auditory acuity should be tested with any clear tone audiometer. While deficits in vision and hearing have not been identified as serious contributors to reading disability, it only makes good sense to remove any of these kinds of problems the youngster might have before attempting instruction.

The results of a pilot test for early diagnosis, based on testing 153 entering kindergarteners, provided evidence that traditional kindergarten programs were not adequately meeting the needs of children in the 1970s (Hillerich, 1976). Kindergarten teachers in a blue-collar community were surprised at the level of language development demonstrated by most of the children they received. On the other hand, since the purpose of early identification ought to be diagnostic with the intent of individualizing, there was surprise at the serious lack of basic language skills that was apparent with a few of the entering kindergarten children.

There was not—and need not be—any attempt to provide norms for this kind of test. The test was a criterion test: The intent was to discover whether or not each child could perform these activities and, if any could not, to provide instruction that would enable them to perform adequately in the language. Educators ought to be less concerned about what percentage of children can or cannot perform such activities and more concerned about whether or not the child at hand can perform them. Therefore, a norm-referenced test would be inappropriate. In fact, as pointed out by Jansky and deHirsch, we can't really talk about norms when we talk about the four and five year old because variation is the norm.

Follow-Up of Early Identification

The pilot tests for early diagnosis just described were revised (Hillerich, 1974) and, with the help of a grant from the Edyth Bush Charitable Foundation, were administered to 916 entering kindergarten children in three school districts. The project was designed, first of all, to test kindergarten children diagnostically the week before school started, then to provide a more individualized kindergarten program based on the results of the diagnostic testing. The effectiveness of this procedure was to be evaluated at the end of first grade in terms of the reading achievement of these children compared with control groups that did not experience the early diagnostic procedure.

While results of reading achievement testing are not in as yet, the effect on the kindergarten program has been reported by the kindergarten teachers and observed by this author. First of all, one might question introducing five year olds to school through a testing procedure. This certainly presented no problem since the kinds of tests described were nonthreatening and success insured: They were tests at which no four or five year old could "fail" in his own eyes. Kindergarten teachers reported that this was the most pleasant introduction they had ever provided for entering kindergarten children. Of the 916 children, one of the comments was that there were only one or two separation problems or cases of crying on the first day of regular kindergarten, as compared with the much greater number that usually occurred.

The testing itself was much less involved than it might sound and took only fifteen minutes per child. Naturally, this kind of testing must be done on an individual basis and, to be most beneficial, ought to be done the week before children actually begin nursery school or kindergarten, so the teacher has results from the very beginning. Further, that testing ought to be done by the teacher, so the child has the advantage of becoming acquainted with that teacher and also because the teacher is the one who will benefit most from the personal insights gained from the testing.

As others had stated in the pilot, kindergarten teachers in this study reported that it was enlightening to see the great deal of language development among most of the children and to discover that a few children came to school with so much less than they had assumed every four or five year old had accomplished.

Once more, the reader is reminded that norms are not the goal in this kind of testing; however, for the reader's benefit, Table 1 indicates averages from the diagnostic testing of the 916 entering kindergarten children.

Table 1. *Average PDQ Test Scores of Entering Kindergarten Children in Three School Districts, 1974–75 (N = 916)*

Subtest	Average Score	Possible Score
Auditory Discrimination	37.1	39.0
Listening Comprehension (Memories)	4.0	6.0
Vocabulary (Picture Names)	31.2	36.0
Relationship Words	11.6	13.0
Recalling Sequence from a Story	48.0%	100.0%
Oral Language Development	5.2/T-unit	—
Following Oral Directions	10.9	12.0
Using Oral Context	6.6	7.0

As shown in Table 1, auditory discrimination was certainly not a problem with most children, nor was the understanding of relationship words, the ability to follow oral directions, or even the ability to use oral context. The oral language development, 5.2 words per T-unit, was about the same as found in other research: Typical kindergarten children might be expected to range somewhere around five to six words per T-unit (Loban; Templin).

Armed with this kind of information about each child in the first week of school, the kindergarten teacher was prepared to carry on a more individualized program, making use of the activities suggested in the early part of this chapter for those children who needed experience in certain areas.

Another thought is in order about this kind of testing: Such testing informs a kindergarten teacher about what the child *can do* and not necessarily about what he *will do* in a group situation; it appears to measure the child's maximum capability. In a few isolated instances, children behaved initially in a way suggesting less competence than the teacher had identified on the test. Having the test results, the teacher did not beome concerned as he might have done without preliminary information about the child. For example, there was one child who, in the first two weeks of school, did not communicate either with the teacher or with peers. Under other circumstances, this may have been cause for concern, but the teacher knew this was a child who had shown an excellent mastery of the English language. Possibly, he happened to be a child who was smart enough not to stick his neck out until he knew what was going on.

SUMMARY

This chapter presented an outline of some of the basic language understandings and skills that are prerequisites for any kind of success in reading. It included various procedures and activities that can be used with children who need more development in these areas. Finally, it reviewed some of the elements that ought to be considered—as compared with the elements that are often considered—if educators are concerned about a diagnostic approach to early identification rather than about the mere prediction of reading success or failure.

Efforts at early diagnosis indicated that most kindergarten children came to school with adequate preparation in the language, and were ready to begin more formalized reading instruction. These efforts also revealed that a few came to school needing a great deal of background development in language before being faced with any kind of skills instruction in reading. These are the kinds of discoveries with which early identification ought to be concerned.

References

Bond, Guy, and Tinker, Miles. *Reading Difficulties: Their Diagnosis and Treatment.* New York: Appleton-Century-Crofts, 1973.

Cohen, S. Alan. "Studies in Visual Perception and Reading in Disadvantaged Children." *Journal of Learning Disabilities* 2(1969):498–503.

deHirsch, Katrina; Jansky, Jeannette J.; and Langford, William S. *Predicting Reading Failure.* New York: Harper & Row, Publishers, 1966.

Durrell, Donald; Nicholson, Alice; Olson, Arthur V.; Gavel, Sylvia R.; and Linehan, Eleanor B. "Success in First Grade Reading." *Journal of Education* 140(1958). Boston: Boston University School of Education, 1958.

Flower, Richard. "The Evaluation of Auditory Abilities in the Appraisal of Children with Reading Problems." In *Perception and Reading,* edited by Helen K. Smith, pp. 21–24. Newark: International Reading Association, 1968.

Fry, Edward. "Are Reading Readiness Materials Necessary in the First Grade?" Paper presented at American Educational Research Association annual meeting. Chicago, February 1965.

Hammill, Donald. "Training Visual Perceptual Processes." *Journal of Learning Disabilities* 5(1972):552–59.

Hammill, Donald; Goodman, Libby; and Wiederholt, J. Lee. "Visual-Motor Processes: Can We Train Them?" *The Reading Teacher* 27(1974):469–78.

Hillerich, Robert L. "Eye-Hand Dominance and Reading Achievement." *American Educational Research Journal* 1(1964):121–26.

———. "An Interpretation of Research in Reading Readiness." *Elementary English* 43(1966):359–64, 372.

———. *PDQ: A Diagnostic Approach to Early Identification of the Pre-Reading Language Needs for Four- and Five-Year-Olds.* Wilmette: Eduscope, 1974.

———. "Predicting Reading Success." Unpublished manuscript, 1976. (Available from 1311 Bourgogne, Bowling Green, OH 43402.)

Hunt, Kellogg. *Grammatical Structure Written at Three Grade Levels.* Champaign: National Council of Teachers of English, 1965.

Jansky, Jeannette, and deHirsch, Katrina. *Preventing Reading Failure.* New York: Harper & Row, Publishers, 1972.

Jensen, Norma, and King, Ethel. "Effects of Different Kinds of Visual Motor Discrimination Training on Learning to Read Words." *Journal of Educational Psychology* 61 (1970):90–96.

Karlin, Robert. "The Prediction of Reading Success and Reading Readiness Tests." *Elementary English* 34(1957):320–22.

Loban, Walter D. *The Language of Elementary School Children*. Champaign: National Council of Teachers of English, 1963.

Muehl, Sigmar. "The Effects of Letter-Name Knowledge on Learning to Read a Word List in Kindergarten Children." *Journal of Educational Psychology* 53(1962):181–86.

Templin, Mildred. *Certain Language Skills in Children: Their Development and Inter-relationships*. Minneapolis: University of Minnesota Press, 1957.

Wepman, Joseph. *Auditory Discrimination Test*. Chicago: Joseph Wepman, 1958.

Wolf, Lois. *Reading Readiness: An Experimental Study of the Effects of Specific Reading Skills Instruction on Sixty-Three Four Year Olds in Winnetka, Illinois*. Master's thesis, National College, 1972.

4

Prereading: Foundation Skills in Decoding

Once children demonstrate the ability to function in the language as suggested in Chapter 3, they are ready to take the next step toward reading success whether they are six years old, five years old, or four years old.

This chapter presents a sequence of skills, the instructional purposes behind them, and suggested teaching activities that will contribute to their development.

Overview of Skills

The skills themselves consist of the ability to use oral context, to discriminate letter forms, to identify beginning sounds, to associate consonant letters with the sounds they represent, and to use oral context along with the letter-sound associations to read a printed word. In addition, whether one wants to classify the balance of this chapter as the end of "prereading" or the beginning of "reading," children also need to develop the habit of left-to-right movement when faced with printed material, and they need to be able to recognize certain high-frequency words.

Some of the prereading skills must be developed prior to others: They have a necessary sequence. Others are interchangeable. It makes sense to begin with the use of oral context, since this is such an easy and natural thing for children to do. Work on letter form discrimination and listening for beginning sounds can be interchanged, since one is not dependent on the other. Obviously, letter-sound association must follow work with both letter form discrimination and work with beginning sounds. Use of these skills to read a printed word must also be the last step in the series.

Left-to-right orientation can be a continuing process and will be discussed in the section devoted to it. Recognition of high-frequency words can be conducted along with the other activities, shortly after children have developed some of the letter-sound associations.

Using Oral Context

This skill is an excellent one with which to begin at the four- or five-year-old level since children who speak and understand their native language already intuitively use oral context as they listen and anticipate words that would make sense. The purpose of this activity with preschool children is not to *teach* them to use oral context; its purpose is, first of all, to make them consciously aware of their ability to use the sense of other spoken words in order to supply a missing word and, secondly, to make them aware that more than one word will make sense if only context is used. Hence, this two-fold purpose prepares youngsters to use printed context in reading, and it makes them aware that they need more than context in order to be certain of the precise word intended. Conversely, it lays a foundation to help them avoid becoming merely context "guessers" or, at the other extreme, it helps them avoid becoming letter-by-letter "sounder outers" of words.

This awareness may begin by merely saying to the children that you are going to tell them something but will stop before you finish. They are to tell you what word they think you were going to say. For example, "At the grocery store I bought some _____." Children may supply any word that makes sense. (See Chapter 3 for activities.)

When children in the group make up sentences for others to complete, they should understand that others need not supply the exact word so long as the words suggested make sense in the context.

As you read a story to children, pause once in awhile before reading a word that is in strong context. Let children supply the word they think you were about to read. Naturally, you would not want to do this so often that they lose interest in the story.

While such practice will undoubtedly increase the vocabularies of some of the children in the group, this is not the prime purpose for practice in using oral context. It is usually better to try for no more than two or three words before going on to the next sentence; there is no need to try to pull from children all possible words that would make sense in a given context.

Discriminating Letter Forms

It is most important that the teacher be aware of *what* must be taught under this heading. Hence, we need some clarification of the current interest in letter names and the relationship between this knowledge and reading success.

Durrell and others reported a series of studies at Boston University that began to establish an influential pattern. Nicholson, testing over 2,000 first-grade children, found that those children were well beyond the point where gross discrimination activities—for example, discriminating geometric forms—were useful; in fact, in her words, traditional readiness programs were "a waste of time."

Olson then followed over a thousand of these same children through February of first grade and found that knowledge of letter names and the ability to write letters correlated .55 with reading achievement. Since that time numerous studies have been reported demonstrating that a simple test of knowledge of letter names is as good as any reading readiness test for prediction of future reading success (McHugh; Johnson; Barrett). Another study indicated a correlation of .69 between knowledge of letter names at the beginning of kindergarten and reading success at the end of first grade (Hillerich, 1966d).

Such findings have led to an unjustified and unwarranted emphasis on teaching letter names to children. While Johnson did verify the correlation, he found no significant difference between the reading achievement of children who were and those were not taught letter names. Silverberg and others compared four classes of kindergarten children: Two classes were taught letter names and two classes had a traditional informal program. These investigators found that the children who were taught letter names learned them, but there was no significant difference in reading achievement between the groups at the end of grade one.

Samuels, in a study that involved one hundred first-grade children, found no significant difference in reading achievement between groups that had been taught letter names and those that had not been taught them.

Jenkins and others compared the ease of learning letter names with the ease of learning letter sounds and the transfer value of each in the case of ninety-six first-grade children. As one might expect, they found that letter names were easier to learn than the letter-sound associations, but it was the latter that had transfer value to reading success.

It should be apparent that beginning readers do not need to know the names of the letters in order to be able to read; however, they do need to know the sound representations for those letters. In fact, Muehl found that too much stress on letter names could become a handicap in reading: Children so drilled tended to go through an intermediate step of naming the first letter of a word before beginning to say it.

Applying common sense to Muehl's findings, the reader should recognize that half of the consonant letters in English have names that do not begin with the sound those letters usually represent. For example, the name of the letter *b* would be quite satisfactory since its name "bee" begins with the same sound the letter usually represents at the beginning of a word. On the other hand, *c, f, g, h, l, m, n, r, s, w,* and *y* do not have names that begin with the sound each of those letters usually represents.

As suggested elsewhere (Hillerich, 1966c), the high correlation between knowledge of letter names and reading success is undoubtedly no more than a demonstration of the past experience and ability of the child—experience or exposure to print and the ability to retain some of the learnings from that experience.

The task of learning to discriminate letter forms is not one of learning letter names, nor is it one of learning to *see* differences in letters. The task is one of attending to the fine detail that differentiates one letter from another. This would include noting such points as the extra hump that distinguishes *m* from *n* or the mere change in direction that differentiates *b* from *d,* and *p* from *q*.

In the process of providing practice in discriminating letter forms, it is only sensible to use the names of letters referred to. However, as already pointed out, excessive drill on the names is not the important goal, since it is ultimately the letter-sound association that is necessary in learning to read.

Work on letter form discrimination should be handled in cycles to provide for variety in the program. In other words, a group of four to six letters should be developed through each stage: Discriminating letter forms, listening for beginning sounds, associating letters and sounds, and through the final stage of using oral context with the letter-sound associations to read printed words beginning with those consonants.

While there is no need to establish associations for *x* or *z* (no primary word begins with *x; zoo* is the only *z* word and children learn this early), the question remains: With what group of letters shall we begin? A number of sequences are justifiable. For example, one might begin by following a sequence based on frequency of use in initial position. If so, based on a list of 3,455 most frequently used words (Hillerich, 1976) and ignoring sound values of letters, the sequence, from most to least frequent, would be:

1. s, c, b, p, t, d
2. f, a, m, r, e, w
3. h, l, g, i, n, o
4. u, v, j, k, y, q

On the other hand, Cohn found that frequency of error and frequency of use were unrelated. Hence, one might look at sequences in order of difficulty. Even here, however, there are choices to be made. For example, Nicholson reported an order in terms of the ability to name lowercase letters:

1. o, s, c, i, p, y
2. k, m, w, e, a, n
3. r, t, j, v, u, f
4. b, h, g, d, l, q

Since we are ultimately concerned with the development of letter-sound associations, perhaps Nicholson's sequence based on the ability to give sounds for the lowercase letters should be used:

1. s, o, t, k, p
2. m, j, b, n, c
3. g, a, h, r, v
4. f, e, d, i, l
5. w, u, y

In the absence of clear research evidence, one is free to select whatever set of four to six letters preferred and to begin instruction in letter form discrimination. Even the traditional practice of separating confusable letters such as *m/n, b/d* is not justified in the research. In fact, Williams found that it was better to teach confusable items together to help children notice the slight differences between them.

Groff suggested the following adapted sequence:

1. t, s, l, c, a
2. f, m, b, r, o
3. h, w, p, v, e
4. d, n, k, g, i
5. j, z, q, x, y, u

Groff's sequence might be followed except for possible questions about the placements of *l, p,* and *v.* Lowercase *l* is one of the most difficult letters for children to recognize; *p* is easy and frequently used; *v* is seldom used in initial position in young children's reading material.

Any sequence for teaching should be based on a combination of factors: (1) discriminability and demonstrability of the sounds is important in the early stages; (2) ease of learning, as reported by Nicholson, ought to be considered; and (3) frequency of use is important if children are to apply their skills. Finally, while letter-sound associations usually are not developed for vowels, the vowels ought to be part of the letter form discrimination activities.

Based on these premises, the following sequence of sets is suggested:

1. s, t, m, p, o
2. b, c, r, f, a
3. d, n, w, g, i
4. h, l, k, j, e
5. y, v, q, u
6. th, sh, ch

The first cycle of letters is *s, t, m, p, o.* The easiest stage in work on letter form discrimination is to use simple one-to-one correspondence. Put these five letters in any sequence in a row, for example, *s, o, t, p, m.* Then, in a row below this sequence, put the same letters in the same sequence with the exception of two letters, which should be transposed, for example, *s, o, t, m, p.* Letter by letter, point to the pairs and ask the children if they are the same or different. Then have a child suggest rearrangement of the second row of letters, so it is exactly like the first.

Practice of this kind can be followed by providing each child with a small set of individual letter cards. Hold up a letter and ask the children to hold up the same letter from their sets. In order to keep the practice as close as possible to reading behavior, it is better to *show* a letter and ask children to find the same letter, rather than to *say* the name of a letter and ask children to find it. In reading, children actually see the letters; they don't hear someone say their names.

Such activities can be followed with individual work. A scrap of newspaper can be given to each child. On the paper, print with a felt marker whatever letter the children are working on. Then have them use crayon or pencil to mark all the examples of that letter they can find.

The emphasis in letter form discrimination should be on lowercase letters, since these are most frequently encountered at the beginnings of words. At this point, however, children should also have experience with the capital forms of the letters and can do some activities that require merely matching the lowercase with the capital form of the same letter.

The following activities may be used with preschool children or in kindergarten to provide additional practice in letter form discrimination:

1. Matching Letters. Write five or six letters on the chalkboard, mixing both capital and lowercase forms. Have individual children connect the lowercase letters with their capital forms.

2. Finding Letters. Use word game sets, such as Scrabble, to have the child find all copies of a given letter form.

3. Race. Two children, each with a small set of letter cards, stand side by side some distance away from the teacher. The teacher will hold up a letter one at a time. The first child to show the new letter takes one step toward the teacher. The winner is the first one to reach the teacher.

4. Fruit Basket. Children form a circle with one child in the middle. Each child has a card with one capital or lowercase letter on it. Duplicate letters are used. The

child in the center holds up two letters and the children with these letters change seats. The leader tries to get a seat also, and the child left standing calls the next letter.

5. Letter Rhythms. Children sit in a circle, each with a letter card. There are two cards for each letter. As the music is played, cards are passed around the circle in time to the music. When the music stops, the teacher calls on one child who stands and shows the card. The child who has the same letter also stands. If a child misses, he sits in the center. If a second child misses, the first one may reenter the circle.

6. Make: Believe Stream. A "stream" goes through the middle of the circle. Letter cards are used for stepping stones and placed across the stream. A child names the letters before he steps on them and tries to get across the stream without falling in, or miscalling, a letter.

7. Go Fish. After four or five letters are introduced, give the children a bowl in which they can "fish" for their letter of the day. Let them find matching letters hidden in the room.

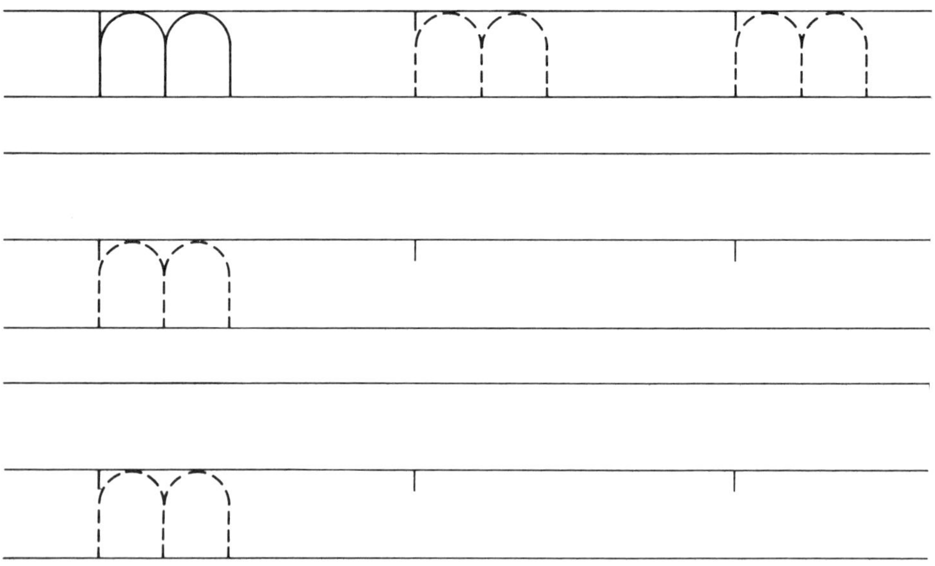

Figure 1. *Practice sheet for letter* m.

A good culminating activity with a given set of letters is to gather the children around an easel or chalkboard. Write the lowercase form of one of the letters studied, for example, *s*. With a box of colored chalk or crayons nearby, ask individual children to come up and make a "green letter *s*," "red letter *s*," and so on. When all have had a turn and it appears they have noticed the detail of that letter formation, a final activity might be to distribute a duplicated sheet on which there may be six to nine opportunities to practice the formation of the letter, as shown in Figure 1.

The purpose of this activity is not to teach handwriting; it is to be certain that with a kinesthetic approach, children are paying attention to the detail of the letter forms under consideration. If this stage—the formation of letters—is to take place in nursery school or kindergarten, the teacher should have a copy of the manuscript style used in first grade, so children begin the formation of the letters in the proper spot.

Identifying Beginning Sounds

As discussed previously (see Chapter 2), children who already speak their native language do not need to be taught to hear differences in sounds. On the other hand, children do need to be taught what is meant by "the beginning" of a spoken word. In fact, there is no reason to think that children in the preschool years even have a clear understanding of what a word is. In the act of saying a sentence, we run words together and often have longer breaks between two syllables in a word than between some sets of words: "She's a nice person" might be said "Shesanice per son." The whole sentence might even seem, to the preschool child, like one glob of sound and be interpreted as one word. That child certainly has no reason to think of spoken words as having beginnings and endings, and—unlike the adult—that child may not have had the advantage of seeing words pointed out in print, where it's very easy to classify a word as a collection of letters separated from other collections of letters by extra white space.

The primary purpose of this activity is to teach children what is meant by "the beginning" of a spoken word. A secondary purpose is to provide practice in classifying words by their beginning sounds. To say that there is no need to teach children to *hear* beginning sounds in no way implies that teaching them what is meant by the beginning of a spoken word is an easy task; it is a very difficult one, but it ought to be easier if we understand what the task is.

A teacher or parent can clarify the meaning of "beginning sound" by using the following principle. Take a picture of a house. Hold it up and say, "Is this a picture of a mouse?" The child will correct, "No, house." Then say, "Oh, is it bouse?" After several changes and corrections, tell the child, "Do you know what I did? I changed the beginning sound." Then take another picture and do the same thing.

Incidentally, be certain children recognize the pictures used and call them by the name you expect. This author once made the mistake with kindergartners of holding up a picture of a hammer and asking "Is this a bammer?" The children agreed that it was!

After changing the names of a few pictures, you will find some children beginning to get the idea, and they can be allowed to change the names of pictures for other children.

In working with beginning sounds, you will use words that begin with the sounds of the four consonant letters already developed in letter form discrimination, in this case, *s, p, m, t*. Children, of course, are not aware of this fact, since you are talking only about sounds, without reference to letters at this point.

In the process of working with beginning sounds through the use of pictures, it is imperative that you identify the names of the pictures for children, since there are few pictures that cannot be called by more than one name. Secondly, in naming the pictures, drop the article so that the beginning sound stands out clearly; for example, do not say "a, house" but say "house." Also, in the process of asking children about beginning sounds of picture names or words, our instructional language must be clear: We never ask children if *house* and *mouse* "sound the same" because they do in the middle and at the end; ask either "Do they begin with the same sound?" or "Do they start the same?"

Finally, as discussed in Chapter 1, consonant sounds should never be pronounced in isolation. Any attempt to pronounce /p/ in isolation will result in /pə/ or even /pəh/. The sound is referred to as "the sound you hear at the beginning of _____." If a child is having difficulty in identifying beginning sounds in the names of two pictures, exaggerate the beginning sound as you pronounce the name or show the position of your mouth to contrast the names.

Once children begin to get the idea of what is meant, move on to activities involving the set of beginning sounds you are going to work on. Further clarification of "beginning" sound will come as children participate in classifying activities. One of the easiest activities is to start with two of the sounds, the sound heard at the beginning of *sun* and of *pipe.* Put a picture of a sun at the beginning of one row in the pocket chart and a picture of a pipe in the next. Mix about six picture cards, three for each of the two sounds, and have the children say the name of a picture and decide if its name begins like *sun* or like *pipe.* Do this by having the selected child say the name of the picture you hold and then the name of each key picture with which to pair the beginning sounds. The selected picture may be placed by the child beside the key picture that has the same beginning sound. The names of the key picture and the newly placed picture should be repeated by the group as a check and for further auditory practice.

Other activities may then follow, where the group will concentrate on one of the beginning sounds at a time. For example, take a set of four picture cards, three with names beginning with the same sound and one with a name that does not. As you put the four pictures in the pocket chart, say their names: *soap, sun, house, sign.* Have the children identify which one does not begin with the same sound as the others. Continue with other sets of pictures.

In working with children on beginning sounds, it is important that we truly note sound and not spelling. For example, the child who says *circus* begins with the same sound as *sun* is correct. Any such matching should be complimented. On the other hand, there is no point in the teacher deliberately providing youngsters with matching words or pictures whose names are spelled differently at the beginning.

Along this same line, while we always accept and compliment the child's statement that *truck* and *tree* begin with the same sound as *tooth,* we should try to avoid setting up situations where consonant clusters begin the name of a picture, since the second consonant sound comes so close that it could interfere with the clarity of the initial consonant sound.

In all the following activities, children should *say* the names of the pictures or objects they are using. This auditory experience is very important in helping to clarify the meaning of "beginning sound" and in providing practice in listening for the different sounds. The activities are arranged in an approximate order of difficulty: It is easier to identify pictures or objects whose names begin with a given sound than it is to think up or to draw the appropriate pictures.

1. Changing Names. While working with a given beginning sound, have all the children change their names to conform with the sound on which they are working. If the sound is that heard at the beginning of *mask,* then children's names become Mob for Bob, Med for Ted, Meth for Beth, and so on.

2. Treasure Hunt Number 1. Have the children see how many things they can find in the room whose names begin with the sound heard at the beginning of the word *sun.*

3. Treasure Hunt Number 2. In various parts of the room, place objects or envelopes, each with a picture in it. Divide children into teams and have a captain for each team. Each captain receives an envelope, and the teams hunt for objects whose names begin with the same sound as the name of the picture on the envelope. The captain checks to see that objects are matched correctly.

4. Sound Page. Give the children a paper with a picture at the top. Have them cut out and paste on the page all the pictures they can find whose names begin with the sound heard at the beginning of the word *sun.* (This activity may be done individually or as a group.)

5. Beginning Sound Lotto Number 1. Paste six pictures on 8 × 11-inch tagboard. Have the children match other pictures to the large card by beginning sound. The winner is the first to cover all six pictures.

6. Beginning Sound Lotto Number 2. Make three large cards, each with a picture whose name begins with a consonant sound. Have twelve smaller picture cards, four for each sound. Children must match the four smaller cards with each large card.

7. Fish. Deal five picture cards to each child. Place the remainder of the deck in a center pile. The first placer asks another player, "Do you have a picture card whose name begins like _____?" (Names picture card in hand.) If a pair is made with the other player's card, the first player gets another turn; if not, he draws a card from the pile and the next player has a turn. Winner is the first player to match all cards.

8. Concentration. Picture cards are placed facedown on the table and players take turns turning up any two cards. If a match is made (same beginning sound), the set of cards is kept by the player and that player continues until no match is made. The winner is the player with the most cards when all are gone.

9. Racing Game. The class is divided into two teams. Two small boxes are placed in the front of the room, each labelled with a different picture. Small objects and/or pictures are scattered around the room. One team finds all the pictures or objects whose names begin with the same sound as the picture on one box. The other team does the same with the picture on the second box. The winning team is the one with the most correct items in their box at the end of a period of time.

10. Magic Sound. Pictures of objects whose names begin with various initial consonant sounds are passed out. The teacher (or child) calls out for all pictures whose names begin like *sun.* All children who have appropriate pictures take turns saying the name of their pictures and skipping around the room.

11. Name Game Number 1. Spread pictures on the floor, one for each child, and say, "Find a picture whose name begins with the same sound as your name."

12. Name Game Number 2. Ask each child to point to all things in the room with names that begin with the same sound as the child's first or last name.

13. Name Game Number 3. The children form a circle. They say their names individually and then name an object whose name begins with the same sound.

14. Knock, Knock. One child is "it" and covers his eyes. Another child stands behind "it" and says, "Someone's knocking at your door. My name begins like _____." If "it" guesses correctly, he stays for another turn; if not, the one who knocked becomes "it."

15. Animal Party. Peter Pig, Sally Seal, etc. all find gifts (pictures) whose names begin with the same sound as their names.

16. Going Fishing. Make construction paper fish that are about five inches long. Paste a picture whose name begins with a consonant sound on each fish. Put a paper clip on each and place them in a cardboard "pond." Make a fishing pole of string and a magnet. Each child "fishes," and when they catch a fish, they say, "I caught a fish whose name begins like _____." (The child gives another word beginning with the same sound.) If correct, the fish is caught; if not, the fish is thrown back.

17. Sound Relay. Place pictures whose names begin with several different consonants on the floor. Line the children up in three or more rows as relay teams. Say, "I'm looking for a picture whose name begins with the same sound as _____." The first child in each row runs to get the picture. The winner is the team with the most cards.

18. Magic Castle. Pass pictures around a circle while music is playing. When the music stops, say, "If you have a picture whose name begins like _____ , you may come to my magic castle."

19. Train Ride. Line up chairs as a train. Play as in activity 18.

20. Sound Hunt. Pass out big pictures, two for each sound. Each child finds a partner with a picture whose name begins like the name of his picture.

21. Hang large magazine pictures (one for each of the consonant sounds under consideration) around the walls. As music plays, the children skip around the room. When the music stops, each child gives a word that begins like the name of the picture he is standing beside.

22. Sound Chairs. Play like musical chairs, except use words instead of music. When a word with the predetermined beginning sound is mentioned, children try to get a chair.

23. Sound Bingo. Use cards with pictures instead of letters in the squares. The caller may either hold up a picture or call out a word, and players cover the picture whose name begins with the same sound.

24. Grocery Store. Distribute pictures of items found in a grocery store. Each child is a clerk and uses his desk as a counter. A designated "shopper" goes from desk to desk asking for all things whose names begin with a certain sound. If the shopper fails to take all appropriate pictures and the clerk notices, the clerk becomes the shopper.

25. Sound Dominoes. Make dominoes with pictures on each end. Play like regular dominoes, matching pictures by beginning sound.

26. Clock. Make a large clock face with slots for picture cards instead of numbers on the face. Insert picture cards and attach one moveable hand. When the hand is

set at a picture, ask a child to give a word that begins with the same sound as the name of the picture.

27. Following-the-Leader. Distribute a picture card to each child and have them form a circle. Select two leaders, each of whom has a different beginning sound on his picture card. Each of the leaders seeks another person whose picture card has the same beginning sound and that person then helps the leader to find others with the same beginning sound on their picture cards.

28. Make-Believe Stream. A make-believe stream goes through the middle of the circle of children. Picture cards are used as stepping stones across the stream. A child tries to cross the stream by giving a word that begins with the same sound as each picture card before stepping on that card. Children who fail to give a word with the proper beginning sound fall in the stream.

29. Drawing a Sound Page Number 1. Newsprint pages may be distributed or this may be done as a group project. This is the same as activity 4, except children *draw* pictures they can think of whose names begin with the same sound.

30. Drawing a Sound Page Number 2. Provide a context sentence and have the children draw pictures whose names begin with the same sound and would make sense in the context given.

　　a. "Draw all the things Carol got at the grocery store whose names begin with the same sound as her name."

　　b. "Draw all the things in a house whose names begin with the same sound as *dog.*"

31. Thinking of Things. Give a key word. Children take turns thinking of things whose names begin with the same sound. When no more words can be thought of, the last successful player gets to name a new key word. (If desired, a score of correct items may be kept for each player.)

32. Going to Boston. Showing a picture card, one player says, "I'm going to Boston and I'm taking something that begins with the sound you hear at the beginning of (show picture)." Any child who guesses correctly takes another card and is "it."

34. Context and Sound. Provide sentences in which children are to use context and a given beginning sound to decide on the missing word.

　　a. "John went for a ride on his new _____ . What makes sense and begins like *wing?*" (*wagon*)

　　b. "We went to visit the farm. While we were there, we petted a _____ . What makes sense and begins like *can?*" (*cow, calf, cat, kitten*)

(NOTE: If the children have difficulty keeping two directions in mind, have them first think of things that make sense and then pick one of those that begins with the given sound.)

Associating Consonant Letters and Sounds

The teaching goal for activities related to associating consonant letters and sounds is to establish with children an immediate response to an initial consonant letter in terms of a key word that begins with the sound for which that letter stands. There is no way to explain why the letter *s*, for example, stands for the sound it does; it is just that all English speakers agree on this point, and the sooner children agree, the sooner they will be learning to read.

The most effective method for developing letter-sound associations is through the use of key pictures, where a letter is superimposed on a picture whose name begins with the sound that letter represents. Figure 2 shows examples of key pictures.

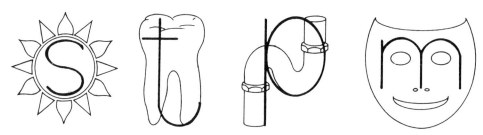

Figure 2. *Key pictures for* s, t, m, p.

The key picture technique was used widely by Laubach in his world literacy campaign. Its effectiveness was demonstrated in a study involving eighty kindergarten children (Hillerich, 1966b). These children were tested at the beginning of kindergarten with seventeen pairs of key pictures in the hope of identifying what kinds of key pictures were most effective: novel pictures or common ones, those that followed the configuration of the letter or those that did not. Children were shown the key pictures in random order and were asked, "What is this a picture of?" They were then *told* the name of the letter while the examiner traced that letter with his finger.

A week to two weeks later the children were retested by being shown just a letter card and asked, "What picture does this remind you of?" While results gave support to the importance of the picture's following the configuration of the letter, the most interesting result was the ability of most children to recall a majority of key pictures from the letter stimulus with no instruction whatsoever.

From this study, we might conclude that the particular kind of picture may not be important, but the use of a key picture is effective in helping children recall a key word. Use of key pictures, of course, requires consistency in the choice of pictures among teachers working with a given child. It isn't so important what picture is chosen for each letter; but if different teachers use different pictures, the effectiveness is lost. The pictures are no longer key pictures but merely different reminders of a beginning sound.

Sound associations will need to be developed for all single consonants except *z* and *x*, as noted previously. They also need to be developed for the digraphs *th, sh,* and *ch*. While many programs include the digraph *wh* as in *wheel*, there are so few people who pronounce the /hw/ that children can undoubtedly use their letter-sound association for the initial *w* and determine the word just as well.

The sets of letters to be used will be the same as those used in work on letter form discrimination and beginning sounds. Begin by showing youngsters a key picture card, such as *sun* with *s* superimposed. Ask children to say the name of the picture, and write the name on the board to demonstrate that the word *sun* begins with the letter *s*. Then point out that the key picture will help them remember that when they see a word beginning with *s,* that word will begin with the same sound as *sun.*

As soon as a key picture has been introduced, it is advisable, to keep it displayed in the room as a reference, so the children who need a reminder can check.

Following introduction of a key picture, the same kinds of activities can be conducted to establish letter-sound associations that were conducted with beginning sounds. The only difference is that the stimulus becomes a letter rather than a picture name. For example, children working on beginning sounds may have made a sound page, where they collected pictures whose names began with the sound they heard at the beginning of the word *sun.* A picture of *sun* was put at the top of the sound page as a reminder for the sound. Now, for letter-sound association, children will collect pictures whose names begin with the sound for which the letter *s* stands. The letter *s* now becomes the reminder at the top of the page.

In addition to adaptations of activities suggested under "Identifying Beginning Sounds," the following may be used:

1. Sound Page. Children collect pictures whose names begin with the sound for which a given letter stands. For example, put an *s* at the top of the page and have the children collect pictures whose names begin with the sound *s* stands for.

2. Collect the Alphabet Cards. Show children an alphabet card. Whoever can name the key picture gets to keep that alphabet card. (Reinforce immediately by showing the key card.)

3. Matching. Paste pictures on a flat board. Provide small letter cards. The child draws a letter card from the pile and places it on the matching picture, for example, *s* on *sailboat.*

4. Clothespin Matching. Make a large cardboard circle and divide it into eight or ten sections with a picture in each section. Also prepare the same number of clothespins (spring type) with a letter on each. The child is to match each clothespin with its proper picture. (This may be made a self-checking activity by using matching symbols or color codes on the backs of the pictures and clothespins.)

5. Electric Matching. Make a game board with pictures down the right side and letters down the left. Put an electric contact beside each letter and picture and connect appropriate letters and pictures *on the back* with copper wire. Set up a battery with a small light bulb and wires to be used as connectors between letter and picture. When the child touches the wires to the proper letter-picture combination, the light will go on.

6. Yarn Board. Make a board as in Activity 5, but put a hole beside each picture. Attach a piece of colored yarn permanently beside each letter. Children can thread the yarn through the hole beside the proper picture. Color coding on the back enables self-checking.

7. Drawing Number 1. Give the child a paper with one letter (about 2×2 inches) on it. The child is to draw a key picture over the letter. Other pictures may then be drawn that have names beginning with the sound for which the letter stands.

8. Drawing Number 2. Make a wooden or styrofoam block with the four letters under consideration written, one on each side of the block. Provide a sheet of paper folded into four sections. A child rolls the block and prints the letter into one of the four blocks. The child then draws a picture whose name begins with the sound for which that letter stands.

9. Spinner Bingo. Make bingo cards with pictures on them and a spinner with letters instead of numbers. Children spin the spinner and cover the picture whose name begins with the sound for which the letter stands.

10. Ala Chutes and Ladders. Make a game board such as used in chutes and ladders, but have each square contain a picture. Use alphabet dice. The children move to the next square that has a picture whose name begins with the sound for which the letter rolled stands.

11. Puzzle. Use rectangular tagboards about 3 × 6 inches. Paste a picture at one end and a letter at the other end of each tagboard. Cut each diagonally to form two-piece puzzles. Color code or mark the backs for self-checking. (NOTE: All puzzles should be cut exactly the same, or else children will match appropriate pieces merely by physical fit.)

12. Dominoes. Make dominoes with a picture at one end and a letter at the other. Children play like dominoes, but match letter to picture.

13. Relay Number 1. Divide the group into two teams. Place two small boxes in the front of the room, each labelled with a different letter. Scatter small objects and/or pictures around the room. One team finds all the pictures or objects that begin with the sound represented by the letter on one box; the other does the same for the second box. The winner is the team with the most correct items in the box.

14. Relay Number 2. Put four letter cards each in two pocket charts in a vertical column on the left side. Pass out picture cards to children, one to each. Divide them into two teams. The first child on each team puts his picture card in the proper row with the letter card. The first team to place all cards correctly wins the relay.

15. Choo Choo. Children line up in two rows to form trains. The teacher is the engineer and holds up a letter card. The first child in each line (the engine) answers with the key picture word. That child then goes to the end to be the caboose and the next child is the engine.

16. Treasure Hunt. Place objects in various parts of the room. Divide the children into teams, each with a captain. Each captain gets an envelope with a letter on it. Teams hunt for objects whose names begin with the sound for which their letter stands, and the captain checks to be certain objects are correct.

17. Spinner. Make a spinner with slots for letter cards. Put letter cards in and spin the needle. Call on a child to give the key picture and a word that begins with sound for which that letter stands.

18. Follow-the-Leader. Two children (leaders) are inside a circle. Other children each have a picture card, while the leaders have letter cards. Leaders find one child with a picture card that matches his letter. This child follows the leader to help find other picture cards to match the letter.

19. Teacher Says. The teacher gives a picture card to each child in a circle. Then she says, "All those whose picture name begins with the sound this letter stands for (hold up letter card) may hop (skip, jump, etc.)."

20. Daily Activities. "All those whose names begin with the sound this letter stands for (hold up letter) may (go outside, get a drink, etc.)."

21. Golf. Divide a large cardboard circle into sections. In each section paste one picture and put four letters around the edge, with a small hole beside each letter. Children may put golf tees into the hole beside the one letter of the four that stands

for the sound the picture name begins with. Again, self-checking is possible through marking the correct hole on the reverse side.

Using Oral Context and Initial Consonant Sound Associations to Read a Printed Word

Once letter-sound associations are developed for a set of consonants, children can be told that now, with your help, they will be able to read some words. Develop sentences that provide good context and then write one of the key words on the board. For example, write the word *paper* on the board and tell the children you will say something but will leave out this word. Then say: "I wanted to make a picture for my mother. I found my crayons, but I couldn't find any _____." They should use the sense of the other words you say and the sound they know that first letter stands for in order to read the word.

At this stage, it is important to be careful about the context and words selected. Be certain the word on the board is the only one that would make sense and begin with the sound for which the first letter stands. For example, it would be unfair to children at this stage of their skill development to put the word *house* on the board and say, "It started to rain, so we decided to go into Johnny's _____." In such a case, *house* or *home* could make sense and begin with the same letter.

In the process of providing practice sentences, omit words in the middle or early part of a sentence as well, so the children don't get the mistaken impression that they should stop when they come to a word they don't know. This can happen if the unknown word is always the last word in a sentence. From the very beginning, children should form the habit of continuing on to get more context in order to help them unlock a strange word.

Following are some example sentences that might be used with children. The word to be written on the board for each sentence has been underlined.

m At night you can see the moon in the sky.
    Rosa always drinks milk for breakfast.

s That boat doesn't have a motor. It has a sail.
    Will you please sit down and be quiet?

p The mother dog had a little black and white puppy.
    Jerry put a penny in his coin bank.

t Jeff puts butter and jelly on his toast.
    Sue called her grandmother on the telephone.

Left-to-Right Orientation

While some educators go to great lengths to help children learn the terms *left* and *right,* such knowledge is not needed for reading: These terms are merely labels. What is necessary for success in reading is the understanding and habit of starting here (the left side) and going this way (toward the right side of the page).

Children will begin to develop this habit if they use work sheets or workbooks. Even without workbooks, left-to-right orientation can begin very early. The adult, sitting side by side with an individual child and reading to that child, has the perfect opportunity to begin left-to-right orientation by running a finger along the lines being read. This will lead the child to follow from left to right.

In working with groups of children, teachers can gain the same advantage by putting stories to be read on transparencies. When the transparency is projected overhead, a finger can again trace along the lines being read and children will follow on the screen.

This use of stories on transparencies has another advantage once children have developed letter-sound associations for some of the consonants and have been given some initial practice in using those associations along with oral context: in the process of reading a projected story, stop once in a while at a word in good context and have the children use their skill to read the word. Children get a sense of accomplishment in doing this reading, but it should never be done so often that enjoyment of the story is destroyed.

Left-to-right orientation may also be developed through the use of experience charts. While some educators have reservations about the language experience approach as a total reading program, these charts can be used effectively to demonstrate several points about reading to children. First of all, they demonstrate that the printed form of language is the same language children have been speaking: It is "talk written down." Secondly, the production and use of these charts demonstrate left-to-right movement. By having the children dictate their story while you write it on a chart, you demonstrate both of these points very effectively. If you work with children who are further along in their reading development, beginning to read on their own but lacking sufficient skill to read the more involved experience charts they might dictate, read the stories back to them for changes or additions and then suggest the charts be preserved until a future time when they might want to look back and read about what they did earlier in the year.

Recognizing High-Frequency Words

The act of reading, even at the very beginning, is not one of merely making noises for printed symbols, nor is it, at the other extreme, a matter of merely learning words. Initially, the act of reading is one of learning to use the two-pronged skill being developed—the skill of using context and consonant sound associations. Even so, we must recognize that the individual who has completely mastered the skill developed thus far cannot be handed a book and be expected to read it. That individual usually has no recognition vocabulary, hence he has no printed context to use to unlock strange words; all the words are strange in their printed form.

A "recognition vocabulary" is sometimes referred to as a "sight vocabulary." It consists of those words in print that are known, or recognized, instantaneously, without recourse to any analysis. "Word recognition" may be contrasted with "word identification," a process that enables the reader to determine what a word is through analysis, that is, through use of skills such as context, phonics, or structural analysis.

A very few different words account for a large percentage of all words on a page of English printed material. For example, it was found that the three most frequently used words accounted for 10 percent of all words written by adults (Horn). It was also reported those same three words (*I, and, the*) accounted for 11 percent of the 380,342 words written by elementary school children (Hillerich, 1966d). The ten most frequently used words in either of these studies accounted for at least 25 perment of all words written by adults or children. These facts mean that the child who recognizes those ten words instantaneously automatically recognizes a fourth of all the words in any book he picks up in English, from *The Cat in the Hat* to *Gone With the Wind*. (See Chapter 5 for more detail about recognition vocabularies.)

Vocabularly is best developed in meaningful context, whether by child or by adult, whether the concern is for meaning or recognition, and whether the language is oral or printed. Hence, rather than take the first ten of the most frequently used words, we should be a little more selective. The following eight words serve a more practical use and account for 18 percent of running words in print: *the, a, is, was, in, on, and, it*.

Children may be introduced to the high-frequency words after they have completed one or two cycles of letters and may carry on activities with these words simultaneously as they pick up another cycle of letters. Introduce the words in meaningful context, just as you have read stories to children from transparencies. For example, the words the, is and in can be put into sentences on a transparency. Tell the children you will read the sentence through and you want them to remember the word that is underlined. Read the sentence a second time and ask them to use the sense of the other words to read the underlined word for you.

In the case of words beginning with consonants for which children have developed sound associations, read the sentence through once and omit the underlined word, then have them use the context and initial sound association to read the underlined word when you come to it the second time.

After each word has been introduced, show the children the word again, this time on a card, and have them repeat it. After all three words have been introduced, put them on cards in a pocket chart as a rebus sentence:

The (picture of a boy) is in the (picture of a house).

Point out to the youngsters that they can read the whole sentence. Have several children do so. Then change the sentence by changing one of the picture cards and have the new sentence read. Invite the children to select picture cards to make new sentences for others to read. Very soon kindergarten children will make sentences with boys in tigers, monkeys in hats, and so on. They think they are playing great jokes, but in reality they are doing exactly what you want: They are getting practice in reading the high-frequency words in meaningful context.

For those children who have gained the mechanics of letter formation, these simple rebus sentences can be transformed into questions by merely moving *is* to the beginning of the group of words. Then by introducing the word *not* on the board, have children write answers in reply to questions put in rebus form. Also encourage them to write rebus sentences of their own in which they draw pictures for the nouns—or even for the action verbs. Writing experience reinforces the recognition vocabulary. The more ways children use a word, the more likely they are to remember that word.

By now, reason for the choice of high-frequency words should be clear. By introducing the article *a,* additional options are provided for rebus sentences; *was* can be substituted for *is.* Eventually *it* can be substituted for a subject noun, and *and* can be used to connect a compound sentence.

SUMMARY

This chapter presented a listing of the basic prereading skills, including their underlying purposes and activities for their development. Those skills are using oral context, discriminating letter forms, identifying beginning sounds, associating consonant letters and sounds, using oral context and initial consonant sound associations, developing left-to-right orientation, and recognizing high-frequency words.

While no one can say when children will—or even should—master these skills, we can say that all children ought to have the opportunity to be exposed to these skills prior to their entry to first grade.

References

Barrett, Thomas C. "Visual Discriminatioin Tasks as Predictors of First Grade Reading Achievement." *The Reading Teacher* 19(1965):276–82.

Cohn, Marvin. "Letter Recognition Difficulties: Their Real Nature." Paper presented at International Reading Association. New Orleans, May 1974.

Durrell, Donald D., et al. "Success in First Grade Reading." *Journal of Education* 140 (1958): entire issue.

Groff, Patrick. " 'Sight' Words and the Disabled Reader," *Academic Therapy* 10(1974): 101–8.

Hillerich, Robert L. "Analysis of Words Used in Creative Writing, Grades 1–6." Unpublished manuscript. Glenview, 1966. a (Available from 1311 Bourgogne, Bowling Green, OH 43402.)

———. "Effectiveness of 'Magic' Picture Cards." *School Bulletin,* Glenview, December 1966. b

———. "An Interpretation of Research in Reading Readiness." *Elementary English* 43(1966):359–64, 372. c

———. "Predictive Value of Letter-Name Test." *School Bulletin,* Glenview, June 1966. d

———. *Spelling for Writing.* Columbus: Charles E. Merrill Publishing Co., 1976.

Horn, Ernest. *A Basic Writing Vocabulary.* University of Iowa Monographs in Education, First Series, No. 4. Iowa City, April 1926.

Jenkins, Joseph R.; Bausell, R. B.; and Jenkins, Linda M. "Comparisons of Letter Name and Letter Sound Training as Transfer Variables." *American Educational Research Journal* 9(1972):75–86.

Johnson, Ronald. "The Effect of Training in Letter Names on Success in Beginning Reading for Children of Differing Abilities." Paper presented at American Educational Research Association meeting. March 1970, Minneapolis.

Laubach, Frank C. *Teaching the World to Read.* New York: Friendship Press, 1947.

McHugh, W. J. "Indices of Success in First Grade Reading." Paper presented at American Educational Research Association meeting. Chicago, February 1962.

Muehl, Siegmar. "The Effects of Letter-Name Knowledge on Learning to Read a Word List in Kindergarten Children." *Journal of Educational Psychology* 53 9(1962):181–86.

Nicholson, Alice. "Background Abilities Related to Reading Success in First Grade." Ph.D. dissertation, Boston University, 1957.

Olson, Arthur V., Jr. "Growth in Word Perception as It Relates to Success in Beginning Reading." Ph.D. dissertation, Boston University, 1957.

Samuel, S. Jay. "The Effect of Letter-Name Knowledge on Learning to Read." *American Educational Research Journal* 9(1972):65–74.

Silverberg, Norman E.; Silverberg, M.; and Iversen, I. "The Effects of Kindergarten Instruction in Alphabet and Numbers on First Grade Reading." *Journal of Learning Disabilities* 5(1972):254–61.

Williams, Joanna P. "Successive versus Concurrent Presentation of Multiple Grapheme-Phoneme Correspondences." *Journal of Educational Psychology* 59(1968):309–14.

5

Reading: In the Beginning

The typical child who has experienced the prereading skills program in or before kindergarten will be ready about the end of kindergarten or beginning of first grade to make use of these skills in actual reading. Of course, there will be some children entering first grade who are well beyond this level and others who have not yet mastered the necessary prereading skills, even though they may have been exposed to them.

Children who have progressed up to this point in their skill development have a considerable foundation for reading. They have gained the following skills and understandings:

1. Development of an adequate oral language, including both sentence patterns and vocabulary;
2. Awareness of their ability to use oral context to anticipate a word;
3. Ability to discriminate minor differences between letter forms;
4. Understanding of what is meant by "the beginning" of a spoken word;
5. Experience in classifying spoken words according to beginning sounds;
6. Association of consonant letters with the sounds those letters represent at the beginning of a word;
7. Ability to apply the skill of using oral context along with the consonant sound association for the first letter of a printed word in order to read that word;
8. Familiarity with the patterns of the literary language from having been read to;
9. Experience with certain high-frequency words, enabling instant recognition of these printed words.

This chapter provides suggestions for extending these skills and for increasing interest in reading. The key to reading success for any child is the enjoyable application of what skill he has, the gradual and successful adding on of additional skills, and repeated praise and documentation for each small step of progress.

The First Book Materials

Children's first book material is usually the first preprimer of a basal reading series. While this doesn't have to be, there certainly is nothing wrong with using a preprimer. Regardless of the material used, it is essential that vocabulary be very limited at this stage; youngsters cannot be faced with too many words they don't know. Even though the children have some recognition vocabulary—the high-frequency words—it still is not adequate enough for them to build sufficient context to use in unlocking other strange words.

With a few words in a sentence, and a sentence or two on a page, the teacher builds background and develops a story through oral discussion. With this context and their knowledge of the high-frequency words, the children should be able to use their skills in unlocking strange words in order to read the printed page.

The first reading of any material, even though limited to a three- or four-word sentence, should always be done silently before children are asked to read orally.

Introducing New Words

New words are introduced in context in most basal readers. However, the way in which a new word is introduced may vary and will reveal much about the philosophy of reading espoused by the program or by the teacher using it.

Word introduction, properly conducted, is one of the most important elements in the teaching of beginning reading. Obviously, if the teacher sees reading as nothing more than making noises for print, then there is no need for word introductions at all; children merely learn the sound correspondences and make the noises for the symbols.

Until children have an adequate recognition vocabulary to provide printed context for them, new words may be introduced in oral context. Printed context should be used as soon as practicable, since this is the form in which the children will meet the words.

According to some philosophies of reading, the teacher introduces a new word—*house,* for example—in the following manner. Notice the purpose underlying this technique. The word *house* might be written on the chalkboard and the following procedures used by the teacher:

"Boys and girls, here is a new word from the story we will read today. What do you call a place people live in? It can be made of wood, or brick, or stone."

Words introduced in this form seem to imply that the teacher is preparing the children to participate in a quiz game. The technique has little if anything to do with developing independent word attack skills.

Another technique is to put this same word on the board and to provide the children with oral context such as "Boys and girls, here is a new word from the story we are going to read. You might see it in a sentence like 'Jerry's family moved to a new _____.' Does anyone know the word?" Usually one or two children will be able to tell the group what the word is. Then the teacher will go on to discuss the word: "Yes, what is the word again? (point) What are houses made of? Who lives in houses? Can birds also live in houses? What is the word?" (point).

New words introduced in this fashion clearly imply that the teacher is trying to build meaning for the word, and is calling the children's attention repeatedly back to the word form. This teacher is attempting to "teach" the word *house,* hoping that when children come to the word *house* in their reading they will remember it.

New words should not be introduced in either of these two forms. Neither is helping children to become independent readers, unless, in the latter case, one expects children to be able to memorize all the words they will ever meet in print.

New words ought to be introduced in something of the following manner. Write the new word on the board and say: "Boys and girls, here is a new word from the story we are going to read. I'll give you the rest of the sentence; you decide what would make sense with what I say and begins with the sound you know this first letter stands for."

When the sentence is given, children might be expected to say *house,* and the teacher is finished with the word introduction.

The purpose for introducing the new word in this manner is clearly to review with the children the skill they are to use when they come to a word they don't know. After being introduced to one or two new words, youngsters may begin their reading with a final reminder about the technique they are to use when they come to a word they don't know.

Such a technique helps children to become independent of us as word introducers. It reviews with them what they need to do independently when they meet a strange word in print.

This purpose for introducing new words also means that it is not necessary to introduce every new word from a story. The skill can be reviewed with any one or two of the new words, and the word introduction should be continued until the children are independently applying the skill that is being taught. Some children may be doing this in the second or third grade. Usually it is wise, even if children appear consistently to use the skill by the end of first grade, to introduce new words again at the beginning of the second- and third-grade years just as a reminder or review.

Extending Consonant Sound Association Skills

Children who have not developed sound associations for the single consonants and the digraphs *sh, ch, th* should be provided with activities suggested in the previous chapter. Others, who merely need additional reinforcement of the letter-sound associations, should continue to use key pictures and can strengthen their associations through the use of consonant substitution exercises.

Write on the board a word the children know, such as *an.* Have them read the word. Then put *f* in front of *an* and remind them that they know the sound for which *f* stands, so they should now be able to read the new word. Change *f* to *m,* and have them read the word.

While this kind of activity will serve as a test or as a review of consonant sound associations, it is not designed to teach children what to do when they come to a strange word; a reader does not look at a strange word and substitute consonant sounds to convert the strange word to a word he knows.

See-Hear-Associate Method

Instead of using key pictures to develop letter-sound associations, some programs use a see-hear-associate method. Children first must learn from a sight approach three or four words that include the element to be taught. Ideally, these should be words that also contain no other elements in common. Then the known words are put before the children and a three-step procedure is followed. For example, to teach the sound association for *m,* the following might be written in a column on the board:

man

me

my

Children are then asked to look at the words (see) and decide how they are alike. Then they are asked to read the words and listen for (hear) the sound that is the same in all three. Finally, they are told by the teacher (associate) to remember when they see the letter *m* that it stands for the sound they hear at the beginning of *man, me,* and *my.*

Such a method has at least two major defects:

1. Children must first be told words as they begin reading, without the benefit of phonic skills.
2. While broad experience with words will certainly strengthen sound associations, this method fails to establish strong associations initially.

In contrast, key pictures can provide the strong associations through a memorable key word. The see-hear-associate method may then be used, after children are reading, as another means of reviewing or strengthening their sound associations.

Ending Consonants

Children will soon need to use their knowledge of consonant sound associations for consonants in positions other than the initial one. Use of consonant sound associations in final position is developed before use of these associations in medial positions.

Children seem to make the transfer from using sound associations in initial position to their use in final position easily. One way to provide initial practice in using ending sounds is to provide oral context in which two words both make sense and begin with the same sound but have different endings. For example, "Mother was making soup in a big _____." Then put on the board the initial letter *p.* Possible words are *pot* and *pan.* If the children respond with only one of the words, ask for another that would make sense and begin with the sound for which *p* stands.

Now finish printing the word *pot* and have the children identify whether the printed word is *pot* or *pan* by reminding them that they know what the sound *t* stands for. They should be able to use that knowledge to decide if the printed word is *pot* or *pan.*

Consonant Clusters

Consonant clusters do not need to be taught as new or separate sound associations as were each of the single consonants. They should be recognized as a combination of two or three known consonants and should be practiced specifically at the time children meet examples in their reading material.

The most common consonant clusters are *bl, cl, pl, sp,* and *br, dr, fr, gr, pr, st, tr.* Additional clusters should be taught as children meet them. These would include *fl, gl, sc, sk, sm, sq, str, tw, thr,* and *cr, scr, sl, sn, spr, sw.*

Blending

While the reading of consonant clusters merely requires the use of two or three known consonant sound associations, some children will have difficulty with them. On the other hand, unless the child has been taught to pronounce consonant sounds in isolation, he will not need to be taught to blend their sounds together. In learning to speak his language, no child has difficulty in blending together the sounds of the language in order to say words. But the child who has used an artificial means of learning to read—isolating the sounds in words—often has a problem in getting those sounds back together so they sound like words he has heard.

We should find ways to avoid isolated sounding of consonants in blending. With children who need some help in identifying the two or three consonants in a cluster, use a blending technique that produces no distortion.

First, we should recognize that it is the final consonant, not the initial consonant, that controls the sound value of a single vowel in a one-syllable word. For example, given the endings *-an* or *-all,* the reader will expect the vowel sounds to be those in *can* or *call,* regardless of the initial consonant or cluster used. On the other hand, given the beginning *ba-* or *be-,* there is no way to know the vowel sound: in the first, it might be the vowel sound in *bat, babe, ball, bar,* and so on; in the latter, it might be *bell, berth,* or *bey.*

By using ending phonograms, we can control the sound value of the vowel and use a pronounceable unit that may be added to in order to produce new words using clusters that we want to review. Write on the board a word the children know, such as *lay,* and have them read that word. Then add *p* and have them use their consonant sound association for *p* to read *play.* This procedure can even be used with consonant substitution: write *back* and have the children read it; change *b* to *l* and have them read *lack;* add *b* and have them read *black.*

Following are a few examples of words that might be used to provide practice with clusters in this reverse kind of blending:

low: blow, flow, glow, slow
ring: bring, spring, string
lay: clay, play, slay
lock: block, clock, flock
rain: drain, grain, sprain, strain, train
ray: pray, spray, stray, tray
led: bled, fled, sled

The following list of phonograms, adapted from Wylie and Durrell, may be used as a source of additional word parts to provide practice with initial consonants or clusters:

/a/: -ack, -ad, -am, -an, -ap, -ash, -at
/e/: -ell, -en, -est, -et
/i/: -ick, -ill, -in, -ing, -ink, -it
/ä/: -ock, -op, -ot
/ə/: -uck, -ug, -ump, -un, -unk
/ā/: -ail, -ain, -ake, -ame, -ate, -ay
/ē/: -eat, -eed
/ī/: -ice, -ide, -ight, -ine
/ō/: -oke, -ore, -old
/ò/: -all, -aw
/ã/: -ar
/ú/: -ook

Phonograms can also be used in another way. They can be used along with the alphabet chart usually found at the front of a classroom to provide the children with an organized method for analyzing the language. Given a phonogram, the children may use the alphabet, letter by letter, to see how many words they can make from the phonogram.

While children often resist pronouncing a nonsense word, if you introduce this latter activity, they may still play with pronounceable units and decide whether or not they have ever heard such a word. If nonsense words are used, it is wise to reinforce the children's natural expectancy that words in reading material should always make sense; we certainly don't want them to be satisfied with saying words whether or not they make sense to them.

It should be recalled that these uses of phonograms are suggested as a means of providing greater familiarity with the nature of the printed language and as a means of reviewing initial consonant sound associations. As indicated in Chapter 1, children do not use phonograms as an independent means of unlocking a strange word when they come to it in their reading.

A second point is undoubtedly in order here: While the use of phonograms leads to words that rhyme, there seems to be no reason to emphasize rhyming words as a skill in beginning reading. The emphasis with phonograms is on the changing part, that is, the beginning letter or letters, not on the rhyming part. On the other hand, to drill on rhyming words—to emphasize the endings of words—seems to be an inconsistency at a time when we are trying to get beginning readers to move from left to right and to use the initial letters first in their efforts to unlock strange words. (This point should not be construed as a criticism of the use of nursery rhymes and jingles, which are read or recited for the fun of the sound and without particular attention to the position of the sound in a word.)

Other Consonant Spellings

In addition to the clusters and the digraphs *ch, sh, th,* some consonant sounds may also be represented by combinations of letters, for example, /n/ is spelled *kn* in *know, pn* in *pneumonia, mn* in *mnemonic.*

Once more, children should be introduced to these forms as they come to them in their reading. They should use the context, and they should have the different spelling called to their attention. However, they should not be told that *k* in the above example is a "silent" letter, as if some letters are quiet and others make noises. They should recognize *kn* as a representation of the sound /n/.

Of most concern are these combinations in initial position, since context and other consonant clues will usually enable decoding of such items as *ll* (*still*) or even *mb* (*lamb*). The major additions for children are the following digraphs:

gn = /n/: gnash, gnat, gnaw, gnome
kn = /n/: know, knew, known, knee, knife, knock
ph = /f/: phone, photo, physical
wh = /h/: whose, who, whole, whom
wr = /r/: write, wrote, written, wrap, wreck, wrong

Inflectional Endings

Inflectional endings should be presented and discussed as they are met in children's reading matter. Children who have had experience with the *-ing* phonogram should have no problem in recognizing that unit at the end of a word.

Plural and past markers (*s, es, ed*) should be taught as meaning units rather than as elements of phonics. There is no point in trying to teach children the three different sounds a plural marker has at the end of English words—/z/ (*plays*), /s/ (*tops*), and /əz/ (*bushes*). The English-speaking child who recognizes *-s* or *-es* as a plural marker will automatically pronounce the ending correctly; in fact, there are many educated adults who are not even aware that the plural marker has three different pronunciations.

The same point applies to the past marker *-ed*. Children do not need to recognize its three sounds either—/t/ (*tossed*), /d/ (*happened*), and /əd/ (*hunted*). Once children recognized *-ed* as a signal that something happened in the past, they will pronounce the past form correctly.

Word Recognition with Beginning Readers

One of the major tasks in teaching reading is to provide lots of experience in reading: Children learn to read by reading. There is no better way to expand a recognition vocabulary than through lots of reading, and the expansion of this recognition vocabulary is one of the principal tasks for the beginning reader.

While there may be a place for enjoyable word games, there should be no use of isolated flash card drills with beginning readers. First of all, it is easier to recognize words in context than it is in isolation. Goodman found that first-grade children missed three times as many words in isolation as in context; second-grade children missed one-third more in isolation, and third-grade children missed one-fourth more words in isolation as they did in context. In another study it was found that, even in reading third-grade material, poor readers at junior high level missed three times as many of the same words in isolation as they did in context (Hillerich, 1975b).

Secondly, vocabulary is best developed in meaningful context. It is the experience of the word in context that helps to build associations and to clarify or amplify meanings. This is true whether applied to the development of a recognition vocabulary among young children or applied to the expansion of a listening/speaking vocabulary among older individuals.

Finally, there are very few words so important that they are worth teaching for themselves. We quickly reach a point of diminishing returns if we try to teach reading strictly as a word-learning process. For example, in a count of 380,342 words used by children in their writing (Hillerich, 1966), the most frequently used word, *I,* was used 16,178 times; the one-hundredth word—still a relatively high-frequency word—was used only 647 times. In other words, if we are merely trying to teach specific words, any one of another hundred could be just about as important as the one-hundredth word.

To put this in a different way, the hundred most frequently used words account for 48 to 61 percent of all words used in print. The next one hundred words expand the percentage by only 6 to 11 percent; the third hundred add 4 to 5 percent.

As pointed out by Dale, vocabulary can be developed by using all the means available: reading, writing, speaking, and listening. Children should be involved in writing experiences as soon as they have mastered the mechanics of letter formation. They should move from rebus sentences to the writing of sentences based on stories they've read; they may use phonograms to make up rhyming couplets, or they may write in response to pictures from greeting cards. Any and every idea, occasion, or object should be used as a jumping-off point for creative writing.

Research indicates that this is not the level to be overly concerned about spelling (Hillerich, 1976); the teacher should provide the spellings for children and should see the basic job as being one of encouraging the youngsters to write and to enjoy it.

Word Recognition with Older Children

How do we deal with older children, those beyond first or second grade, who are having difficulty with reading? We know they have been exposed to important words in meaningful context hundreds of times. These children need intensive work in word recognition as well as in the development of whatever skills they are lacking. What word list should be used with these children to assure they will be learning the most important words?

Of course, one might question the use of any word list. The assumed purpose of a word list is to expose children to the "most important," that is, the most frequently used, words. However, if children are reading English material, how can they avoid being exposed to the most frequently used words? By definition, the "most frequently used words" are the words that must be used most often in any English communication.

However, for checking, testing, or just for added insurance, many teachers like to have a basic word list. To that end, Hillerich (1974) reported a study of the words most frequently used by children and adults. He began with four different word counts from natural writing. This use of word studies based on original, uncontrolled writing seemed necessary since too many word lists are made from basal readers, which are made from word lists, which are made from basal readers, ad infinitim.

The following word counts were used as the basis for the study:

1. Carroll et al. tabulated 5,088,721 words from 1,045 textbooks, grades three through nine.

2. Hillerich (1966) tabulated 380,342 words used by children, grades one through six, in creative writing.

3. Kucera and Francis tabulated 1,014,232 words from fifteen categories of adult printed material.

4. Rinsland tabulated 6,012,359 words used by children, grades one through eight, in writing.

From a composite of the 500 words most frequently used in each of these studies, those words that were common to all four studies and within the first 300 in frequency of use were selected. It was found that only 190 words met these criteria. The 190 words were then compared against fourteen different word lists in an effort to explain their differences.

Differences among the word lists did not seem to reflect the date the list was compiled: It would be difficult to say that any list was dated. This finding should surprise few people. Horn reported that, even of the 5,000 most frequently used words, less than 4 percent entered the language in the last hundred years; less than 10 percent in the last two hundred. In fact, he found more of these words were in the language *before* 1099 A.D. than came into the language since 1799 A.D.

Actually, differences in word lists seemed clearly to reflect the source of the list. For example, word counts based on school texts tended to include—within the first 300 in frequency—many direction words (*draw, circle, mark,* etc.) not found so important on other kinds of lists.

Since the 190 words ("Starred Starter Words") were drawn from reading and writing vocabularies of both children and adults, they should be an appropriate basic vocabulary. Among the lists checked against the starter words and the composite was the Dolch list of 220 words a list that has been widely used as a basic vocabulary for poor readers. This comparison of the Dolch list against the composite seemed to refute the criticism of datedness sometimes made of the Dolch list. However, the Dolch list did clearly reflect its source, the beginning readers of the late 1920s.

More important were the considerable differences in words included on the Dolch and the Starter Words lists, reflecting the differences in sources. Forty-three of the 190 Starter Words were not on the Dolch list of 220 words; conversely, sixty-two of the Dolch words were not even among the most frequently used 240 words from the composite.

Which list is more accurate? One way to answer that question is to evaluate the percentage of running words in different studies that can be accounted for with each list. This evaluation (Hillerich, 1973) is reported in Table 1.

As shown in Table 1, the Starter Words list provide about 2 percent more coverage in running words, regardless of the kind of material checked against and in spite of there being thirty fewer starter words as compared with the Dolch words. Incidentally, as one might expect, this table also shows that fewer different words are used by children in writing than are used in adult printed material, or even in elementary textbooks.

Table 1. *Percent of Running Words Accounted for by Hillerich's Starter Words and Dolch's Basic Sight Vocabulary*

	Hillerich 190 words	Dolch 220 words
Hillerich (children's writing)	70.0%	67.5%
Rinsland (children's writing)	67.5%	65.6%
Kucera and Francis (adult print)	53.2%	51.7%
Carroll et al. (textbooks, grades 3–9)	56.9%	55.3%

In using any basic word list, the teacher is helped by knowing what might be expected of typical children. To provide this kind of information, the 190 Starter Words were administered to six hundred children in three different school districts during January of the school year. There were two hundred children each in grades one, two, and three. Table 2 lists the Starter Words in order of frequency of use, based on the composite list. Words known by 50 percent or more of the first graders in midyear are marked with an asterisk.

As shown in Table 2, eighty-nine words were known by 50 percent or more of the first graders in January. All words except *through* were known by 50 percent or more of the second-grade children by midyear. All words except *through, every,* and *were* were known by 75 percent of the third graders.

One of the most interesting facts shown in Table 2 is the pattern of words known by the first graders. The children tended to know the most frequently used of the starter words; the average first grader in January tended not to know the less frequently used words—the later columns on the list. This is just another verification that children learn to read by reading. The more frequently a child is exposed to a word, the more likely he is to recognize that word.

Finally, as demonstrated by McDaniel and Moe, there seems to be no need to have different basic lists for children from different socioeconomic or ethnic backgrounds. These investigators examined words used in creative writing by white, black, and Spanish-surname second graders of different socioeconomic backgrounds. The authors found the high-frequency words consistent across ethnic groups and socioeconomic levels. One can hardly use English without using *the, a,* and *and.*

Table 2. *The 190 Starred Starter Words in Order of Frequency of Use*

Midyear Norms, based on individual recognition testing in three school districts.
* = Grade 1 (N† = 186)—89 words were known by 50 percent or more pupils.
      Grade 2 (N† = 208)—all words were known by 50 percent, except <u>through</u> (47 percent)
      Grade 3 (N† = 208)—all known by 75 percent, except <u>through</u> (71 percent), <u>every</u> (61 percent), <u>were</u> (50 percent).

* the	as	could	want	water	next
* and	were	* has	way	also	may
* a	would	* look	* work	before	* Mr.
* to	* so	* get	which	* off	give
* of	* my	* now	* good	through	show
* in	* out	* see	well	right	once
* it	from	our	came	ask	something
* is	* up	* two	new	most	* room
* was	* will	* into	* school	should	must
* I	* do	* did	* too	don't	didn't
* he	* said	over	been	than	always
* you	* then	* how	think	three	* car
* that	what	* down	* home	found	told
* for	* like	back	* house	these	why
* on	her	just	* play	saw	small
they	* go	year	* old	find	children
* with	* them	* little	long	tell	still
* have	time	* make	* where	* help	head
* are	* if	who	only	every	left
* had	* some	after	much	again	white
* we	about	people	* us	another	let
* be	* by	* come	* take	* big	world
* one	* him	* no	name	night	under
* but	* or	because	* here	thought	same
* at	* can	first	say	last	kind
* when	* me	more	got	away	* keep
* all	* your	many	around	each	* am
* this	* an	know	any	never	best
* she	* day	made	use	while	better
* there	their	thing	place	* took	soon
* not	other	went	put	men	four
* his	very	* man	* boy		

From "Word Lists—Getting It All Together" by Robert L. Hillerich, *The Reading Teacher* 27, no. 4 (January 1974):357. Reprinted by permission.
†*N* = Number of subjects tested.

Practice Materials

Teachers often use practice materials in the form of workbooks or duplicating masters to provide additional practice of the skill being taught. Several points should be kept in mind in selecting and using these materials.

First of all, any such materials are merely practice materials for a given skill. This means that they are the middle step of a three-step process: The skill must first be taught; then comes the additional practice with a work sheet or workbook page to reinforce that skill; nothing is accomplished unless the third step is also taken—showing the children how that skill can be applied in an actual reading situation. After all, the goal of any teacher is not to help children become "good in phonics;" it is to help them use phonics as one tool in order to become "good in reading."

A second consideration before using any practice materials is the evaluation of those practice materials. Just because a duplicated sheet or a workbook page comes next in the program being used does not mean that it is a good practice page, that it develops the skill for which it claims to be designed, or that your particular children need further practice in that skill. Before the practice material is used, it ought to be examined by the teacher for at least the following points:

1. Do my children need further practice in this skill? If not, the material is busy-work and the children will gain more by reading library books or doing some creative writing.

2. Is this the best way for them to get needed practice? If not, use a better method or material.

3. Does the workbook page actually provide practice in the skill it claims? If not, better look for an alternative.

4. Is this an important skill for reading improvement or is it busywork? If it is busywork, skip it and move on to helpful activities.

5. Are the mechanics of doing the page more difficult than the skill it is trying to provide practice in? If so, either simplify the mechanics or find other material.

In just a brief review of some games and practice pages, some strange examples were found (Hillerich, 1975a). One workbook page, part of a major basal reading series, purported to give practice in using context and initial consonant sound associations to read a strange word (certainly a worthwhile skill!). Using nonsense symbols instead of the letters used by the publisher, following are just two examples from an entire page:

1. Sue took a ride on her @_____ .   #¢*$¢%
2. Ted's dog was looking for a #_____ .   @%$&¢@%

The first letter for each word was provided and every word, listed on the right side of the page, began with a different first letter. Just as the reader here can determine which "word" fits in each of the blanks, so the child could decide every word on the page, without reading a thing, strictly by visual matching.

Visual matching is also all that is necessary in some of the self-checking puzzles children are given. If the skill is to match a letter with a picture whose name begins with the sound for which the letter stands, this is a worthwhile skill. But if the two correct pieces are the only two that fit together, all the child needs to do is to find the physical fit! This problem can be corrected by making all pieces fit equally well; the self-check can be a color code on the back of the pieces.

Sometimes worksheets or games provide good practice, but not in the skill they claim. For example, the following was supposed to provide practice in using context and sound associations for initial consonant clusters:

Dottie and her friends waited at the bus _____ .

star   stop   still

Obviously, children must use the printed context, but the decision about the missing word requires the use of every part of the words *except* the initial cluster, since all three words begin with the same cluster. If the intent was to give practice in initial clusters, the word choices should have been something like *plop, stop, slop.* It is the part of the word in which children are to have practice that must be varied if they are to get the appropriate experience.

Correction of work sheets or workbook pages ought to be immediate and must involve the children who did the pages. Emphasis in the process should be on why a response was marked, not on whether it was right or wrong. If handled in this manner, the correction of work sheets becomes a learning process for children and a diagnostic process for the teacher.

One interesting method of handling work sheets or workbook pages is to pair two children of about the same ability on one page. The two together must decide on the response to be marked. This again puts the emphasis on why a particular answer will be chosen, rather than on the routine checking off of answers, followed by finding out from the teacher which is correct.

Actually, many practice situations can—and should—be turned into teaching situations. For example, a group of children may be weak in their use of printed context. Make sentences or take a portion of a story and delete every tenth word or so. Have the children decide what words would make sense in the blanks. (If practice is needed in the use of context plus initial consonant, leave the initial consonant for each blank.) After the children have completed the exercise, "correction" can become "teaching" if discussion of answers includes discussion of why a given word was selected: "What words in the sentence gave you clues to the missing word?"

No reading skill is worth teaching unless the children see how it helps them when faced with the printed page. There are already too many disabled readers who can do phonics pages better than their teachers. In teaching or giving practice in any isolated skill, the immediate follow-up ought to be a demonstration of how that skill can be used in reading the printed page. If such application is not possible, further consideration ought to be given to the importance of such an activity as a "skill" in reading.

This need for children to see how to use skills in actual reading is the reason for the stress on the word introduction technique described previously: It is a constant reminder to children of how they are to apply their skills when they come to a word they don't know.

Avoiding Questionable Practices

Two very questionable practices sometimes encountered in reading programs are matters of teaching "configuration" and "finding little words in big words." While the former may merely waste time, the latter can be completely misleading.

Children taught to find little words in big words will be confused more often than they are helped. Just a quick check of a few basic words gives some indication of the problem:

name = am	another = a not her
because = be use	came = am
down = own	find = in
good = go	head = he
house = ho use	

Configuration is another matter entirely. First of all, there is such a phenomenon. The experienced reader can move much more quickly and efficiently through a page of regular print than through a page printed entirely in capitals; the ascenders and descenders provide for quicker recognition of familiar words. Even the adult, however, does not make configuration a major clue to word recognition (Williams et al.).

Children use initial letters as their first cue to word identification, then final letter, then other letters. Configuration or shape of the word is a final and minimal clue (Williams et al.; Marchbanks and Levin). In fact, Gorelick found that training in configuration contributed nothing to reading achievement.

Undoubtedly, the adult's use of configuration is combined with the use of context and is a matter of familiarity with print. Certainly, boxes drawn on the board contribute nothing to children's word recognition skills. For that matter, without context, what adult could say what the following "words" are: ⌐⎯⌐   ⌐⎯⌐   ?

The Role of Oral Reading

From the very beginning, no child should be expected to read materials orally that have not been read silently. The only exception to this statement is in the case of an oral reading test. Even the adult does not relish reading material orally without first having the opportunity to look that material over in advance. The same principle ought to be applied with children.

A second point is that all oral reading ought to be purposeful. Children should not be expected merely to take turns reading around the group.

These comments are in no way intended to minimize the importance of oral reading with the beginning reader. Children just learning to read need to associate the printed word with the oral language they have been speaking and hearing; these children need the reinforcement of hearing the words pronounced. Hence, the first-grade teacher might be forgiven if he runs out of strong purposes for reading that same sentence after about the tenth time. On the other hand, much of the beginning reading material is in the form of conversations between characters, so at least half a dozen different children can be asked to read the same sentence the way they think the character said it.

Further practice in oral reading can be attained through a variety of activities. Children may be asked to find a part in a story to verify a point and to read that orally. They may dramatize a story by taking the parts of characters and reading their parts directly from the book. As soon as they are into library books, children should have an opportunity to share by reading to the rest of the group a small portion of a book they enjoyed. Purposes for reading may be to read the funniest part, the most exciting part, an unusual way of saying something, a sentence that has a strange or interesting word, or just anything that happened to appeal to the reader.

Whenever possible, the oral reading should be done from a book that others do not have in hand. After all, who appreciates being read to from a selection that he also has in front of him and can read?

Reading to Children

It is questionable whether there is ever a time that children are either too young or too old to be read to. Certainly, there is no such time at the elementary school level.

First of all, as pointed out in Chapter 2, it is important to read to young children in order to acquaint them with the patterns of the literary or printed language. In doing this reading, once you have selected a story appropriate to the interests of the group's age level, that story ought to be read without paraphrasing. It does no harm for children to hear a word now and then that might not be in their listening vocabularies. For example, this author has read *Once a Mouse* by Marcia Brown to four and five year olds. Children can follow and enjoy the story, and talking down to them often detracts from that story.

A second purpose for reading to children is to increase their interest in reading. Before children have learned to read, this might be done with books of all kinds, from the nonsense of Dr. Seuss to the fun of *A Fly Went By* by Mike McClintock, or the humorous solutions to problems faced by Frances in the Hoban books. Large picture books, including Caldecott Award winners and runners-up, not only make excellent reading to children but they also provide the picture books for children themselves to "read." Nor should Mother Goose and poetry be forgotten at this level.

As children begin reading, some of the beginning-to-read books can be read to them and made available to them as they develop the basic skills necessary to read these books themselves. Reading a book to children only increases their desire to read it themselves.

While a few such books are listed in Chapter 9, major sources of beginning-to-read books are Follett's "Beginning-to-Read Series" and "JUST Beginning-to-Read

Series," Harper & Row's "I Can Read Series," and Random House's "Beginner Books."

Finally, factual books and picture dictionaries should not be forgotten at this level. The former ought to be reasonably uncluttered, such as Macmillan's "Beginning Knowledge Series," where each book contains only about a dozen common examples of whatever natural object or creature it deals with.

Picture dictionaries should also be available, and they should be in alphabetical order, so children recognize that there is order to dictionaries. Examples are discussed in Chapter 8.

As children progress in their reading skill, the level of the books read to the group ought to progress accordingly. Picture books such as most of the Caldecott winners and runners-up are seldom read by children other than for pictures, since the reading level is such that by the time children can read them they will not; the books then have too much the format of a "baby" book.

A third purpose for reading to children is to begin the development of the reading comprehension skills discussed in Chapter 7. When a story is read to children, that story should be discussed. Depending upon the length of the story, it may be discussed part by part or, with younger children and a short book, in total. This discussion is aimed primarily at increasing enjoyment of the story, but it is also an opportunity for the teacher to range through various comprehension skills at the listening/speaking level. Such practice in the use of these skills at an oral level paves the way for the use of these skills later in actual reading.

SUMMARY

This chapter has outlined the progression of skills as children move from the foundation of prereading skills into actual reading. Using the word introduction technique, teachers constantly remind children how they are to apply the skills they have learned in a reading situation.

The remaining jobs are to expand the use of consonant sound associations to positions other than the initial one and to consonant clusters, and to build a recognition vocabulary through considerable experience with reading. All skills developed must be taught for application if children are going to use them in reading.

References

Carroll, John B.; Davies, Peter; and Richmond, Barry. *The American Heritage Word Frequency Book.* Boston: Houghton Mifflin Co., 1971.

Dale, Edgar. "Vocabulary Development: A Neglected Phase of Reading Instruction." Paper presented at the annual meeting of International Reading Association. Detroit, May 1972. (ERIC Document Reproduction Service No. ED 063 597)

Dolch, Edward W. *A Manual for Remedial Reading.* Champaign, Ill.: Garrard Publishing Co., 1939.

Goodman, Kenneth. "A Linguistic Study of Cues and Miscues in Reading." *Elementary English* 42(1965):639–43.

Gorelick, Molly C. "The Effectiveness of Visual Form Training in a Prereading Program." *Journal of Educational Research* 58(1965):315–18.

Hillerich, Robert L. "Analysis of Words Used in Creative Writing, Grades 1–6." Unpublished manuscript. Glenview, 1966. (Available from 1311 Bourgogne, Bowling Green, OH 43402.

————. "Make and Take—But Reflect and Reject Too!" *Illinois Reading Council Journal* 3(1975):15–18. a

————. "The Pacemaker Readability Study: A Recognition Vocabulary for Upper Grade Students Reading at Third Grade Level." In *Pacemaker Core Vocabulary,* pp. 5–10. Belmont: Fearon Publishers, 1975. b

————. *Spelling: An Element in Written Expression.* Columbus: Charles E. Merrill Publishing Co., 1976.

————. "Starter Words: A More Efficient Beginning Vocabulary." *Illinois Reading Council Journal* 2(1973):3–5.

————. "Word Lists—Getting It All Together," *The Reading Teacher* 27(1974):353–60.

Horn, Ernest. "The Validity and Reliability of Adult Vocabulary Lists." *The Elementary English Review* 16(1939):134.

Kucera, Henry, and Francis, W. Nelson. *Computational Analysis of Present-Day American English.* Providence: Brown University Press, 1967.

McDaniel, Ernest, and Moe, Alden J. "High-Frequency Used in the Writing of Second-Grade Students from Varying Socioeconomic and Ethnic Backgrounds." *Education* 93(1973):241–45.

Marchbanks, Gabrielle, and Levin, Harry. "Cues by Which Children Recognize Words." *Journal of Educational Psychology* 56(1965):57–61.

Rinsland, Henry. *A Basic Vocabulary of Elementary School Children.* New York: Macmillan Co., 1945.

Williams, Joanna P.; Blumberg, Ellen L.; and Williams, David V. "Cues Used in Visual Word Recognition." *Journal of Educational Psychology* 61(1970):310–15.

Wylie, Richard, and Durrell, Donald. "Teaching Vowels through Phonograms." *Elementary English* 47(1970):787–91.

6

Vowels:
What Can Be Taught?

Any discussion of the decoding skills for primary children must ultimately deal with what can be taught about vowels. Hence, this chapter will review the research in terms of evidence drawn from analyses of the language itself and from the results of attempting to teach generalizations about vowels to children.

What Are Vowels?

A very natural first step, if we are going to talk about vowels, is to decide what they are. The term *vowels* may refer either to the vowel letters *a, e, i, o, u* or to the fifteen sounds usually represented in the dictionary as vowel sounds.

In terms of sound, reading teachers have traditionally referred to "long" and "short" vowel sounds. This particular terminology ought to be rejected on several counts. First, the terms *long* and *short* are not descriptive: They have nothing whatsoever to do with the "length" of the vowel sounds referred to. Second, this classification fails to account for those sounds that are neither long nor short.

More accurate terminology has been indicated from studies of the language. Linguists classify all vowel sounds into one of two categories, based on whether they are single phonemes or combinations of phonemes.

A phoneme is the smallest sound unit of a language that distinguishes one sound from another. For example, *bit* and *pit* are minimal pairs in English; they differ by only one phoneme, the initial /b/ and /p/. Similarly, *pin* and *pen* are minimal pairs, differing only by the vowel phonemes /i/ and /e/.

The two classifications for vowel sounds in a linguist's system are "simple" and "complex" vowels, sometimes referred to as "checked" and "glided." Both sets of terms are descriptive of the nature of the sounds and are linguistically honest. A simple (checked) vowel is a single phoneme, such as /i/ in *pit*. The complex (glided) sounds are combinations of phonemes. For example, one of the easiest to identify as a complex vowel sound or a combination of phonemes is the three-phoneme vowel sound /ȯi/, as in *boy*. In this case, the vowel sound begins in the position for /ȯ/ (*paw*), glides forward and up in the mouth through /i/ (*pit*), and concludes with the /y/ glide.

Figure 1 shows the fifteen vowel sounds usually identified in a dictionary, according to the position in which each is formed in the mouth. In the case of complex vowel sounds, the phonemes combined to form those sounds are indicated in parentheses. Sample words are provided, and all sound notations follow the G & C Merriam system for diacritical marks.[1]

---

1. G & C Merriam diacritical marks are used throughout for sound notations for two reasons. First, linguists have not agreed upon a uniform system of symbols for vowels. Second—and

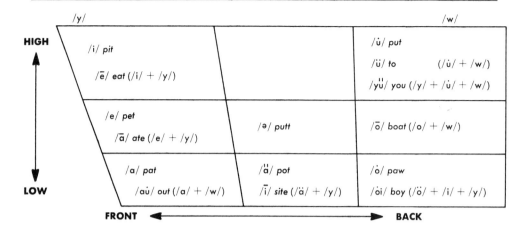

Note. Arrows indicate direction of glide; for example, /ē/ begins as /i/, then glides up and forward.

Figure 1. *Formation of simple and complex vowels in the mouth.*

Reading Versus Spelling

We must consider whether an examination of the language is to be from a reading viewpoint or from a spelling viewpoint. While the two might be mutually reinforcing, they are entirely different activities. In the case of spelling, the individual must have a word (sound) in mind and must decide what is the likely letter or combination of letters to represent that sound. In the case of reading, the individual begins by seeing a letter or sequence of letters and must decide on the sound for which that representation stands.

Furthermore, in reading one does not pay attention to every letter in a word. To do so would be a serious handicap. In spelling, one must attend to every letter and in the proper sequence in order to spell the word correctly.

Generalizations also differ in reading and in spelling. For example, if one wanted to begin with a reasonable generalization in spelling (and about the only vowel generalization that is safe), that teacher would begin by showing children that the vowel sound /a/ (*pat*) is spelled *a*. For spelling, this generalization is true about 98 percent of the time. On the other hand, to assume the reverse is true would be very misleading: In reading, *a* represents /a/ only about 42 percent of the time.

Since this is a book about the teaching of reading, the discussion will focus on the nature of language from that viewpoint. How regular is the correspondence between symbol and sound in English? One could evade the issue by merely stating one of

more important—children and teachers use dictionaries and there is no need for them to be encumbered with two systems of sound notation.

the basic tenets of linguistics: The written word is only the representation of speech —there is no rule of language that states there must be a one-to-one correspondence between symbol and sound.

If children are to be taught to read, however, we ought to identify and help them to identify patterns that might exist. Such patterns do exist when dealing with consonants. While even these have exceptions, from a reading standpoint, *b* usually stands for the sound heard at the beginning of *bear*. Geminate consonants present little more of a problem.

How True Are Vowel Generalizations?

The early 1960s saw a spate of reports about the validity of vowel generalizations being taught to young children. Best known of these studies is probably that of Clymer. He examined the teacher editions of four basal reading programs at the primary level and listed the phonic and structural rules to be taught that were common to all four programs. Clymer found forty-five generalizations, which he then applied to the words used in the pupil books of the four series. Arbitrarily determining that a rule ought to be true 75 percent of the time if it is to be taught to children, Clymer reported on the "utility" of the rules, that is, the percent of time each was true of words in the basal series studied.

Pertinent here are the twenty-four rules dealing with vowels. Clymer found only six of the twenty-four true as much as 75 percent of the time. In fact, one of the common rules, "when two vowels go walking, the first does the talking," was true only 45 percent of the time. A child who faithfully applied that rule would be wrong more often than right.

The following six rules, with Clymer's numbers, were found true at least 75 percent of the time:

No. 5   The *r* gives the preceding vowel a sound that is neither long nor short (*horn*). 78 percent

No. 8   Words having double *e* usually have the long *e* sound (*seem*). 98 percent

No. 10   In *ay* the *y* is silent and gives *a* its long sound (*play*). 78 percent

No. 16   When *y* is the final letter in a word, it usually has a vowel sound (*dry*). 84 percent

No. 19   When *a* is followed by *r* and the final *e*, we expect to hear the sound heard in *care* (*dare*). 90 percent

No. 44   When there is one *e* in a word that ends in a consonant, the *e* usually has a short sound (*leg*). 76 percent

As shown, three of these six rules barely reached the 75 percent criterion, and of the six, two are of very doubtful value. Rule 5 merely tells a child what a sound is *not,* and rule 16 provides a choice of all fifteen vowel sounds!

One question that might be raised about the Clymer study is its limitation to a primary vocabulary. However, Bailey applied Clymer's list of rules to the vocabulary of middle-grade basal readers with much the same results. A further verification was reported by Emans (1967a), who applied the Clymer list of generalizations to a random sample of 10 percent of the words beyond fourth grade level on the Lorge Thorndike list.

Burrows and Lourie tested the rule for two adjacent vowels ("when two vowels go walking") on the 5,000 most frequently used words in the Rinsland list. They found that 1,728 of the words had adjacent vowel letters, but only 668 followed the rule.

Such findings can lead in two opposite directions. Some educators might be satisfied to say the vowel rules are not worth teaching. Others might search for better rules.

Taking the latter course, Fry recognized the weakness of the general rule about two vowels together and suggested teaching each of the digraphs as a separate rule. Carried to its logical conclusion, such a route could lead to over two dozen rules that —even if learned—would account for a minority of the problems faced with vowel representations.

Burmeister (1968) followed the same tack in attempting to improve on the existing rules by combining evidence from other studies. She later (Burmeister, 1971) reported evidence for a new rule for words in a final vowel-consonant-*e* pattern. With some strange combinations (*cake* and *care* as /ā/; *have* and *are* as /a/), she managed to work out a rule that was true 85.6 percent of the time: "When a word ends in a single vowel and single consonant *e,* the *e* is silent, and the vowel usually represents its own long or short sound—try the long sound first."

Fuld attempted to refine a rule for vowel sounds in the vowel-consonant-consonant (VCC) pattern. Using words taken from the primary level of five reading series, she found that 613 of 1,450 words were in the VCC pattern. Applying the rule that the vowel would have its "short" sound, she found the rule true—or "so close it would not prevent recognition"—in 431 words, 70 percent of the cases.

In the same vein as Fry, Emans (1967b) suggested a proliferation and expansion of rules to replace the general ones that applied to many words but were seldom true. For example, Clymer's rule 16 stated, "When *y* is the final letter in a word, it usually has a vowel sound (*dry*)." This useless rule was true 84 percent of the time. Emans suggested adding the qualification excepting *ay,* in which case the *y* is "silent." In so doing, he raised the utility of the rule to 100 percent, but he didn't make it any more helpful to the child.

It is readily apparent that the broad general rules apply to many words but aren't true very often. In the effort to proliferate the general rules into more accurate and specific ones, what is accomplished? For example, several specific vowel rules can be suggested that are true 100 percent of the time in a primary vocabulary: *ee-e* represents /ē/ (*freeze*), *ei-e* represents /ē/ (*receive*), and *eo* represents /ē/ (*people*). The only difficulty with such rules is that they each apply to only one word in Fitzgerald's list of 2,650 most frequently used words.

Rather than continue an examination of efforts to "patch up" existing rules about vowels, let's take a look at analyses of language that have gone beyond basal reader vocabularies. Are there facts about the "real world" of language that lend credibility to some vowel generalizations? How "regular" are the symbol-sound relationships for vowels?

The Nature of Vowel Symbol-Sound
Correspondences in English

As pointed out by Dewey's review of research (1971), various claims have been made about the "regularity" of English symbol-sound relationships: At one extreme is Hotson's claim that, since five-hundred symbols are used for forty sounds, English is "8 percent phonetic"; at the other is the claim by Spaulding that English is almost completely phonetic if one considers that 94 percent of the most used 1,000 words can be spelled correctly using seventy phonograms controlled by twenty-six rules.

Falling between these claims is the report by Moore, based on a study of 3,000 most frequently used words. This study, reported by Hanna and Moore, resulted in the claim that the English language was found to be 80 percent "regular" and that nearly three-fourths of the vowel phonemes were "regular" in 57 to 99 percent of their occurrences.

Horn reported results of his analysis of 10,000 words from his basic writing vocabulary. While he was in basic agreement with Moore on the most frequent spellings of most of the vowel sounds, he disagreed with the percentages and number of different spellings. He strongly disagreed with the term *regular* for a representation of a sound when that spelling occurred less than 50 percent of the time.

Horn also pointed out that, within the 10,000 words he examined, it would be most difficult to find a "regular" spelling for a sound since one-third of the words examined had more than one pronunciation.

Groff reported an analysis of the sound-symbol relationships in the *New Iowa Spelling Scale*. He took every fifth word from the more than 5,000 words. Even though he considered all variant sounds of a vowel letter as "phonetic" spellings ("the *a*'s in *fate, chaotic, care, add, account, arm, ask, sofa,* and *baby* were all considered phonetic" [p. 47]), he still found that 75 percent of the words were "nonphonetic." On the other hand, in a letter by letter analysis, he found that only 18.8 percent of the letters were "nonphonetic."

A large scale computerized study was completed at Stanford University (Hanna et al.), analyzing 17,000 words to determine the relationship between sound and symbol in English. From this study comes the often quoted statistic that English is 84 percent "regular" in its sound-symbol relationships. However, that 84 percent is based on several questionable factors and is also only part of the story.

First of all, the computer was programmed for 203 rules—more than most children can be "programmed" for. More important in our consideration here were some of the elements of the programming. For example, the schwa sound is the most frequently used vowel sound, comprising about 25 percent of all the vowel sounds represented on a page of text. This sound is also the most variable in its representation, with at least twenty-six different spellings. Hence, the computer was programmed with eight different spellings for the schwa sound. It shouldn't have been difficult for the computer to respond correctly when asked how to spell "schwa spelled *e*," "schwa spelled *o*," and so on.

Finally, the 84 percent was the result of input of the 17,000 words *phoneme by phoneme*. It is important on this point to recall that two out of three phonemes in running English text are consonants, and consonants tend to be much more consistent in their sound representations. For example, the three-phoneme word *been* (/bin/) results in 67 percent "regularity," since the two consonant phonemes represent their usual sounds: $b = $ /b/ and $n = $ /n/. However, *ee* is an infrequent representation of /i/. Such handling of the study would tend toward 67 percent regularity, even if there were *no* sound-symbol relationships among vowels.

A major finding from the Stanford study is the result when the 17,000 words were fed into the computer as whole words. Then the computer, even with its 203 rules, was able to spell with only 49.9 percent accuracy. Hence, rather than refer to English as being 84 percent "regular," if we want to talk about regularity at all, it should be in terms of 50 percent correspondence between sound and symbol. Children are asked to read and to spell words, not phonemes!

Many of the same questions or criticisms Horn raised in connection with the Moore report could be raised with the Stanford study. It is not our purpose here to do such a complete analysis. The reader who is interested in more technical concerns with the study is referred to Cahen and others, Reed, or Roberts.

Rather than present more conclusions and arguments from others, we would like to present data from three analyses of the English language and allow the reader to make his own interpretation about the possibility of rules about vowels. All three studies are summarized in terms of the fifteen vowel sounds usually presented in a dictionary pronunciation key.

The first study (Hillerich, 1965) is probably more pertinent to our subject of primary reading instruction since it is a tabulation of vowel sounds and their representations in the 1,942 base words from Fitzgerald's list of 2,650 most frequently used words. The tabulation excluded variant forms of words in order to avoid excessive duplication. It also does not include the final vowel in 303 of the words in which schwa plus /r/, /l/, /n/, or a syllabic consonant form the last syllable, as in *battle, writer,* or *broken.*

The second study is the Stanford study (Hanna et al.), which included 17,000 different words. In order to make the studies comparable, Hanna's twenty-two-vowel sound classifications had to be regrouped into the fifteen-sound classification. Hanna classified a number of similar sounds separately, apparently because of the spelling and to lead to a higher percentage of accuracy by the computer. For example, *all, arm,* and *off,* classified separately by Hanna, have been combined under /ȯ/, since all three contain that same vowel sound.

In the third study, Dewey analyzed 10,119 words. His tabulation had to be adjusted to combine the vowel sounds in the words *alms* and *not* under /ä/ to fit within the fifteen-sound classification.

Some of the differences among the three studies are due to differences in dialect among the speakers, as well as to Hanna's use of "spelling pronunciation," that is, pronunciation as it would be in the isolated pronunciation of each word. Hillerich used *Webster's Third New International Dictionary* (1961) and selected the pronunciation closest to the Midwest dialect.

Since Hanna and Dewey used more traditional dictionaries, a major difference in the studies will be in the frequency of the schwa sound. The older dictionaries differentiate the vowel sound at the beginning of *about* from the vowel sound at the beginning of *up*, indicating the former as /ə/ and the latter as /u/ because it is in an accented syllable. Since publication of the *Third International,* G & C Merriam dictionaries have consistently recognized the sound by the same symbol /ə/, whether in an accented or unaccented syllable, reasoning that when a sound is the same, the symbol used for it should be the same, regardless of the kind of syllable that sound is in.

A final difference in classifications has to do with the subject of this section: Since there is no one-to-one correspondence between symbol and sound, how does one classify the *b* in *lamb* or *doubt,* or the *e* in *chance?* Dewey assigned half values to each letter. While such a system does not seem very satisfactory, it is better than some of the inconsistencies observed in the Stanford study.

Hillerich tried to handle the problem by assigning consonant letters to consonant sounds when they seemed to have no connection with vowel sounds, as in *lamb* and *doubt.* Final *e* clearly is part of the spelling of the vowel sound in vowel-consonant-e (VCe) words such as *cape, ate, Pete.* However, unlike the usual handling in the Stanford study, Hillerich assigned the final *e* in words like *chance* or *change* to the spelling of the final consonant sound, since *e* indicates the /s/ and /j/ sounds for *c* and *g.* In other words, when two consonants (nondigraphs) intervened before the final *e,* the *e* was usually part of the spelling of the final consonant sound and was so assigned in the data.

All three studies are presented in Tables 1, 2, and 3. These tables may be used either for reading or for spelling. From a reading standpoint, each table shows the number of cases in which a given grapheme represented each of the vowel sounds. Using Table 1 for reading, entry would be from the left-hand column ("Spelling"). For example, if the reader sees the letter *e,* that person might want to know what sound *e* represents. Finding *e* in the left column, the reader would move across that row. Each numeral in the row indicates the number of cases in which the vowel sound at the top of the column was represented by *e.* In these data, *e* represented /i/ 9 times, /e/ 241 times, and so on.

To use the table for spelling, enter with the sound representations at the top of the page and move down the column to find the various ways that sound was spelled. For example, to find the spellings of /e/ (*elf*), locate that sound at the top of the second column of sounds and move down the column to find that sound spelled *a* in twenty cases, *a-e* in eight cases, *ai* in thirteen, and so on.

A comparison of Tables 1, 2, and 3 indicates that the larger word counts naturally include a greater variety of spellings for the vowel sounds.[2] However, they are in reasonable agreement about what the spellings are and the proportions of each. Efforts to find a generalization from the foregoing tables might begin by selecting the most frequently occurring graphemes and examining them in terms of their most frequent sound representation. Results of such an exploration are presented in Table 4.

Table 4 indicates a reasonable amount of agreement among the three studies in terms of percentages of sounds represented by each of the graphemes. The outstand-

---

2. Tables 1–3 are reproduced from Robert Hillerich, *Spelling: An Element in Written Expression.* Columbus: Charles E. Merrill Publishing Co., 1976.

TABLE 1. HILLERICH COUNT: SOUND-SPELLING CORRESPONDENCE FOR VOWELS

Key Word	pin	elf	bat	top	saw	foot	cup	ape	eel	kite	boat	oil	owl	moon	few
Sound	/i/	/e/	/a/	/ä/	/ȯ/	/u̇/	/ə/	/ā/	/ē/	/ī/	/ō/	/ȯi/	/au̇/	/ü/	/yü/
Spelling															
a	1	20	197	6	71		113	60							
a-e	9	8	1	1	1		9	62							
ai		13					1	34							
ai-e								1							
aigh								1							
au			2		8										
au-e					2										
augh					4										
aw					9										
ay		2						18	9						
e	9	241					140		71						
e-e	2	1					1		3						
ea	9	27		1			7	3	53						
ea-e									2						

TABLE 1. HILLERICH COUNT—CONTINUED

Key Word	pin	elf	bat	top	saw	foot	cup	ape	eel	kite	boat	oil	owl	moon	few
Sound	/i/	/e/	/a/	/ä/	/ȯ/	/u̇/	/ə/	/ā/	/ē/	/ī/	/ō/	/ȯi/	/au̇/	/ü/	/yü/
Spelling															
eau															2
ee	6								55						
ee-e									1						
ei							1		3						
ei-e									1						
eigh								10		1					
eo									1						
ew											1			8	2
ey								2							
eye										1					
i	219						86		16	48					
i-e	6						7		5	65					
ia							1			1					
ia-e	2														

TABLE 1. HILLERICH COUNT—CONTINUED

Key Word Sound	pin /i/	elf /e/	bat /a/	top /ä/	saw /ȯ/	foot /u̇/	cup /ə/	ape /ā/	eel /ē/	kite /ī/	boat /ō/	oil /ȯi/	owl /au̇/	moon /ü/	few /yü/
Spelling															
ie	2	1					1		7	7					
ie-e									4						
iew															1
igh										13					
io							1								
iou							1								
o	1			84	60	2	135				72			7	
o-e					1		9				41			4	
oa											17				
oe							1				3			1	
oh											1				
oi										1		9			
oi-e												2			
oo						18	2				1			19	

106

TABLE 1. HILLERICH COUNT—CONTINUED

Key Word	pin	elf	bat	top	saw	foot	cup	ape	eel	kite	boat	oil	owl	moon	few
Sound	/i/	/e/	/a/	/ä/	/ȯ/	/u̇/	/ə/	/ā/	/ē/	/ī/	/ō/	/ȯi/	/au̇/	/ü/	/yü/
Spelling															
oo-e														3	
ou				3	1	2	18				8		24	3	15
ou-e													2	1	
ough					5						2			1	
ow				4							26		10		
oy												5			
u	2	1				6	127							11	15
u-e						2	7							4	7
ua				1			2								
ue		1												5	2
ui	3													2	
ui-e										1				1	
uy										1					
y	5								119	15					
y-e										1					

107

TABLE 2.   HANNA COUNT: SOUND-SPELLING CORRESPONDENCE FOR VOWELS

Key Word	pin	elf	bat	top	saw	foot	cup	ape	eel	kite	boat	oil	owl	moon	few
Sound	/i/	/e/	/a/	/ä/	/ȯ/	/u̇/	/ə/	/ā/	/ē/	/ī/	/ō/	/ȯi/	/au̇/	/ü/	/yü/
Spelling															
a	4	158	4192	80	683		1606	1002							
a-e	187	51	147		34		3	790							
ae		1							5						
ah					4										
ai	15	50	1				9	208							
ai-e		3						18		1					
aigh								4							
ao					2										
au					150		1				3				
au-e					9			1			2				
augh					12										
aw					75										
aw-e					2										
ay		1						131		3					
ay-e								1							
e	69	3320			5		2742	16	1765						
e-e	28	113					143	6	62						

Table 2. Hanna Count—Continued

Key Word	pin	elf	bat	top	saw	foot	cup	ape	eel	kite	boat	oil	owl	moon	few
Sound	/i/	/e/	/a/	/ä/	/ȯ/	/u̇/	/ə/	/ā/	/ē/	/ī/	/ō/	/ȯi/	/au̇/	/ü/	/yü/
Spelling															
ea	50	152			18		32	14	245						
ea-e	1	1					2		30						
eau											6				5
ee	42								249						
ee-e									9						
ei	13	6					2	14	16	6					
ei-e								2	6	3					
eigh								18							
eo		3					10	9	2						
et								9							
eu						1	6							4	28
eu-e															1
ew											3			22	38
ew-e															1
ey	40	1						14	6	1					
ey-e										7					
eou							8								

TABLE 2. HANNA COUNT—CONTINUED

Key Word	pin	elf	bat	top	saw	foot	cup	ape	eel	kite	boat	oil	owl	moon	few
Sound	/i/	/e/	/a/	/ä/	/ȯ/	/u̇/	/ə/	/ā/	/ē/	/ī/	/ō/	/ȯi/	/au̇/	/ü/	/yü/
Spelling															
i	5349						1459		38	554					
i-e	339						7		44	555					
ia	3						2								
ia-e															
ie	43	4					22		33	26					
ie-e	4						4		23						
ieu															4
iew															6
igh										88					
o	1			1558	435	17	2044				1876			37	
o-e				20	21		48				370			12	
oa					9						127				
oa-e											3				
oe									5		13				
oh											4			4	
oi												92			
oi-e							2					8			

110

Table 2. Hanna Count—Continued

Key Word	pin	elf	bat	top	saw	foot	cup	ape	eel	kite	boat	oil	owl	moon	few
Sound	/i/	/e/	/a/	/ä/	/ò/	/ů/	/ə/	/ā/	/ē/	/ī/	/ō/	/öi/	/aů/	/ü/	/yü/
Spelling															
oo						114	7				9			173	
oo-e														12	
ou						25	388				29		227	29	
ou-e							1				10		54	3	
ough					15						8		4	2	
ow				4							124		119		
ow-e											1		2		
oy												48			
oy-e										1		1			
u	3	2				200	1743							93	814
u-e	3					11	60							34	256
ue														16	27
uo														2	
ui	16													6	8
ui-e														4	
uy										3					
y	1801						29			211					
y-e	1									23					

111

TABLE 3. DEWEY COUNT: SOUND-SPELLING CORRESPONDENCE FOR VOWELS

Key Word	pin	elf	bat	top	saw	foot	cup	ape	eel	kite	boat	oil	owl	moon	few
Sound	/i/	/e/	/a/	/ä/	/ȯ/	/u̇/	/ə/	/ā/	/ē/	/ī/	/ō/	/ȯi/	/au̇/	/ü/	/yü/
Spelling															
a	15	10	1536	315	107		1105	650							
a-e	94		23	22	4		51	355							
a-ue								1							
aa				1											
ae									1						
ah				1											
ai	15	4						244							
ai-e								11		1					
aigh								5							
ao					1										
au			3	15	38						4				
au-e					7			1			1				
augh					8										
aw					34										
awe					1										
ay		1						90							
aye								1							

Table 3. Dewey Count—Continued

Key Word	pin	elf	bat	top	saw	foot	cup	ape	eel	kite	boat	oil	owl	moon	few
Sound	/i/	/e/	/a/	/ä/	/ȯ/	/u̇/	/ə/	/ā/	/ē/	/ī/	/ō/	/ȯi/	/au̇/	/ü/	/yü/
Spelling															
e	803	2941		2			1051	3	205						
e-e	4	96					27	24	46						
e-ue		4													
ea		105		11			30	20	266						
ea-e							1		27						
ea-ue									1						
eau								1			1				3
ee	6							1	175						
ee-e									6						
eh								1							
ei	3							6	13						
ei-e									11						
eigh								19		4					
eo							1		3		1				
eu							6							1	3
eu-e															1
ew											5			12	19

113

TABLE 3. DEWEY COUNT—CONTINUED

Key Word	pin	elf	bat	top	saw	foot	cup	ape	eel	kite	boat	oil	owl	moon	few
Sound	/i/	/e/	/a/	/ä/	/ò/	/ù/	/ə/	/ā/	/ē/	/ī/	/ō/	/òi/	/aù/	/ü/	/yü/
Spelling															
ey	22							12	3						
eye										4					
ha							1								
hau					1										
hi	1														
ho				6											
hou													4		
i	3807						330		16	302					
i-e	151								14	324					
i-ue									3						
ia	3														
ia-e	2														
ie	121	5							36	49					
ie-e									14						
ieu															2
iew															8
igh										74					
i-o							3			3					

TABLE 3. DEWEY COUNT—CONTINUED

Key Word	pin	elf	bat	top	saw	foot	cup	ape	eel	kite	boat	oil	owl	moon	few
Sound	/i/	/e/	/a/	/ä/	/ȯ/	/u̇/	/ə/	/ā/	/ē/	/ī/	/ō/	/ȯi/	/au̇/	/ü/	/yü/
Spelling															
io															
o	2			1022	219	14	891				755			26	
o-e				21	10		44				183			15	
o-o							3								
o-ue			5			2					1				
oa					3						72				
oa-e											4				
oe							2		1		13			5	
oeu														1	
oh											1				
oi	1			1			1					66			
oi-e							7					7			
oo						54					6			88	
oo-e														6	
ot											2				
ou						8	168				21		150	36	
ou-e											4		40	4	

TABLE 3. DEWEY COUNT—CONTINUED

Key Word	pin	elf	bat	top	saw	foot	cup	ape	eel	kite	boat	oil	owl	moon	few
Sound	/i/	/e/	/a/	/ä/	/ȯ/	/u̇/	/ə/	/ā/	/ē/	/ī/	/ō/	/ȯi/	/au̇/	/ü/	/yü/
Spelling															
ough					9						7		6	2	
ow				5							106		56		
owe											1				
oy												32			
re							10								
u	4	1				288	904							78	186
u-e	3					87	19							28	81
u-ue							1								
ua			3	8											
ue		5				13	2	1						9	14
ugh						1									
ui	16								1	1				10	5
ui-e										5				1	
uo							1								
uy										6					
y	885						1			73					
y-e										11					
ye										2					

116

Table 4. The Most Frequently Occurring Graphemes, Their Most Frequent Sound Representation, and the Percentage of Times They Represent that Sound

Grapheme	Number of Sounds Represented	Hillerich (1,942 words)			Hanna (17,000 words)			Dewey (10,119 words)		
		Number of Occurrences	Most Common Sound	Most Common Sound (%)	Number of Occurrences	Most Common Sound	Most Common Sound (%)	Number of Occurrences	Most Common Sound	Most Common Sound (%)
a	7	468	/a/	42.1	7,725	/a/	54.3	3,738	/a/	41.1
a-e	5	91	/ā/	68.1	1,212	/ā/	65.2	549	/ā/	64.7
e	6	461	/e/	52.3	7,917	/e/	41.9	5,005	/e/	58.8
ea	6	100	/ē/	53.0	511	/ē/	47.9	432	/ē/	61.6
i	4	369	/i/	59.3	7,400	/i/	72.3	4,455	/i/	85.5
i-e	4	83	/ī/	78.3	945	/ī/	58.7	489	/ī/	66.3
o	7	361	/ə/	37.4	5,968	/ə/	34.2	2,929	/ä/	34.9
o-e	4	55	/ō/	74.5	471	/ō/	78.6	273	/ō/	67.0
u	6	162	/ə/	78.4	2,855	/ə/	61.1	1,461	/ə/	61.9
u-e	4	20	/ə/	35.0	364	/yü/	70.3	218	/ü/	40.0
			/yü/	35.0						
y	4	139	/ē/	85.6	2,041	/i/	88.2	959	/i/	92.3

ing difference is the grapheme *y,* which Hillerich classifies as /ē/ (*baby*), whereas the other two researchers classify it as /i/.

Other than for the possible acceptance of a generalization that *y* represents /ē/ or /i/, depending upon dialect, one would be hard pressed to justify any other generalization based on the facts about language presented in Table 4. For example, each of these frequently occurring graphemes represents from four to seven different sounds, and the most frequently represented sound never occurs even 75 percent of the time in all three studies.

The most frequently occurring graphemes are of little help toward a generalization because of the number of different sounds they represent and because of the low frequency with which they represent even their most common sound. Hence, we might take a different tack and look for graphemes that represent only one sound, that is, graphemes with 100 percent utility. Table 5 presents the list of graphemes that represent only one sound in at least one of the studies. Indicated within parentheses in Table 5 are the number of different sounds represented by the grapheme when such was found in one or more of the studies.

As shown in Table 5, there are only nine (asterisked) graphemes that consistently represent one sound in all three studies. Those nine, if stated as rules, would be true 100 percent of the time. The only difficulty is that the nine rules would account for only 0.5 to 1.1 percent of all the words in the three studies.

Slightly more efficient coverage can be achieved by reducing the nine rules to the two graphemes that occur with any degree of frequency at all, *aw* and *igh.* These two graphemes, taught as rules (*aw* = /ȯ/ and *igh* = /ī/), would be true 100 percent of the time and would account for 0.4 to 0.8 percent of the cases in these studies. Put another way, if one feels it is worthwhile, the teaching of these two rules would account for twenty-two words from the primary list of 1,942 words, or 0.8 percent of those words.

Even here, however, a word of caution is in order if we are to think from the standpoint of a child in the early stages of reading. If *aw* is taught as consistently representing /ȯ/, which it does in nine words, the youngster could be mislead in words such as *await, awake, award, away, awhile, awoke.* Likewise, the inexperienced reader, drilled on the fact that *igh* represents /ī/, may not be alert enough or experienced enough to distinguish the *igh* from *aigh* and *eigh.*

A summary of the evidence from Tables 1 through 3 is presented in Table 6. As shown, fifty-seven to eighty-seven different graphemes are used in English to represent the fifteen vowel sounds. From a spelling viewpoint, one would have to look at the 142 to 200 different grapheme/phoneme combinations, since these fifty-seven to eighty-seven graphemes represent different sounds, and different graphemes are also used to spell the same sound.

The second part of Table 6 summarizes the evidence previously discussed: The single graphemes *a, e, i, o,* and *u* represent a large percentage of the vowel sounds. However, while they are most frequently used, they are also variable in that the five graphemes represent twenty-eight to thirty different sounds, an average of 5.6 to 6.0 different sounds per grapheme.

Finally, Table 6 summarizes the evidence for those seeking graphemes representing only one sound: 37 to 52 percent of all the graphemes represent only one sound

Table 5. *Numer of Occurrences of Graphemes with One Sound Representation on at Least One of the Studies (Figures in Parentheses Indicate Number of Sounds when More Than One Is Reported)*

Grapheme	Hillerich	Hanna	Dewey	Grapheme	Hillerich	Hanna	Dewey
a-ue	–	–	1	hou	–	–	4
aa	–	–	1	i-ue	–	–	3
ae	–	(2)	1	ia	(2)	2	3
ah	–	4	1	* ia-e	2	3	2
ai-e	1	(3)	(2)	ie-e	4	(3)	14
* aigh	1	4	5	ieu	–	4	2
ao	–	2	1	* iew	1	6	8
augh	4	12	8	†* igh	13	88	74
au-e	2	(3)	(3)	io	1	–	2
†* aw	9	75	34	iou	1	–	–
aw-e	–	2	–	o-o	–	–	3
awe	–	–	1	oa	17	(2)	(2)
ay-e	–	1	–	oa-e	–	3	4
aye	–	–	1	oeu	–	–	1
ea-e	2	(4)	(2)	* oh	1	4	1
e-ue	–	–	4	oi	(2)	92	(4)
eau	2	(2)	(2)	oi-e	2	(2)	7
ea-ue	–	–	1	* oo-e	3	12	6
* ee-e	1	9	6	ot	–	–	2
eh	–	–	1	owe	–	–	1
ei-e	1	(2)	11	oy	5	(2)	32
et	–	9	–	oy-e	–	1	–
eo	1	(3)	(3)	re	–	–	10
eu-e	–	1	1	u-ue	–	–	1
ew-e	–	1	–	ugh	–	–	1
ey	2	(5)	(3)	uo	–	2	1
ey-e	–	7	–	* uy	1	3	6
eye	1	–	4	ui-e	(2)	4	(2)
eou	–	8	–	y-e	1	(2)	11
ha	–	–	1	ye	–	–	2
hau	–	–	1				
hi	–	–	1				
ho	–	–	6				

*Represent one sound in all three studies. Account for 0.5–1.1 percent of all words.
†Graphemes with any degree of frequency at all. Account for 0.4–0.8 percent of all words.

Table 6. *Representations of the Fifteen Vowel Sounds*

	Hillerich (1,942 Words)	Hanna (17,000 Words)	Dewey (10,119 Words)
Vowel Sound Occurrences (Total Number):	2,772.0	41,155.0	23,041.0
Number of Different Graphemes:	57.0	69.0	87.0
Average per Sound:	3.8	4.6	5.8
Number of Different Grapheme/Phoneme Combinations:	142.0	190.0	200.0
Average per Sound:	9.5	12.7	13.3
Percent of Vowel Sounds Accounted for by the Most Common Graphemes (a̲, e̲, i̲, o̲, u̲):	65.7	77.4	76.3
Number of Occurrences:	1,821.0	31,865.0	17,588.0
Total Number of Sounds Represented by the Five Graphemes:	28.0	30.0	30.0
Average Number of Sounds per Grapheme:	5.6	6.0	6.0
Number of Graphemes Representing Only One Sound:	25.0	26.0	46.0
Percent of All Graphemes:	43.9	37.7	52.9
Number of Occurrences Accounted for:	79.0	359.0	292.0
Percent of All Occurrences:	2.8	0.9	1.3

each. The difficulty here is that this large number of different graphemes account for only 0.9 to 2.8 percent of all vowel sounds represented in the three collections of words.

Summary: How "Regular" Is English Orthography?

By "regular" do we refer to the percent of phonemes that are spelled in the most common way? This is the direction Hanna took with the 17,000 words and found that phoneme by phoneme, the computer was able to spell with 84 percent accuracy.

This view, when applied to vowels, is of little help. The five most common representations (*a, e, i, o, u*) account for 65.7 to 77.4 percent of the vowel appearances, but they also represent twenty-eight to thirty different sounds.

By "regular" do we refer to the percent of letters that represent only one sound? If, so, at first glance it would appear that the spellings of vowel sounds are fairly regular: Depending on the study used, 37 to 51 percent of the graphemes represent just one sound each. Unfortunately, the total number of cases accounted for by this large percentage of consistent representations is only 0.9 to 2.8 percent. In other words, a good number of the graphemes have one sound representation, but they account for very few occurrences of the vowel sounds.

By "regular" do we mean the percent of sounds spelled only one way? If so, then there is absolutely no regularity! In terms of any study, there is no sound that is spelled in only one way.

By "regular" do we mean the percent of words spelled in the most common way? If so, then the Hanna study itself clearly answers that question. Of the 17,000 words, only 49.9 percent were spelled in the regular fashion as based on 203 rules.

In summary, any rule about vowels can be classified into one of two categories: either it is a very broad rule that applies to many words but isn't true very often, or it is a very specific rule that is true most of the time but applies to very few words. In either event, are such rules worth teaching?

The Effectiveness of Teaching Vowel Rules to Children

All of this examination of the nature of the English language answers only part of the question about the value of teaching vowel generalizations. The answer cannot be resolved finally without a look at the evidence on what happens when vowel generalizations are taught to children. Are they better readers as a result?

A considerable number of studies exist that are in agreement that the teaching of vowel generalizations does not contribute to spelling success (Hillerich, 1976a). This is true even though phoneme to grapheme correspondence (spelling) has been demonstrated as easier than the reverse—grapheme to phoneme correspondence (reading) (Hardy). However, research studies that deal specifically with evaluation of the effectiveness of teaching vowel generalizations in reading are scarce.

As stated in Chapter 1, global kinds of comparisons between extreme phonic programs versus those that delay phonics are of no help because so many other variables enter into them. And certainly, this author has no desire to imply that there is a question as to whether children should or should not be taught phonics. The emphasis in the earlier chapters dealing with the development of consonant sound associations certainly suggests the importance of that kind of phonics. On the other hand, within the area of phonics, all kinds of practices take place; and the question being raised is, How effective are the phonics rules we teach about vowels?

Ibeling reported a study of six hundred children in grades two, four, and six. All children used the same reading program, but the experimental group received supplementary instruction with phonics workbooks. In terms of reading achievement, Ibeling found no significant difference in the two groups except at grade four, where reading comprehension was significantly higher for the group that did not receive the supplementary phonics.

An investigation of the effectiveness of teaching vowel generalizations to first-grade children compared two school districts comparable in terms of the children's IQ, socioeconomic level, their teachers salaries, and so on (Hillerich, 1976). With a total of 722 first graders in the two school districts, the effectiveness of teaching vowel generalizations was compared with no teaching of these generalizations.

At the end of the year, the children were tested on a thirty-item test of vowel generalizations using nonsense syllables. Children who had been taught vowel generalizations scored significantly higher on the nonsense syllables than did those children who were not so taught. It was interesting that a correlation of scores for children in the two districts was .92, suggesting that the relative difficulty of the vowel generalizations related more to the nature of the language than to whether or not teaching had taken place. More evidence on that point was apparent since four of the six most frequently missed nonsense syllables, and four of the five least frequently missed, were common to both groups of pupils.

Reading achievement was tested at the end of the year with the *Stroud Primary Reading Profiles,* Level 1. Results indicated a significant difference in reading achievement (.05) in favor of those children who had not been taught about vowels. Most interesting in the breakdown of the five subtests was the lack of difference in any subtest except one; in the subtest of reading comprehension, there was a significant difference (.01) in favor of the children who had not been taught about vowels, suggesting that such children might be concentrating more on meaning.

If the teaching of vowel generalizations in first grade does not contribute to reading success, why do we assume that it will do so in second grade? This question was also investigated (Hillerich, 1970). Six second-grade teachers agreed to participate in the study and were assigned to one of three treatment groups. Basal reading program and school district were the same for all three treatments.

In the first treatment, two teachers taught the basal reading program just as the manual directed, including a considerable number of lessons on vowel generalizations. The second treatment group of two classes used the same program but stopped short of developing a generalization about any of the vowel sounds. Children worked only at the hearing level, identifying a vowel sound and then finding other words with the same vowel sound but never going to the point of attempting to generalize that a given letter or letters represented a certain vowel sound. The third treatment group of two classes was taught absolutely nothing about vowels during the second-grade year.

Reading achievement at the end of the year was tested with the *Stroud Primary Reading Profiles,* Level 2. Results indicated that the children in treatment group two (hearing level) scored significantly higher (.01) than did the group taught about vowels. The group taught nothing about vowels was also higher in reading achievement than those taught about vowels, but the difference was not significant.

Such evidence brings us back full circle to Chapter 1 and indications reported there about the importance of an auditory emphasis in beginning reading. Treatment group two, which had worked on the vowel sounds without generalizations, was truly emphasizing an auditory approach. While further research is needed from a reading viewpoint, the effectiveness of this auditory approach from a spelling standpoint has been demonstrated in a number of studies (Hillerich, 1966 and 1971; Bredin).

No vowel rule is more than partially true: In the words of basal reader manuals, they are true "sometimes but not always," "usually," and so on. This being the fact, the teaching of vowel rules must also be considered from the point of the child. What happens if the child is taught a rule, limited to contrived vocabulary that keeps the rule true for a while, and then faced with the real world of variability in reading material?

This point has been brought out in a number of research studies. Levin and Watson compared two groups of third-grade pupils. One group was given two lists of words: the first contained a one-to-one correspondence between letter and sound; the second was a list with typical "irregularities." The second group was presented with two lists of words also, but both were "irregular." Results indicated that the second group did better on the second list than did the first group; children in the first group seemed to develop a "mind set" for consistency and to have more difficulty when then faced with the natural inconsistencies of the language. Williams and Ackerman reported this same kind of mind set.

What Should Be Taught about Vowels?

Based on the evidence presented thus far, analysis of the language leads to few if any generalizations to be taught about vowel symbol-sound relationships. The limited evidence available from the teaching of vowel generalizations to children also raises a major question about the effectiveness of such teaching.

Hislop and King also verified the finding that children taught those generalizations score higher on a test of nonsense syllables. These authors pointed out, however," the majority were unable to explain how they had arrived at their pronunciation" (p. 412). This writer found the same thing to be true in testing kindergarten children who had learned to read before they came to school. These children could score as well as typical second or third graders on the test of nonsense syllables, but naturally could not verbalize vowel rules or reasons to explain how they knew the pronunciation of the syllables.

Such findings imply that reading experience will lead to some intuitive generalizations about vowel representations. It may be much more effective if these generalizations remain intuitive rather than be verbalized. Apparently, children who were taught to verbalize the rules suffered in comprehension (Hillerich, 1967), a finding that has been rather consistent in comparisons of extreme phonics programs with those placing less emphasis on phonic rules. Are children taught the rules more concerned about recalling the rule and decoding the word than they are about using context and reading with understanding?

Actually, we might look on the lack of regular symbol-sound relationships for vowels as somewhat of a benefit. Children who learn to read in languages, such as Spanish, that do have nearly a one-to-one correspondence between symbol and sound learn very easily to say all the words but may easily become word callers rather than comprehenders of their reading. The lack of regularity of the vowels in

English almost forces the reader to use context and therefore to read for comprehension.

Furthermore, English orthography seems partially designed on a morphological rather than a phonological basis, that is, variant forms of printed words keep a base spelling even though pronunciation may be different. This characteristic, referred to by Venezky as "morphophonemic alteration," assists recognition of *angel* in *angelic* or *athlete* in *athletic* despite a different pronunciation of the vowel sounds in each of the pairs.

There is even some question about the retention of rules, even if they can be developed. For example, Gagné and Wiegand reported a study of ninety-six fourth graders who were taught three, five, seven, and nine rules relating to consonant-vowel-consonant patterns in words. These investigators found virtually complete retention of the three and five rules on immediate recall tests. However, there was only 20 percent retention after three days.

Teaching about Vowels—The "Exploration Method"

Based on the evidence from language and from working with children, an "exploration of possibilities" rather than the teaching of rules seems in order. In other words, recognizing the importance of an auditory emphasis, the teacher will call children's attention to a particular vowel sound, possibly use a key picture to help them recall that vowel sound, and then will have them explore material they can read in order to find other example words that contain that vowel sound.

The initial identification of the vowel sound may have to begin all the way back at the same level as was used in developing recognition of the consonant sounds; that is, say three words, two of which have the same vowel sound and one which does not, or have the children begin by collecting pictures whose names contain the same vowel sound as a key picture presented to them.

While no specific sequence of vowel sounds is necessary, the teacher may want to begin with complex vowel sounds, since they are usually easier to discriminate auditorily than simple vowels; for example, compare the minimal pairs *tame/team* with *ten/tin*.

Following is a sample procedure for the vowel sound /ā/, as in *ape*. Once children at second grade or above are capable of identifying whether a word has that sound, the teacher may begin by giving them a key word (for example, *ape*) and having them examine a page from the story they have just completed in their readers to find all the words that contain /ā/.

The children will make lists of the words found. In an ensuing discussion, make a composite of the words on the board, sorted by the spellings of /ā/. The list may look something like the following:

/ā/ as in *ape*

a	*ai*	*a-e*	*aigh*
able	aim	bake	straight
lazy	paint	age	
	chain		

Following this compilation, suggest that children use their free time to find additional words with the same sound from library books or other printed material. In a day or so, the group may be brought together to share the words they have found. The resulting discussion may extend the original composite on the board to something like the following:

/ā/ as in *ape*

a	*ai*	*a-e*	*aigh*
able	aim	bake	straight
lazy	paint	age	
April	chain	ate	

ai-e	*eigh*	*ay*	*ey*	*ea*
raise	eight	play	they	break
	weigh	day		

Classes may then try the reverse process, finding words with *a* and sorting according to the sounds represented by that letter.

Such experience has a number of values. First of all, obviously no generalization will be drawn other than the fact that /ā/ is spelled in a variety of ways or a variety of letters may represent the vowel sound /ā/. Secondly, this kind of approach is truly a discovery method: It doesn't "stack the cards" with a few preselected items that will force children to the generalization we want them to learn; it opens the door to the whole world of language. Third, this approach has its own built-in adaptation to individual differences. Every child can participate. The bright child will collect fifty words and fifteen different spellings; the slower child will collect fifteen words and five different spellings. All can benefit from the ensuing discussion of the findings. Finally, this kind of activity has implications for future use of a dictionary, which will be discussed in Chapter 8.

For teachers who use this approach, Table 7 provides a list of the possible sounds represented by each of the graphemes. Such lists should never be *taught* to children, since the process of exploring language is much more important. In fact, teachers ought to join with their pupils in this kind of exploration.

SUMMARY

Examination of the language indicates that rules about vowels either must be so general that they have many exceptions or so specific that they apply to very few words. Hence, from the nature of language, the value of teaching rules about vowels can be questioned.

Limited research evidence on the effectiveness of teaching vowel rules to children indicates that such teaching fails to contribute to reading success. In fact, it suggests that children seem more concerned about the rule than they are about the meaning of what they read. In fact, it suggests that children who face the irregular nature of the language from the beginning have a better "mind set" for the language than do

Table 7. *Representations of Vowel Sounds*

Letter	Sound	Example Word	Letter	Sound	Example Word
a	/a/	bat	aw	/ȯ/	saw
	/e/	any	awe	/ȯ/	awe
	/i/	spinach	ay	/e/	says
	/ä/	father		/i/	yesterday*
	/ə/	along		/ā/	may
	/ȯ/	all		/ē/	quay
	/ā/	favor		/ī/	bayou
a-e	/a/	have	aye	/ī/	aye
	/e/	care	e	/e/	elf
	/i/	message		/i/	pretty
	/ä/	are		/ä/	sergeant
	/ə/	immediate		/ə/	enough
	/ā/	ape		/ā/	cafe
ae	/e/	aesthetic		/ē/	be
	/ā/	maelstrom	e-e	/e/	where
	/ē/	aegis		/i/	here
ah	/a/	dahlia		/ə/	science*
ai	/a/	plaid		/ā/	suede
	/e/	said		/ē/	these
	/i/	fountain*	ea	/e/	bread
	/ə/	captain		/i/	dear
	/ā/	pain		/ä/	heart
ai-e	/e/	millionaire		/ə/	pageant
	/ā/	aide		/ā/	steak
	/ī/	aisle*		/ē/	meat
aigh	/ā/	straight	ea-e	/e/	cleanse*
ais-e	/ī/	aisle		/ē/	leave
ao	/ȯ/	extraordinary		/i/	mileage*
au	/a/	laugh	eau	/ō/	beau
	/ə/	epaulet		/yu̇/	beauty
	/ȯ/	fault	ee	/i/	been
	/ō/	chauffeur		/ā/	matinee
	/au̇/	glaucoma		/ē/	eel
au-e	/ȯ/	cause	ee-e	/e/	sneeze
	/ā/	gauge	ei	/ē/	their
	/ō/	mauve		/i/	weird
augh	/ȯ/	taught		/ə/	foreign
				/ā/	vein

* = Hanna classification

126

Table 7 (Continued)

Letter	Sound	Example Word	Letter	Sound	Example Word
	/ē/	either	ia-e	/i/	carriage
	/ī/	stein	ie	/e/	friend
ei-e	/ā/	beige		/ə/	mischief
	/ē/	receive		/ē/	chief
eigh	/ā/	weigh		/ī/	tie
	/ī/	height	ie-e	/i/	sieve
eo	/e/	leopard		/ə/	patience*
	/ə/	luncheon		/ē/	believe
	/ē/	people	ieu	/ü/	lieu
	/ō/	yeoman		/yü/	adieu
eou	/i/	courageous	iew	/yü/	view
et	/ā/	bouquet	igh	/ī/	high
eu	/u̇/	pleurisy	io	/ə/	religion
	/ü/	maneuver	iou	/ə/	religious
	/yü/	feud	is	/ī/	island
ew	/ō/	sew	is-e	/ī/	isle
	/u/	grew	o	/i/	women
	/yu/	few		/ä/	top
eu-e	/yü/	deuce*		/ə/	son
ewe	/yü/	ewe		/ȯ/	off
ey	/e/	eyrie		/u̇/	wolf
	/i/	monkey*		/ō/	go
	/ā/	they		/ü/	do
	/ē/	key	o-e	/ə/	come
	/ī/	geyser		/ä/	gone*
eye	/ī/	eye		/ȯ/	gone
ho	/ä/	honest		/ō/	note
i	/i/	pin		/ü/	move
	/ə/	easily	oa	/ȯ/	broad
	/ē/	ski		/ō/	boat
	/ī/	bicycle	oa-e	/ō/	loathe
i-e	/i/	give	oe	/ə/	does
	/ə/	promise		/ē/	amoeba
	/ē/	machine		/ō/	hoe
	/ī/	kite		/ü/	canoe
ia	/ə/	parliament	oh	/ō/	oh
	/ī/	diamond	oi	/ȯi/	oil

* = Hanna classification

127

Table 7 (Continued)

oi-e	/ə/	porpoise			/i/	busy
	/ȯi/	choice			/ə/	cup
ois	/ē/	chamois			/u̇/	put
oo	/ə/	flood			/ü/	rumor
	/u̇/	foot			/yü/	unite
	/ȯ/	door	u-e	/ə/		minute
	/ü/	moon		/u̇/		sure
oo-e	/ü/	choose		/ü/		rule
os	/ō/	apropos		/yü/		use
ot	/ō/	depot	ua	/ä/		guard
othe	/ō/	clothes	ue	/e/		guess
ou	/ə/	couple		/ə/		guerilla
	/ȯ/	cough		/ü/		due
	/u̇/	should		/yü/		cue
	/ō/	soul	ueue	/yü/		queue
	/au̇/	out	ui	/i/		build
	/ü/	group		/ü/		fruit
ou-e	/ō/	cantaloupe	ui-e	/ī/		guide
	/au̇/	mouse		/ü/		bruise
	/ü/	route	uo	/ü/		buoy
ough	/ȯ/	ought	uu	/yü/		vacuum
	/ō/	though	uy	/ī/		buy
	/au̇/	bough	y	/i/		bicycle
	/ü/	through		/ə/		oygen
ow	/ä/	knowledge		/ē/		baby
	/ō/	know		/ī/		sky
	/au̇/	owl	y-e	/i/		apocalypse*
ow-e	/au̇/	browse*		/ī/		style
owe	/ō/	owe	ye	/ī/		rye
oy	/ȯi/	toy	yew	/yü/		yew
	/ī/	coyote	you	/yü/		you
oy-e	/ȯi/	gargoyle	yu-e	/yü/		yule
u	/e/	bury				

* = Hanna classification

those who receive an initial impression that symbol to sound correspondences are consistent.

On the other hand, the vowel letters do exist in print and ignoring them won't make them go away. While more research is needed, an "exploration method" avoids misleading generalizations and seems to contribute to both reading and spelling improvement. Such an approach has an auditory emphasis, makes children more conscious of the symbols and sounds of language, and makes them aware of possibilities in terms of sound-symbol relationships. Finally, this kind of approach keeps the focus on using context and reading for the author's meaning, as opposed to trying to recall the rules and being concerned about saying the words.

References

Ackerman, Margaret. "Acquisition and Transfer Value of Initial Training with Multiple Grapheme-Phoneme Correspondences." *Journal of Educational Psychology* 64(1973): 28–34.

Bailey, Mildred. "The Utility of Phonic Generalizations in Grades One through Six." *The Reading Teacher* 20(1967):413–18.

Bredin, Dorothy. "Evaluation of Third Grade Spelling." Skokie: *School District Bulletin,* June, 1972.

Burmeister, Lou E. "Final Vowel-Consonant-*e.*" *The Reading Teacher* 24(1971):439–42.

———. "Usefulness of Phonic Generalizations." *The Reading Teacher* 21(1968):349–56, 360.

Burrows, Alvina T., and Lourie, Zyra. "When 'Two Vowels Go Walking.' " *The Reading Teacher* 17(1963):78–82.

Cahen, Leonard S.; Craun, Marlys J.; and Johnson, Susan K. "Spelling Difficulty—A Survey of the Research." *Review of Educational Research* 41(1971):281–301.

Clymer, Theodore. "The Utility of Phonic Generalizations in Primary Grades." *The Reading Teacher* 16(1963):252–58.

Dewey, Godfrey. *English Spelling: Roadblock to Reading.* New York: Teachers College Press, 1971.

———. *Relative Frequency of English Spellings.* New York: Teachers College Press, 1970.

Emans, Robert. "The Usefulness of Phonic Generalizations Above the Primary Grades." *The Reading Teacher* 20(1967a):419–25.

———. "When Two Vowels Go Walking and Other Such Things." *The Reading Teacher* 21(1967b):262–69.

Fitzgerald, James A. *A Basic Life Spelling Vocabulary.* Milwaukee: Bruce Publishing Co., 1951.

Fry, Edward. "A Frequency Approach to Phonics." *Elementary English* 41(1964):759–65, 816.

Fuld, Paula. "Vowel Sounds in VCC Words." *The Reading Teacher* 21(1968):442–44.

Gagné, Robert, and Wiegand, Virginia. "Some Factors in Children's Learning and Retention of Concrete Rules." *Journal of Educational Psychology* 59(1968):355–61.

Groff, Patrick J. "The New Iowa Spelling Scale: How Phonetic Is It?" *Elementary School Journal* 62(1961):46–49.

Hanna, Paul, and Moore, J. T. Jr., "Spelling—From Spoken Word to Written Symbol." *Elementary School Journal* 53(1953):329–37.

Hanna, Paul R. et al. *Phoneme-Grapheme Correspondences as Cues to Spelling Improvement.* Washington, D.C.: U. S. Office of Health, Education, and Welfare, 1966.

Hardy, Madeline et al. "Developmental Patterns in Elemental Reading Skills: Phoneme-Grapheme and Grapheme-Phoneme Correspondences." *Journal of Educational Psychology* 63(1972):433–36.

Hillerich, Robert L. "Comparison of Two Approaches to Spelling Instruction." Unpublished manuscript, Glenview, 1966. (Available from 1311 Bourgogne, Bowling Green, OH 43402.)

————. "Grapheme/Phoneme Correspondence for Vowels." Unpublished manuscript, Glenview, 1965. (Available from 1311 Bourgogne, Bowling Green, OH 43402.)

————. "Predicting Reading Success." Unpublished manuscript, 1976. a (Available from 1311 Bourgogne, Bowling Green, OH 43402.)

————. "A Second Comparison of Two Approaches to Spelling Instruction." Unpublished manuscript, 1971. (Available from 1311 Bourgogne, Bowling Green, OH 43402.)

————. *Spelling: An Element in Written Expression.* Columbus: Charles Merrill, 1976. b

————. "Teaching about Vowels in Second Grade." *Illinois School Research* 7(1970): 35–38.

————. "Vowel Generalizations and First Grade Reading Achievement." *Elementary School Journal* 67(1967):246–50.

Hislop, Margaret J., and King, Ethel M. "Application of Phonic Generalizations by Beginning Readers." *Journal of Educational Research* 66(1973):405–12.

Horn, Ernest. "Phonetics and Spelling." *Elementary School Journal* 57(1957):424–32.

Ibeling, Fred. "Supplementary Phonics Instruction and Reading and Spelling Ability." *Elementary School Journal* 62(1961): 152–60.

Levin, Harry, and Watson, J. *A Basic Research Program on Reading.* Ithaca, New York: Cornell University Cooperative Research Grant No. 639, 1963.

Moore, James T., Jr. *Phonetic Elements Appearing in a Three-Thousand-Word Spelling Vocabulary.* Ph.D. dissertation, Stanford University, 1951.

Reed, David W. "A Review by a Specialist in Dialectology." *Research in the Teaching of English* I(1967):207–15.

Roberts, A. Hood. "A Review by a Specialist in the Uses of Computers in Linguistic Research." *Research in the Teaching of English* I(1967):201–7.

Venezky, Richard. "English Orthography: Its Graphical Structure and Its Relation to Sound." *Reading Research Quarterly* 2(1967):75–105.

Williams, Joanna. "Successive versus Concurrent Presentation of Multiple Grapheme-Phoneme Correspondences." *Journal of Educational Psychology* 59(1968):309–14.

7

Comprehension Skills: From the Beginning

Placement in this book of the comprehension skills after the basic decoding skills in no way implies a sequence, or that the teacher of reading will first teach the decoding skills and eventually begin to teach comprehension skills. Development of the comprehension skills should begin before *any* reading instruction takes place.

To clarify this point, perhaps we might even suggest that there are no such things as "reading comprehension skills." All of the skills called reading comprehension skills are really thinking skills applied to reading. The child who cannot draw conclusions or make judgments at an oral level in listening to a selection certainly cannot be expected to do so in reading.

The development of comprehension skills actually begins long before a youngster enters school. These skills begin in the process of the child's learning his native language, and certainly they begin, as applied to literary materials, with the first story read to the child. Nor do these skills end with mastery at the elementary level; they are the same skills, developed at more sophisticated levels, in the high school (Burmeister).

To avoid duplication, development of comprehension skills at the listening level is not separated from their development in reading. The parent, preschool or nursery school teacher, and kindergarten teacher should look upon the following sequence of skills as appropriate to be developed through discussion of stories read *to* children. The teacher of children who are at the primary level of reading development will look upon these skills as a sequence to be developed through selections read *by* children. Techniques used will be the same in either case.

Levels of Comprehension

While wording may vary and specific skills may differ slightly, there is reasonable agreement among those in the field of reading on the reading comprehension skills. First of all, there is agreement on the fact that comprehension is not a single skill, but rather is a large collection of skills. The reader may be competent in some and lacking in others at any given level of reading maturity.

Secondly, the comprehension skills may be classed into three major categories: literal comprehension, inferential comprehension, and critical reading. The first level, literal comprehension, consists of recognizing and recalling just what was said by the author. Inferential comprehension requires going beyond what the author said to interpret what was meant by what was said. Critical reading requires the reader to bring personal experience and values to bear on what was said and meant. Dale put it cleverly when he referred to the three levels of comprehension as "reading the lines, . . . reading between the lines, . . . reading beyond the lines" (p. 1).

In addition to the comprehension skills that must be developed from the very beginning, study skills must be introduced by the latter part of the primary grades to children who are beginning to get into the content areas. These skills include the ability to locate information, to read for various purposes, to organize information, to evaluate information, and to retain it.

Teacher Questioning Techniques

Children are most often given practice in the comprehension skills through teachers' questioning techniques. Several problems exist in this respect. First, the word *practice* was used advisedly in that too often children are given *practice* in comprehension skills but are given little in terms of instruction in those skills. The method for *teaching* any of these skills is essentially the same: Children are given a lesson in which the teacher will explain or illustrate the particular skill to be developed; then they will be given initial practice to see if they understand the skill and can use it; the teacher will then do whatever clarifying or reteaching is necessary; and finally, children will apply the skill in actual reading situations, not just on practice pages.

A second concern is the evidence that teachers allow two to three times as long for bright children to answer a question as they do for the slow child to answer. Does this mean we want to give the slow child a turn, but we don't really expect an answer?

A third problem relates to the questioning techniques used. The evidence on questions asked by teachers from elementary through high school indicates that 70 to 97 percent of the questions asked are of a literal, factual nature (Godbold; Guszak; Ives).

If one accepts the goal in this skill development as one of increasing children's sophistication in handling written materials, then the percentage of questions devoted to literal as opposed to inferential questions ought to be reversed. Discussions in elementary school usually should begin at the inferential level and, if there is a disagreement that seems to be based on some misunderstanding of fact, then one ought to drop back to the literal level to clarify the facts as stated by the author.

In the process of discussing stories with children, let's not lose sight of what ought to be the primary purpose for such discussions, that is, to increase children's enjoyment of what they read. Such enjoyment is not enhanced if the tenor of the questions is strictly at the literal level: "What street did the character live on? What color coat did he wear? What was the name of his third cousin's uncle?" The implication often is that the more picky the detail, the more sophisticated the thinking required. Certainly, this is not so.

Since comprehension skills are developed through questioning techniques, one way to avoid the literal level is to minimize—if not completely discard—*who, what, when,* and *where* questions. Most questions ought to begin with "Why?" "What do you think?" "Why do you think?" Then they should be followed with "How did you know?" Such a technique will get youngsters to draw inferences and will help them see *how* they drew those inferences.

Another way of looking at questioning techniques is in terms of the organization in Bloom's taxonomy. Bloom departed from the traditional three levels of comprehension to describe levels of thinking in the cognitive domain. His six levels are presented in Table 1, along with his definitions of each level, a "plain English" interpretation, and a series of example questions. The levels move from the lowest level ("Knowledge") at the bottom of Table 1 to the highest, or most sophisticated, level ("Evaluation") at the top.

Table 1. *Levels of Questioning*

Level	Definition	Plain English	Example Question
Evaluation	Judgment: right/ wrong; good/bad	So what?	Would you rather have lived then or now? Why?
Synthesis	Problem solving: original; abstract	Put it back in a new way.	Present a skit based on the first Thanksgiving.
Analysis	Problem solving: analyze elements or principles	Break it down into parts.	Because of the people involved, what problems might have arisen at the first Thanksgiving?
Application	Problem solving: concrete; identify issues and use skills and generalizations	How can I use the information?	How was the first Thanksgiving different from today?
Comprehension	Translation: change form of information	What does it mean?	In your own words, tell how the people dressed.
Knowledge	Memory: recall or recognize information	What did it say?	Who was present at the first Thanksgiving?

As shown in Table 1, each higher level presumes accomplishment of lower levels. In terms of the taxonomy, most teacher questions have been at the pure "knowledge" level. At worst, even for a check of literal comprehension, we must move up to the second level, comprehension, to avoid mere verbalization. For example, suppose we want to check a child's comprehension of the sentence "She found a penny." Most often two questions would be asked: "Who found a penny?" or "What did she find?" Naturally, the answers are "She did" and "A penny."

Such responses demonstrate nothing but pure recall and represent nothing more than saying back the words. For example, given the same pattern, "The stripling unearthed a krone," any child who could read the words could respond in the same pattern to the questions "What did the stripling unearth?" and "Who unearthed a krone?" Such a child need not have any understanding of what a stripling or a krone are. All that child is demonstrating is an understanding of the structural patterns of English. At the ridiculous extreme, we can ask the same pattern of questions of "The gip gapped a gop" and get accurate recall answers, even though the sentence is nonsense.

The remainder of this chapter will list the comprehension skills and suggest the kinds of questions and techniques that might be more effective in developing these skills.

The Comprehension Skills

The following outline of skills is relatively complete at the literal and inferential levels. It is limited at the critical reading level to those skills thought to be appropriate for children at the primary level. While precise placement is almost impossible, we have chosen to err by inclusion rather than omission; some of the critical reading skills should be developed only minimally by the end of the primary grades. Similar listings of these skills may be found in the works of Barrett, Burmeister, Harris and Sipay, Heilman, Tinker and McCullough, and Zintz.

I. Literal Comprehension

   A. Word Meaning
1. Using phonic skills
2. Using structural skills
3. Using picture context
4. Using printed context
5. Using a dictionary (see Chapter 8)
6. Recognizing synonyms, antonyms, homophones, homographs
7. Identifying words with multiple meanings
8. Recognizing the effect of stress on meaning

   B. Sentence Meaning
1. Using typographical aids
2. Identifying referents for pronouns and adverbs

   C. Detail—Recognizing and Recalling

   D. Main Idea—Recognizing and Recalling
1. Topic of a paragraph
2. Main idea of a selection

   E. Sequence—Recognizing and Recalling
1. Plot development
2. Character development
3. Argument

F. Comparisons—Recognizing and Recalling

G. Cause/Effect Relationships—Recognizing and Recalling

II. Inferential Comprehension

A. Drawing Conclusions

B. Main Idea

C. Comparisons

D. Cause/Effect Relationships

E. Making Judgments

F. Identifying Character Traits

G. Predicting Outcomes

H. Interpreting Figurative Language
   1. Simile
   2. Metaphor
   3. Personification
   4. Idiomatic expressions

III. Critical Reading

A. Distinguishing Reality from Fantasy

B. Distinguishing Fact from Opinion

C. Identifying Slant and Bias

D. Determining Author's Competence

E. Determining Author's Purpose

Developing Literal Comprehension

The teacher may develop comprehension skills at the prereading level by reading to children and using the techniques listed for each skill. Most of the skills are developed through questioning, and instruction takes place when follow-up of the question either has the children identify, or identifies for them, the clues used in order to arrive at the appropriate response.

At a reading level these skills are most often developed through the use of a selection from a basal reader, although this doesn't have to be the case. In any event, before the children read the selection to bc used, that selection ought to be introduced to them. The introduction should provide any necessary background children may need in order to understand the story. Most often the story content is within the experience of the children and the introduction is nothing more than a brief motivating statement just to get youngsters into the reading: "What do you think will happen? Let's read it and find out."

Especially in factual material, some clarification of purpose should be made. In a literary selection the purpose is most often to find out what happens. In factual material, the purpose for reading must be clarified because no one, including the adult reader, ever gets everything out of a selection; we all read for particular purposes, whether consciously or not. Secondly, if children have had the typical experience identified in studies of questioning techniques, they are most likely to read every selection for detail because that's the kind of question they are expecting to get. Finally, if the selection to be read is a factual one, the research evidence indicates that discussions are more fruitful and retention is enhanced if clear purposes are established in advance of the reading.

Word meaning. Word meaning requires using the basic decoding skills previously discussed: recognition vocabulary, phonic skills, structural skills such as identifying past and plural markers, and context. In addition, readers at more advanced levels will need to use a dictionary (see Chapter 8) for meanings of words not in their listening/speaking vocabularies. They will also be identifying words with multiple meanings and will have to recognize the effect of stress on words such as *CONtest* and *conTEST*.

Reading programs often provide for experiences in the ability to recognize synonyms, antonyms, homophones, and homographs. Actually, the first two are not necessary for reading, but are important for writing when the writer wants to think of another word that means the same or the opposite of a given word. Homophones are words that have the same pronunciation but differ in derivation, meaning, or spelling; examples are *pair, pare, pear.* Homophones present no problem in reading, but they do present serious problems in spelling. For example, no reader, upon seeing *pair,* even thinks of the other two homophones. On the other hand, in deciding to spell *pair,* the writer could easily become confused with the spellings of the other two homophones.

Homographs are words that are spelled the same but differ in derivation, pronunciation, or meaning; examples are *wind, wind.* These usually present no problem in reading either, if the individual is using context. For example, is the word in the context of "The *wind* blew" or "Please *wind* the watch"?

Sentence Meaning. Part of the skill in getting at the meaning of sentences, in addition to making use of word meaning, requires making use of typographical aids such as punctuation or special type.

In the former case, children should be taught to interpret end punctuation, commas as short pauses in speech, and even ellipses when they come to them in their reading material. The interpretation of the latter can be taught only through the use of context and, in general, as an indication of omission or interruption. Sometimes ellipses are used to indicate that a speaker was interrupted, sometimes instead of *etc.,* and sometimes to indicate a change of thought or direction.

Likewise, teaching children to interpret special type requires the use of context. Boldface type is used to attract attention or to indicate emphasis. Italics may also be used for emphasis or to indicate that the writer is referring to a word rather than to what the word represents, for example, "How do you spell *cat?*"

Comprehending sentences also requires interpretation of pronoun and adverb referents. It is strange that children seem to have no difficulty at the oral level in this interpretation, but do have considerable trouble in reading-practice materials. Could their problem be merely the mechanics of the practice material itself? In the absence of further research, we must provide instruction and practice in this skill.

Children may be given sets of sentences containing pronouns and adverbs and asked who or what each refers to.

Example: Mother called from the kitchen, "John, will *you* come in *here* to talk with *me?*"
Who does *you* refer to?
What does *here* refer to?
Who does *me* refer to?

Detail. As stated previously, children already get too much practice in recognizing and recalling detail. There are times when this skill is important, but its importance is clearly outweighed by the amount of practice usually given. When children are to read a selection in order to recall detail, they should be given that purpose in advance: "Let's read this paragraph and see how many different colors the author talks about."

Main idea. Identifying the topic of a paragraph or the main idea of a selection of several paragraphs is a difficult skill for young children. They have a tendency to repeat the entire selection, whereas application of this skill requires abstracting from several ideas to make a succinct summary statement.

This skill can be initiated at the listening level by reading a little story such as the following to prereaders:

We had fun at Mary's house. She got lots of presents. She blew out all the candles on her cake. I liked Mary's birthday party.

Ask the children what they would call this story if they were going to give it a name. This technique of having children identify a name or title of a selection when the main idea is stated is one means of identifying the main idea at the literal level.

This same technique can be applied when children read a selection of several paragraphs to identify the main idea. Another technique that can be used with single paragraphs or with selections is to have children analyze, sentence by sentence or paragraph by paragraph, to decide what each is about.

Regardless of the technique used or the size of the selection, reinforcement of the skill takes place when the teacher asks the children *how they knew,* having them go back to verify their decision.

Sequence. Recognizing or recalling sequence most often begins with a sequence of events. It can also be developed at higher levels with sequence of character development, sequence of arguments, and so on.

Of all the comprehension skills, this seems to be the one that is given the most unrealistic practice on work sheets or workbook pages. To begin with, this skill is used when a person has read or heard something rather lengthy and wants to have "pegs" on which to hang the story so it can be retold. In other words, that person wants to have in mind three or four major events or items that will serve as a mental outline in the proper sequence for retelling the story. There is no excuse, first of all, for giving children a selection that has no real sequence and, secondly, for giving them a dozen or fifteen petty details to rearrange in the proper sequence.

Appropriate practice can be given by providing a selection that does have a sequence, having the children read the selection, and then having them either recall "what happened first, what happened next, . . ." or having them recognize from a collection of three to five jumbled major events the proper sequence. Any teacher taking such a realistic approach will find that most children do not have difficulty in recognizing or recalling a sequence of events.

Comparisons. At the literal level, children should be asked how characters, events, or situations were the same or different when this sameness or difference was stated specifically in the selection. To go beyond what is specifically stated would be to go beyond the literal meaning. Children can enjoy these kinds of comparisons, especially with characters from library books. Have them compare different dogs, mice, horses, or children they have read about.

Cause/effect relationships. For this skill to be at the literal level, the cause/effect relationships must have been stated in the selection read. The teacher can help children by calling their attention to special words used to indicate relationships; examples are *because, as a result, when, after,* and so on.

Developing Inferential Comprehension

This is the level at which most questioning and teaching time should be spent. At the inferential level, the reader is not provided with the answer to the questions that might be asked. Inferential comprehension requires making use of what is said, plus intuition and experience. It is somewhat like working a math problem: The reader is given this fact and this fact and must put them together to come up with a conclusion not stated.

Drawing conclusions. Drawing conclusions can begin on a very simple level with a riddle-type paragraph such as the following:

> I ride on a big red truck. I usually have a coat and boots on. My truck has ladders and hoses on it. We hurry to fires. Who am I?

If anything more than practice is to take place, it is necessary to take the children back to the selection to point out the clues they used to decide this was a fire fighter.

Also at a simple level, because of the number of clues, would be a paragraph such as the following:

John was bigger than any person in his class. He was also the fastest runner in the school. You should see him throw a football! He was just made captain of the football team.

A very simple and obvious question to ask is, "Do you think John is a good football player?" followed by "What makes you think that?"

At a more sophisticated level, use any library selection that children enjoy. One that can be read to younger children and read by better primary readers is "I Met a Man Down in the Well" by John Ciardi.

Not all conclusions are clear-cut, and children should not get the impression that there is only one right answer. Perhaps a story is about a character on the way to a party. He may get hurt on the way so that walking is difficult. Even though the party will include running games, the character wants to see friends and has a very positive attitude about the party. Will the character have a good time at the party? The positive attitude suggests "yes," but the injury implies "no." The important part of conclusion-drawing experience is to have children verify the conclusions they draw; it is not to arrive always at a preconceived answer.

Main idea. The same procedures used in recognizing or recalling the main idea at the literal level can be used at the inferential level. The only difference is that the inferred main idea is not stated in the selection read. It must be deduced by the reader based on clues given in the selection. For example, even the simple paragraph about Mary's birthday party could be read to children with the last sentence omitted; the children should be able to infer the main idea about Mary's birthday party.

Inferred sequence. This is a skill seldom used and seldom provided for. It is needed in a selection, for instance, where two characters have been playing in a lot when they notice a big bully coming down the street. The next paragraph might take up the story with the two characters dashing down an alley with their materials in hand. To get at inferred sequence, the question would be, "What must have happened between their sighting the bully and the boys' running down the alley?"

Inferred comparisons. This skill is developed in the same manner as at the literal level, except that the comparisons to be made would be ones not specifically stated in the story. For example, after reading a description of the behavior of two characters in one situation, students might be asked how they think the characters would be alike or different in some other hypothetical situation. If the characters were in two different situations, the roles might be reversed and inferred behaviors compared.

Inferred cause/effect relationships. In this case, youngsters are asked to identify cause/effect relationships when they aren't given the clue words as in literal relationships. For example, the selection read may indicate that "The weather was too dry for crops. The shortage of corn led to . . . ." Here a question could be asked about why there was a shortage of corn, since the selection did not state in so many words that there was a shortage *because* of poor weather conditions.

Making judgments. A judgment requires that the individual bring his own values to bear on a situation. Questions to be asked would be questions such as "Do you think . . . ?" or "Why do you think . . . ?" For example, in the story of *Goldilocks and the Three Bears,* "Do you think Goldilocks should have gone into the house when no one was home? Why? (or Why not?)"

Identifying character traits. Often character traits are brought out in the process of other questions, since this category relates closely to making judgments. Children may be asked what kind of person they think the character was and why they have this view. Greater depth can also be achieved through comparisons of characters and through placing characters in new, hypothetical situations where children will infer behavior and justify their inferences.

Predicting outcomes. Practice in predicting outcomes should not occur until a story has been completed. Too often, if we interrupt a story in order to ask youngsters what they think is going to happen, we imply that the author's conclusion is *the* answer. If we do this kind of questioning, we are encouraging convergent thinking, the idea that there is only one correct answer.

Children should have a chance to read the complete selection, and they can still have practice in predicting outcomes by responding to a changed situation. The question would be, "What would have happened if . . . ?" By changing an event, we open up a whole new set of circumstances and encourage divergent thinking, that is, thinking toward a number of different answers.

At the early levels, this skill ought to be developed with considerable freedom of response. Gradually, if this is truly to become a skill, the predictions should be based more and more on an understanding of the characters or the situations in which they are behaving. In other words, youngsters should be brought back to clues and understandings from the selection to justify the predictions.

Interpreting figurative language. At the primary reading level, about the only figurative language children will meet are similes, metaphors, personifications, and idiomatic expressions.

A simile is really a literal, not inferential, matter and usually presents no problem to children. They are told literally how one thing is being compared with another. For example, to borrow from Tresselt, "The cars looked like raisins in the snowdrifts."

A metaphor presents a different problem. Because of their tendency to interpret literally, children have difficulty with metaphors. Stated as a metaphor, the preceding simile becomes "The cars were raisins in the snowdrifts." In this case, children are likely to envision raisins in snow, cars shaped like raisins, or who knows what?

Interpretation of metaphors can be taught in a step-by-step process. "How could cars and raisins look alike?" From the balance of the context, "How did the author intend for us to compare them?"

One of the best ways to help youngsters with metaphors is through creative writing. After a few examples of similes from their reading, have them write some similes. Then have them convert the similes to metaphors. Having engaged in the process themselves, they will find it easier to interpret metaphors when they meet them.

Personification is usually not a difficult figure for children to interpret. For example, they readily understand the sentence, "The trees reached out their branches." Usually understanding of personification can be brought about by asking youngsters why they think an author said something that way, asking if trees really could reach out, and what the author was comparing the trees to. Once more, creative writing can be a great help in the interpretation of personification. If children use the figure themselves, they are more likely to understand it when someone else uses it.

Idiomatic expressions must be interpreted on the basis of a knowledge of those expressions. Anyone from a different language background is going to have difficulty interpreting English idioms. While context can be of some help, experience with the idioms is the only sure way to cope with them. Young children can have an enjoyable time listening to or reading the Amelia Bedelia books by Peggy Parish. Amelia is a maid who interprets everything literally: she dresses the chicken, draws the drapes, and puts out the lights. Children might then enjoy writing selections or drawing pictures depicting literal interpretations of idioms.

Developing Critical Reading

While we most often think of critical reading skills as being extensive and sophisticated, evidence has been presented that children at the primary level can begin learning and using some of the critical reading skills and that, if they are taught these skills, they can read more critically than children who are not so taught. Wolf, Huck, and King found this was true for as low as second-grade children and regardless of intelligence levels.

Distinguishing reality from fantasy. At the prereading level, discussing with children and helping them to distinguish reality from fantasy is a beginning toward distinguishing fact from opinion. As you read stories to children, ask if an event could really happen or if it was make-believe. One-sentence activities can be described and classified by children as real or make-believe. Young children usually have no difficulty in recognizing as fantasy an escapade of a person they know: "Johnny jumped over the roof of my house." Their "problem" lies in dealing with a fantasy character they know; the character's attributes become real for that character and therefore reality: "Mighty Mouse jumped over the roof of the house" is obviously not fantasy—Mighty Mouse does that all the time!

Distinguishing fact from opinion. By second grade, children can get practice in understanding and distinguishing fact from opinion. First, they must be taught the understanding that a statement of fact is one that can be verified objectively; it is a statement about which we can eventually answer "true" or "false." On the other hand, a statement of opinion is one that can never be answered thus, but only with "I agree" or "I disagree"; it can never be objectively verified.

Children usually don't have difficulty with true statements of fact, such as "It is 70 degrees in this room." They will often have difficulty with false statements in the form of a fact, such as "It is 175 degrees in this room."

Opinion statements can be understood with a little practice. "It is too cold in here" can never be verified objectively; for some it may be too cold, for others too hot. Children can discuss the opinion, "There are too many people in this class." How many are "too many"?

Determining slant and bias. Kimmel, using twenty-two samples and nine types of writing from seven different newspapers, attempted to identify what major critical reading skills are needed by a mature reader. He found that adequacy/completeness, fact/opinion, and slant/bias were the three major evaluations required to read these papers critically. With the possible exception of the evaluation for adequacy/completeness, which requires a background of experience, the other two can be taught at the primary level. As Wolf, Huck, and King showed, second graders can be taught to detect the use of *all, some, none, always, never.*

While this is not the age at which to go into the various propaganda techniques, young children are certainly familiar with television advertising and can use some of those commercials to examine false reasoning that may exist. One of the best ways to develop an understanding of the techniques used in advertising is to have children make up their own products and ads for them, imitating commercials or ads they have seen. Then the group can examine the ads to see what words were used to persuade and what techniques might have been even more convincing.

Even something as supposedly sophisticated as understanding the connotation and denotation of words can begin at the primary level: Children can begin to develop skill in understanding how writers use words to slant or bias a selection. Provide children with a paragraph containing blanks for adjectives, such as the following:

Connotation of Words

A _____ boy walked down the _____ street. He saw a _____ pig. It was _____ . He took it to a _____ house. The _____ lady who lived there was _____ . She thought the boy was _____ and told him he belonged in a _____ place.

First read the "dull" paragraph, using the word *something* for all blanks where predicate adjectives should be. Then have the children suggest a list of pleasant, "nice-sounding" describing words that can be used in the blanks. Have them read the filled-in paragraph. Then, using the same paragraph, have the children think of all the ugly, nasty, unpleasant describing words they can think of and put some of those in the blanks. Have them read the paragraph again.

After they have completed several such paragraphs, children can write their own good- or bad-sounding paragraphs, making them as extreme as possible. Having done this themselves, children can more easily interpret when an author is attempting to slant a selection in a given direction. Have the children check to find all the words used that might be leading them in the direction the author is seeking.

Logic is an important part of critical reading. While Wolf et al. demonstrated that youngsters could test the validity of a syllogism, they found that primary children had difficulty if the first major premise was false. It could be questioned whether time is well spent with syllogisms at the primary level.

Determining author's competence. Judging an author's competence is another of the critical reading skills. If background about the author is provided to them, youngsters can begin to make judgments about whether this is an author who is qualified to write on a particular subject. Begin with easy contrasts, such as questioning who is better qualified to write about the care of pets, an animal doctor or a football player. Contrasts can gradually be refined to compare two authors in terms of studies, years of experience, and so on. Then have children apply the skill by making judgments about some of the authors they read.

Determining author's purpose. In dealing with the author, children at the primary level can also be helped to discuss and identify the underlying purpose an author apparently had in writing a particular selection. Was it to convince the reader of a point of view, merely to entertain, or to present both sides of an issue?

Literary Appreciation

The primary purpose for the discussion of any selection is to increase children's enjoyment of that selection. Hence, first of all, they should have an opportunity to give an emotional response to the material: "Did you like it? Why (or why not)?" Needless to say, children should have the right and the opportunity to express a dislike for a selection just as much as any adult does.

Many of the questions at the inferential level should help to increase children's appreciation for selections read. For example, appreciation deals with the amount of empathy the reader develops for characters in a story. This identification with characters or incidents in a story might be brought out in some of the questions asked at the inferential or critical reading levels: "Why do you think the character did that? What would you have done? Why?"

An awareness of the language used by the author ought to be developed early at the primary level. This awareness of language includes recognition and interpretation of the figurative language discussed in the previous section. It should also include an awareness of rhythm in certain selections, whether poetry or prose, such as that used by McCloskey: "The giggling gull teetered on the tip of the tiller and laughed fit to split." Children can appreciate such language when it is read orally.

It probably goes without saying that there is no need for children to know or to identify the terms given to these devices. However, they do need to become aware of the ways authors use words to appeal to our ears as well as to our minds.

Alliteration, as demonstrated by the McCloskey sentence, is a device of which children should become aware. These devices can also be further developed through children's creative writing, where again they can deepen their awareness and understanding of an author's language by becoming producers themselves. Beginning with an alphabetical list of animals, children can find an alliterative describing word for each. Then they may pick an animal about which to develop an alliterative sentence: "The sneaky snake slipped slowly."

Onomatopoeia is another device best developed through children's writing. They may collect words that sound like the action or situation expressed: *crunch, munch, splash, tinkle,* and so on.

Another device particularly enjoyed by youngsters is the repetitive building found in all kinds of children's material, from "The House that Jack Built" to *A Fly Went By* by McClintock. Becoming aware of this technique helps children understand why they like or don't like a particular kind of story and enables them either to seek or to avoid more of the same kind.

Humor comes in all forms. Even first graders can recognize the humor in some kinds of puns, such as that in *The Biggest Bear* by Ward, when Johnny tells Grandfather Orchard there is a bear in the orchard. Grandfather replies, "Better a bear in the orchard than an Orchard in the bear."

While there is no need to become technical, by the upper primary level, children should be made aware of some of the genres of literature. Already discussed was the ability to distinguish fact from fantasy. Next children should be led to recognize poetry as opposed to prose, the general class of folk tale/fairy tale as distinguished from more realistic fiction, and biography.

Appreciation is largely developed through mutual enjoyment and having fun with selections read, whether they be in basal readers or in library books. True appreciation is not likely to be developed by pressuring children to read a variety of types if they don't want to. There are devices and gadgets intended to lead children to a "balanced" fare of reading. Certainly at the primary level, this should not be a concern; the concern is to keep children reading, regardless of what it is they like to read. After all, even when the development of literary taste may become a goal, how does one develop understanding or appreciation of "good" literature if that reader has had no experience with "poor" literature?

Study Skills: The Beginnings

The basic study skills only begin at the primary level since their use in a variety of factual materials depends on a background of experience not usually possessed by the primary child. However, some of these skills do begin, and certainly the foundation in attitudes is established at this level.

In broad terms, the study skills might be classified as the ability to (1) locate information, (2) read for various purposes, (3) evaluate information, (4) organize information, and (5) retain information.

Locating Information

Locational skills include the use of special aids, such as card catalogs, biographical dictionaries, almanacs, encyclopedias, time tables, atlases, and so on. They also include knowing various parts of a book: table of contents, glossary, and index. Of these skills, certainly primary children should become aware of a table of contents and should learn its purpose and use.

The ability to use alphabetical order, basic to the use of most of the aids, will be discussed in connection with using a dictionary in Chapter 8.

Reading for Various Purposes

There need be no apology for making the language arts and math an almost exclusive focus in the first two or three years of school, with content reading providing merely another type of reading. However, by third grade the content areas are usually introduced with more seriousness. Even here, the variety of skills usually developed in middle grades do not need to be introduced, but the foundation is laid and basic attitudes are developed that will carry over to higher levels.

To begin with, the teacher must be aware of some of the problems faced by children reading in the content areas of social studies and science. Among these problems are the common words children meet that now have new meanings: they know what *fruit* is, but in science it has a different meaning; they have eaten from a *table,* but not from a table of facts in social studies. Actually, it is easier for children to understand a completely new term than to meet a familiar term with a different meaning. Care must be taken to help clarify the new meanings for common words.

Children meet technical terms, such as *plateau, hemisphere,* or *igneous.* They also meet abstract words such as *peace, democracy,* or *freedom.* What meaning do these words have for a third grader—or an eighth grader, or adult for that matter?

Even the use of side headings, marginal notes and other aids found in most social studies texts must be taught. Unless children are taught how to use these aids, they add to confusion (Christensen and Stordahl).

Greatest of all is the problem of the rapid presentation of concepts. In social studies especially, concepts tend to be presented rapidly and with little supporting detail or explanation. The teacher working with children in social studies or science must be concerned with understanding rather than with how rapidly those children move through the material: The task is not to "cover the book" but to attempt to "uncover" some of the content. At the elementary level at least, the content areas should be viewed primarily as vehicles for developing the study skills rather than as collections of facts, or even of understandings and concepts, to be mastered by children.

In the content areas especially, children must have clear purposes established for their reading as well as clarification of any new concepts or terms they may meet. A great deal of discussion must take place after the reading and, whenever possible, children should be provided a variety of other material on the same subject to provide the kind of broad detail that will help to make the concepts meaningful for them. Without this kind of care, slow children will get nothing from the content and bright children will learn only to operate at the lowest level, that is, to verbalize back the words they memorized from the selection—a habit that will continue to undermine their ability to learn at higher levels.

One purpose for reading is to follow directions. Children need specific teaching about how directions should be read. Such reading will lead them to understand that the entire set of directions should be read through to get an idea of what the directions are about, what materials are needed, and what the end product will be. Then a step-by-step rereading follows.

Initial instruction may begin with an example such as a variation of the party game, Can You Follow Directions? Take children through the steps to demonstrate the importance of reading the entire selection before beginning. Then have them complete other examples.

Can You Follow Directions?

1. Read everything carefully before you do anything.
2. Put your name in the top right corner of this paper.
3. Put a circle around the word *paper* in number 2.
4. Now call out, "I'm doing it!"
5. Jump up, then sit down and continue working.
6. Put an X in the bottom left corner of this paper.
7. On the back of this paper, add 23 and 28.
8. Out loud, count from one to ten.
9. Draw three small circles in the top left corner of this paper.
10. Put an X in each circle.
11. Call out loud, "I am following directions!"
12. Now that you read everything, do only sentences one and two.

Practice of other kinds may be given, such as directions for making simple designs from squares or circles. More elaborate directions may also be prepared, such as that shown in Figure 1.

This same method of reading should be taught in connection with the reading of math word problems. Math teachers at upper levels often complain that children "don't know how to read" and hence can't do the word problems in math. Actually, the difficulty doesn't lie in the children's reading skills but in the fact that too often they haven't been taught how to read math problems. For example, this author has put a problem such as the following on the board for upper grade and junior high classes to work:

Mary went to the grocery store. She bought two pounds of apples for 49¢ a pound, ½ dozen eggs at 90¢ a dozen, a quart of milk for 48¢, and three loaves of bread at 24¢ a loaf. How much was the milk?

With the exception of one or two students who will sit and smile, those children would divide, multiply, and add to arrive at a total figure. Was it because they could not read the words or could not comprehend the sentences? Obviously, it was because they did not read the problem as they should have.

The task in reading a math problem is essentially the same as that in reading to follow directions—and children need to be taught this. The reader must first read the entire problem through to get an idea of what it is about and to discover what the question is that must be answered. Then the reader will go back and reread,

To see what is in the picture you will
need four colors: red, yellow, green,
and black.
  If a word in the picture names an
animal, make it red.
  If the word names something we do,
make it yellow.
  If the word names a place, make it
green.
  If the word names a person, make it
black.

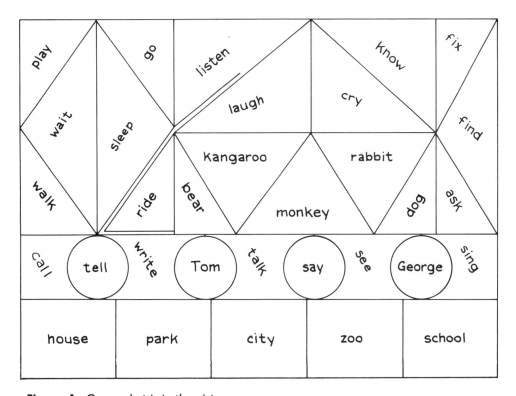

Figure 1. *Guess what is in the picture.*

step by step, to pick out the details that must be used. Examples such as those following may be used as models for further practice.

Practice Reading In Math

Tina went to buy some groceries at the store. She saw apples for 45¢ a pound, candy
for 79¢ a box, oranges for 60¢ a dozen, bread for 29¢ a loaf, and milk for

48¢ a quart. If she bought only a dozen oranges, how much did her groceries cost?

John also went to the store. He bought six apples for 12¢ each, two bottles of milk for 48¢ a bottle, a box of candy for 45¢, and five pounds of potatoes for 20¢ a pound. How much did John pay for the candy?

By upper primary levels, children should also be introduced to the reading of graphs and tables. Teaching here consists primarily of going through examples, step by step, to learn how tables or graphs are organized and what kind of information can be gotten from them. For example, present children with a table such as shown in Table 2. They should be asked what the table is about, as indicated in the title of the table. Then questions of detail can follow: "What is listed on the left side? What do the numbers stand for? What is the area of Lake Huron? Which is the smallest lake?" Such questions will lead children to interpret the table. Facts that can be used to develop tables or graphs can be gleaned from any edition of *The World Almanac and Book of Facts.*

Table 2. *Water Surface Area of the Great Lakes within the United States*

Lake Superior	20,700 square miles
Lake Michigan	22,400 square miles
Lake Huron	9,100 square miles
Lake Erie	4,980 square miles
Lake Ontario	3,600 square miles

Usually, the bar graph and line graph are the extent of types of graphs to be introduced at this level. Facts shown in Table 2 can also be converted to a bar graph as shown in Figure 2. The bar graph should be used along with the table after the appropriate clarifying questions have been asked about both. Then the children can compare to see that a bar graph provides the best format for comparative sizes, while the table gives a more precise indication of the exact number of square miles.

Children may already be familiar with a line graph or bar graph as a result of their recording of spelling progress or some other activity. If not, this would be a good application to contribute to understanding; the actual construction of a graph increases the ability to interpret the graphs of others.

A line graph is usually used to show a relationship, growth, or decrease of some sort. The line graph shown in Figure 3 indicates the pattern of sunset for one year in the state of Illinois. Again, clarifying questions consist of identifying the title of the graph, identifying what the figures are along the left vertical axis and the bottom horizontal axis, and some interpretive questions: "In what month was sunset latest? When was it earliest? What time did it set on February 1?"

The balance of the study skills—organizing, evaluating, and retaining information—are not developed formally at the primary level. Such youngsters are not expected to take notes, outline, or reorganize information. In fact, too often children are introduced to the use of an encyclopedia too early and are thereby encouraged to plagiarize, since they are unable to internalize the kind of material they are expected to read in the encyclopedias.

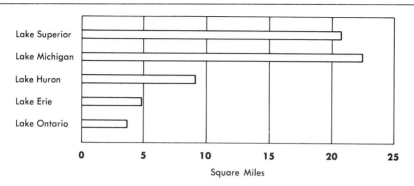

Figure 2. *Water surface area of the Great Lakes within the United States.*

On the other hand, some of the foundation for these skills is laid in that children are taught to identify the topic of a paragraph and the main idea of a selection—skills basic to outlining. Furthermore, in any discussion of content materials, children should be led to support their views with detail from their reading.

SUMMARY

Comprehension is not a unitary skill; it is a large collection of skills. This chapter has presented the comprehension skills as thinking skills and has outlined methods for teaching those comprehension skills appropriate to the primary level.

It should be reiterated that the inferential and critical reading skills—the second and third levels of comprehension—are not just for bright children. Every child

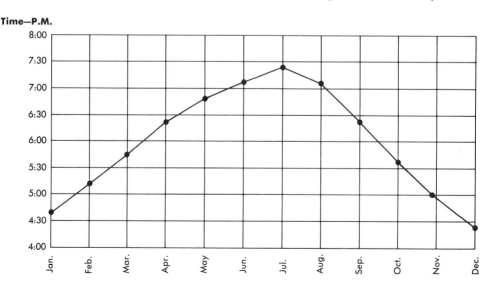

Figure 3. *Time of sunset in Illinois on the first of each month.*

should be taught and given practice in the inferential and critical reading skills at his level of reading.

Comprehension skills are usually developed through a questioning technique, and they must be specifically *taught* by bringing out *how* given questions can be answered. Furthermore, after children have been taught and given practice in a comprehension or study skill, they must then be given an opportunity to apply that skill in a real reading situation. They will not transfer skill from a practice page or an isolated instructional session to use in reading unless that transfer is taught in application.

While the study skills are not a major part of primary reading instruction, content reading is introduced and the foundation is laid for the more sophisticated skills to be taught in middle grades and later. Hence, it is imperative that children develop appropriate attitudes from the very beginning—attitudes of wanting to understand; that they not be satisfied merely with recalling the words.

Finally, whatever content reading these children do is seen as a vehicle to provide opportunity for practice of the study skills. The content is not of major importance in and of itself.

References

Barrett, Thomas. "Taxonomy of Cognitive and Affective Dimensions of Reading Comprehension." In "What Is 'Reading'? Some Current Concepts," by Theodore Clymer. In *Innovation and Change in Reading Instruction,* edited by Helen M. Robinson, pp. 19–23. Chicago: National Society for the Study of Education, 1968.

Bloom, Benjamin S., ed. *Taxonomy of Educational Objectives, Handbook 1: Cognitive Domain.* New York: David McKay Co., 1956.

Burmeister, Lou E. *Reading Strategies for Secondary School Teachers.* Menlo Park: Addison Wesley, 1974.

Carin, Arthur A., and Sund, Robert B. *Developing Questioning Strategies.* Columbus: Charles E. Merrill Publishing Co., 1971.

Christensen, Clifford, and Stordahl, Kalmer. "The Effect of Organizational Aids on Comprehension and Retention." *Journal of Educational Psychology* 46(1955):65–74.

Ciardi, John. *I Met a Man.* Boston: Houghton Mifflin Co., 1961.

Dale, Edgar. "The Critical Reader." *The Newsletter* 30(1965):1.

Godbold, John V. "Oral Questioning Practices of Teachers in Social Studies Classes." *Educational Leadership* 28(1970):61–67.

Guszak, Frank. "Teacher Questioning and Reading." *The Reading Teacher* 21(1967): 227–34.

Harris, Albert J., and Sipay, Edward R. *How to Increase Reading Ability,* Chapter 17. New York: David McKay Co., 1975.

Heilman, Arthur W. *Principles and Practices of Teaching Reading,* Part IV. Columbus: Charles E. Merrill Publishing Co., 1972.

Ives, Josephine P. "The Improvement of Critical Reading Skills." In *Problem Areas in Reading,* by Morrison Coleman. Reading Conference Proceedings, 1965, Providence, Rhode Island.

Kimmel, Thomas. *What Critical Reading Skills Are Important in Evaluating Informative and Persuasive Writing, as Represented by News, Opinion, and Advertisements in Print?* Master's thesis, National College, June 1973.

McClintock, Mike. *A Fly Went By.* New York: Random House, 1958.

McCloskey, Robert. *Burt Dow: Deep-Water Man.* New York: Viking Press, 1963.

Tinker, Miles A., and McCullough, Constance. *Teaching Elementary Reading.* New York: Appleton-Century-Crofts, 1975.

Tresselt, Alvin. *White Snow, Bright Snow.* New York: Lothrop, Lee & Shepard Co., 1956.

Ward, Lynd. *The Biggest Bear.* Boston: Houghton Mifflin Co., 1952.

Wolf, Willavene; Huck, Charlotte S.; and King, Martha L. *Critical Reading Ability of Elementary School Children.* Columbus: Ohio State University, 1967.

Zintz, Miles V. *The Reading Process,* Chapters 11–13. Dubuque: William C. Brown, Co., Publishers, 1975.

8

Dictionary Skills: Moving to Maturity in Reading

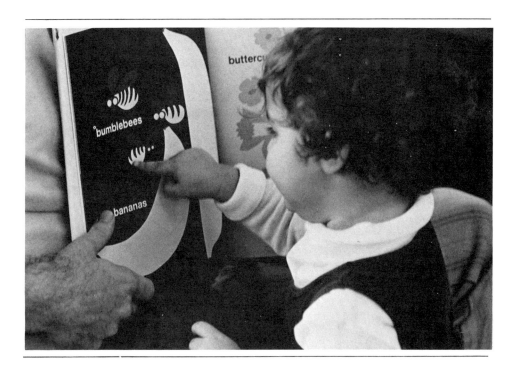

Efficient use of a dictionary is essential for anyone hoping to be effective either as a reader or as a writer. A great number of specific skills are subsumed under the ultimate goals of dictionary usage; nevertheless, those ultimate goals are the ability to use a dictionary effectively for pronunciation, for meaning, and for spelling.

As pointed out in the discussion of the role of phonics in Chapter 1, the basic phonic skills are helpful when individuals are reading material that is within their listening/speaking vocabularies, that is, when they know the meanings of the words and those words are strange only in their printed form.

By the time the typical child reaches third grade, he is beginning to be exposed to words not within his listening/speaking vocabulary. At that point, only context and the dictionary will be helpful in determining the meanings of those strange words. Hence, formal dictionary skills are usually taught at about third grade; however, "dictionary readiness," the preliminary development of those skills, begins at the preschool or kindergarten level.

Dictionary Readiness

Dictionary readiness should begin in the preschool years or in kindergarten with picture dictionaries. At this level, children use a dictionary as a picture book. They obviously do not have words in mind that they do not "know," since no one can think of a word that he doesn't know. These young children are not reading, so the only way they learn words and get meanings for them is through the oral language as they pick up those words. Hence, at this level, children do not use a dictionary for pronunciation or for meaning.

Through the use of picture dictionaries, children can get the understanding that there is an order to a dictionary and that the order is alphabetical. After they are introduced to reading, youngsters may also use picture dictionaries as spelling dictionaries when they are writing. To use picture dictionaries effectively for spelling, children must become familiar with alphabetical order. At this level it is better not to drill on that order, but rather to teach children how to use the alphabet chart at the front of the classroom as a guide to finding words in an alphabetical order.

A second essential point, is that if children are to use picture dictionaries as spelling dictionaries, they must understand the reversal of a skill they should be learning for reading: From a reading standpoint, they are learning that the letter *m* stands for the sound they hear at the beginning of *man;* from a spelling standpoint, they should also learn that a word beginning with the sound they hear at the beginning of *man* is most likely to begin with the letter *m*. Then, using the alphabet sequence at the front of the room, they can find words beginning with the letter *m*.

At this readiness level, it is important that the picture dictionaries used be arranged in alphabetical order, so children do become acquainted with this order. Two good picture dictionaries are *Rand McNally Picturebook Dictionary* by Hillerich, English, Bodzewski, and Kamatos (Rand McNally and Co., 1971) and *My First Dictionary* by Oftedal and Jacob (Grosset and Dunlap, Inc., 1973 printing). Such picture dictionaries can also be helpful, when children are beginning to write, to stimulate ideas about which to write.

Basic Dictionary Skills

Usually by the time children are reading at about a second-grade level, they are ready to begin learning some of the more formal dictionary skills. Then they are also ready to move beyond the picture dictionary stage.

At this transition level, dictionaries do not need to contain pronunciations. The child is still interested in finding words already heard or seen in order to find what the meanings are. Two good transition dictionaries are the *Beginning Dictionary* edited by Halsey and Morris (Macmillan Co., 1975) and *The Ginn Beginning Dictionary* edited by Morris (Ginn and Co., 1973).

By third grade children are typically ready for more advanced skills, including the pronunciation of words, and should be provided with more sophisticated beginning dictionaries, such as *Webster's New Elementary Dictionary* for Grades 3 through 6 (American Book Company, 1970) or *Thorndike-Barnhart Beginning Dictionary* for grades 3 and 4 (Scott, Foresman & Co., 1972).

Dictionary understandings and skills to be developed by the end of primary level include the following:

1. Overview of the dictionary. This would include understanding how words are arranged in alphabetical order; the uses of a dictionary for meaning, pronunciation, and spelling; the elements of a dictionary page, including entry words, guide words, pronunciations, and pronunciation key; other elements of the dictionary at hand, such as the tables or charts it might contain.

2. Basic locational skills. These would include effective knowledge of alphabetical order; use of guide words; understanding of entry words, including base words, inflected forms, prefixes, and suffixes; and the ability to locate and use inflected forms and their cross-references.

3. Use of a dictionary for meaning. This would include use of the locational skills plus use of context; understanding of the order of definitions in the dictionary; knowledge of how to locate and get meanings for homographs and homophones; and the ability to get meanings for prefixes and suffixes, as well as the ability to interpret cross-references for inflected forms of words. Usually, parts of speech and etymologies are not referred to at the primary level.

4. Use of a dictionary for spelling. In addition to the locational skills required for using a dictionary for meaning, children must have had experience with the possible spellings of words, and they must be given specific practice in using educated guessing to try to find unknown words in a dictionary entry list.

5. Use of a dictionary for pronunciation. Children must be taught to recognize the special spelling for pronunciation that follows the entry word; they must also be

taught the location and use of the dictionary key; and they must gain conscious control of stress in their pronunciation of words. Usually, at this level, they do not have to deal with variant pronunciations of a given word.

Teaching the Locational Skills

Children who have had experience with picture dictionaries are already somewhat familiar with alphabetical order. In learning alphabetical order, children should first be given practice in determining what letter comes before or after a certain other letter. There is no value in developing understanding of alphabetical order in a sing-song sequence from *a* to *z*. Such experience becomes a handicap when children must decide what letter comes before *y* and they have to begin rethinking the alphabet from *a*.

Children should be given chunks of alphabet, such as illustrated in Figure 1, to provide practice in determining what letter comes before or after another.

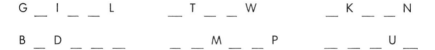

Figure 1. *Fill in the missing letters.*

Following such initial practice, youngsters may be given lists of four to six words, all of which differ by first letter, to be put in alphabetical order. There is some evidence (Styer) that the use of nonsense words is helpful in this initial practice, since it is purely a mechanical activity, and children should not be distracted by the meanings of words; in fact, they don't even need to be able to read the words in order to alphabetize them.

Words to be used for practice should be put on the board or practice sheets in column form. Initially, it seems helpful to use a large sheet of chart paper or similar material to cover all but the initial letter of each word, so children can focus on the point where they need to make decisions. Then, as they learn to alphabetize by first letter, they can be introduced gradually to use the second letter in the same manner; that is, they can see, when only the first letter of each word is visible, that several words begin with the same letter. Now they must look further to make a decision about the alphabetical rank of the words.

Figure 2 shows samples of nonsense words that might be used as children move from the simple level of alphabetizing—where all initial letters differ—to the more advanced stage of second-letter alphabetizing (Hillerich).

Such practice will not assure efficient use of a dictionary unless it is applied *in* a dictionary. One activity that might help children to apply the skill is to have them work in pairs. One child holds a closed dictionary with the spine facing the holder. The one holding the dictionary says a word, for example, *moon,* and the partner tries to slip an index card into the pages at the point where the book should be opened to find the word *moon.* Then roles are exchanged. This activity can be performed as a contest, if desired, in which case a record is kept of the number of pages between the inserted card and the page on which the word is actually found. Then the player with the lowest number of points (pages removed from the word) becomes the winner.

Easiest	More Difficult	Most Difficult
gone	gome	stute
tubel	tubel	sabin
nemet	nemet	sulet
tackit	tackit	smat
acud	gaite	seil

Figure 2. *Arranging words in alphabetical order.*

In teaching children to use guide words in a dictionary, the first point is to teach them where the guide words are located and what function they serve. Guide words are a convenience to aid the user in rapidly finding entry words. They may be located as pairs of words at the top of each page, as one word on each facing page, or as vertical pairs on each page or on alternate pages. In other words, dictionaries differ in their handling of guide words, and children should learn to find out how the guide words are arranged in the dictionary they are using.

The underlined words below are the guide words on a dictionary page. Put a check (✓) beside each word you would find on this page of the dictionary. Put an X beside each word you would not find on this page.

bake   come

_____ been
_____ cake
_____ baby
_____ clue
_____ center
_____ cone

The underlined words below are the guide words on a dictionary page. Put a check (✓) beside each word you would find on this page. Write B if the word comes before this page. Write A if the word comes after this page.

school   second

_____ scull
_____ same
_____ scissors
_____ sea
_____ seed
_____ second

Figure 3. *Exercises for using guide words.*

Children should also understand that guide words can save time in looking up words; then they should be given practice in their use. Such practice should progress from the simple activity of using a different letter for each word to be checked against the guide words, to a collection of words that all begin with the same letter as the two guide words. As a further application of this skill, have the children use the guide words or guide letters in a telephone directory to look up different last names. Figure 3 provides an example of a beginning and a more advanced practice exercise with guide words (Hillerich).

Children usually are not introduced to run-on entries* at this level, but they should understand that, in addition to base words, they can also find prefixes and suffixes in a dictionary. For example, if children look up the form *in* in a dictionary, they will find the base word *in* as an entry, and they will also find *in-,* which is a prefix. If they find a dash preceding the group of letters in an entry, they should recognize that entry as a suffix, for example, *-ness.*

By the upper primary level, children should also become acquainted with the handling of inflected forms in a dictionary: "regular" plurals and past forms are not given in a dictionary as entries. At this point, some clarification must be made of what are considered "regular" forms. Again, dictionaries differ, so children need to become familiar with the dictionary at hand in order to determine what are "regular" and "irregular" inflected forms.

In the process of learning to handle inflected forms, children must also become familiar with the use of cross-references in a dictionary. For example, the child who looks up an irregular inflected form such as *ran,* will most likely find that entry is not followed by a pronunciation and meaning, but by a cross-reference such as "See RUN" or "Past form of RUN." Therefore, children must be given practice to know that definitions of such forms are given with the present tense of that word, that is, with the base form.

Using a Dictionary for Meaning

Children should be taught to use a dictionary for meaning before they are expected to use it for pronunciation. The ability to use a dictionary for meaning requires using the locational skills plus the use of context: There are very few words that do not have more than one dictionary meaning; therefore, context must be used to determine which of several meanings is the intended one.

To begin using a dictionary for meaning, children must first of all gain a further understanding of whatever dictionary they have at hand; that is, they should have some idea of how that dictionary arranges the order of definitions. Some dictionaries arrange definitions in an historical sequence, some by meaning, others according to what they consider the frequency of use.

The easiest step in teaching use of a dictionary for meaning is to begin with a familiar word used in an unfamiliar sense; for example, "Jeff's father built a *run* for the dog." Children know some of the meanings for *run,* but this is probably an unfamiliar use for the word. They will have to use a dictionary plus the context to decide what the word means in this sentence.

Children at this level should also be given practice in using a dictionary to look up homographs and homophones. Since homographs are different words, youngsters must become aware that there will be two entries for a given spelling, for example, *lead/lead* or *pool/pool.*

In contrast, homophones usually don't present problems in meaning so much as they present problems in spelling. Obviously *red* and *read* will be separate entries in

---

*A variation of part of speech of the main word. Often listed in bold at the end of the entry, but without pronunciation or definition. For example, **gambler** *n* after the definition of **gamble.**

the dictionary. In order to handle homophones effectively, the child must be aware of the two or three different spellings of the homophones and then must use the dictionary to check that the correct homophone is being used.

Etymology and parts of speech are usually not included among dictionary skills to be taught at the primary level. However, again, as with the locational skills, children should be given practice in locating prefixes and suffixes and must also understand the use of cross-references if they are to get at meanings of inflected forms of words.

Using a Dictionary for Spelling

Of all the dictionary skills, using a dictionary for spelling is undoubtedly the poorest and the least taught of all the dictionary skills. St. John reported a survey of 580 sixth graders who were asked their major problems in using a dictionary. The most outstanding problem indicated was "I can't find a word if I can't spell it." Children must be *taught* how to find a word when they don't know how to spell it!

In order to use a dictionary effectively for spelling, obviously the locational skills must be used, but much more is required. The initial step is to present the children with a word that begins with a regular consonant spelling. For example, ask, "With what letter do you think the word *meander* begins? In what section of a dictionary would you start to look for that word?"

By the latter part of the second or early part of the third grade, if children have had the experience of exploring the language for possible spellings of vowel sounds as suggested in Chapter 6, the teacher may move the next step and orally give children an unknown word they can look up in the dictionary to check for spelling.

At this level, words should begin with regular consonant spellings. For example, present the children orally with a word such as *moult*. Ask them where they would begin to look for that word in a dictionary. They should recognize that it likely begins with the letter *m*. Then ask what spelling they think the /ō/ has, and have them check their dictionaries for that spelling. If they don't find the word there—for example, they may have suggested *m-o*—ask what other spelling the /ō/ might have. Continue in this manner until they find the word. Such practice—an application of educated guessing—is the only way anyone can learn to use a dictionary effectively for spelling.

At the upper primary level, children can be given some words that begin with variant consonant spellings in initial position after they have had some experience with those spellings from a reading standpoint. For example, they should be familiar with the *kn* spelling of /n/, as in *know*. Hence, they should be able to look up the spelling of a word such as *knee*. Context should be given in the event a child finds *nee*.

Using a Dictionary for Pronunciation

Based on their survey of authorities, Mower and Barney reported a considerable list of dictionary skills considered important. Of those listed as most important, the first four related to pronunciation skills in a dictionary. In 1944, House reported that elementary students, through eighth grade, could not interpret diacritical markings effectively. The same point could be reported today.

In order to use a dictionary for pronunciation, children must have control of the locational skills, but they must also understand (1) how the sound notation is indicated, (2) how to use the pronunciation key, (3) how stress is indicated, (4) how syllabication is marked for pronunciation and how that differs from the syllabication for the entry word, and (5) how to *apply* these skills in pronouncing a strange word. Normally, at this level children do not have dictionaries that indicate variant pronunciations, nor do they need to use run-on entries for pronunciation.

Usually, it is not difficult for children to understand how the sound notation— the special spelling after the entry word—indicates the pronunciation of a word. Some dictionaries use slash marks and some use parentheses to enclose that special pronunciation spelling.

Children should examine the dictionary and be shown where the key is located. In some dictionaries, it may sometimes be at the bottom of facing pages, sometimes only at the bottom of alternate pages, or sometimes at the side or in the middle of the page. They need to know where the key is located in the dictionary they are using, and then they can very easily be shown that the key contains the specially marked vowel letters and a word they know that has the vowel sound indicated by the specially marked vowel letter. None of this is difficult for children to learn.

Furthermore, it is not difficult to show children how stress or accent is marked in the dictionary they have. Some dictionaries use the traditional marking, placing the stress mark after the accented syllable; others place the stress mark before the accented syllable.

To begin teaching children to use a dictionary for pronunciation, use one-syllable words or nonsense words. Put a nonsense word, such as /mȯn/, on the board. Have the children open their dictionaries to any page for the pronunciation key. They should have no difficulty in deciding the pronunciation of initial /m/ or final /n/; the problem lies in determining the pronunciation of /ȯ/.

Children usually have no difficulty in understanding that the symbol /ȯ/ is located in the dictionary key, nor is it difficult for them to recognize the key word beside that symbol, which might be *moth*. The difficulty children have in pronunciation arises at this point: their problem lies in isolating the vowel sound in the key word *moth,* applying it to the strange word they want to pronounce, and pronouncing the vowel sound in the context of the sounds /m/ and /n/.

Obviously, the ability to do this is an oral/aural skill. It cannot be practiced with pencil and paper. If children are going to be successful in using a dictionary for pronunciation, much oral practice should be given in the form just demonstrated. Children will be better prepared to use a dictionary for pronunciation if they have explored the language for the possible spellings of vowel sounds because they will have had much auditory practice in listening for and saying each of the vowel sounds in the language.

A next step in learning to use a dictionary for pronunciation is to learn to deal with multisyllabic words. The same skills developed thus far will be used; in addition, children must be able consciously to control their stress on syllables in words. This also is an oral/aural skill, and a very difficult one with which to begin.

Previous to using a dictionary to pronounce strange words, children have auto-matically, as they have learned a new word orally, placed the stress on the proper syllable. While they do this intuitively with known words, they have not gained con-scious control over the use of stress in pronounced words. One of the best ways to begin developing this conscious control is to use familiar words where stress shifts, for example, 'rec ord/re 'cord or 'pres ent/pre 'sent. Have children deliberately shift stress from one syllable to the other as you point to the first or last syllable.

In the second stage of development, write the pronunciation of two-syllable non-sense words on the board and have the children use their knowledge of the pronunciation key and their control of stress to pronounce the two-syllable words correctly.

Experience with the pronunciation of nonsense words should then lead to the use of a dictionary to pronounce strange words. Write on the board a real word with which you know children are not familiar, such as *forsooth, bison,* or *bizarre.* Have them look up the word and decide—orally—how to pronounce those words.

There should be no effort to teach children to memorize a dictionary key. The important point in learning to use a dictionary for pronunciation is to be able to *use* the key in whatever dictionary the individual has.

Structural Analysis: Syllabication and Affixation

Syllable rules and some prefixes and suffices are usually taught at the primary level in reading and spelling programs. There is a great deal of question about the value of the former; the latter has a very restricted range of value in terms of adding to skill in reading.

Syllabication

There is no doubt that children should be taught what is meant by a syllable. This is important since children will be meeting words of more than one syllable as they progress in their reading. And they should realize that such long words can be pro-nounced in chunks. Hence, understanding of the term *syllable* and practice in listen-ing for the number of syllables in a word can be helpful for reading success.

This practice is usually provided initially by saying a word with exaggerated syl-labication, for example "hap-ē-ness." Ask, "How many parts do you hear in that word?" Children can be given this kind of practice by listening to the pronounced word and tapping their desks or clapping in unison with the number of parts they hear in the word being pronounced.

Children may also be given practice in identifying compound words, that is, words made up of two known words, such as *snowflake, sunshine, raincoat.* How-ever, as pointed out in Chapter 5, this has nothing to do with identifying "little words in big words," which is a misleading practice.

After this point, little can be taught about syllables that is helpful in reading. For example, children are usually next taught the rule that when they see two consonants between two vowels (VCCV pattern), they are to syllabicate between the two consonants, for example, *yel / low*. In one reading program they are taught to divide after the two consonants, *yell / low*. Actually, the latter is more accurate from a reading standpoint, since the act of reading is the act of converting the printed word to the spoken word (either actually or mentally). Hence, the pronunciation syllabication should be used, and the pronunciation of *yellow* is indicated /'yel-ō/; there is no /l/ in the final syllable.

Traditionally, reading programs have been teaching the syllabication of the boldface entry word as the rule for syllabication in reading. Yet, that entry word is syllabicated according to the writing convention, not according to the way the word is shown in the dictionary to be pronounced. On the other hand, to take a word such as *yellow* and to use the conventional spelling with syllabication after the double *l* (pronunciation syllabication) is confusing because one never sees the pronunciation syllabication applied to regular spelling; it is applied only to the special spelling used for pronunciation.

Actually, from a reading viewpoint, it makes no difference where one considers the word syllabicated: It takes a well-trained ear to hear whether the word *yellow* is pronounced "ye-lō," "yel-lō," or "yel-ō." The point was well made by the linguist Wardhaugh, who said, "Syllabication has no 'truth' value" (788). In other words, it is fine to have children determine how many syllables they hear in a word, but there is no point in having them attempt to determine the precise point of division of the syllables. As Wardhaugh continued to indicate, syllabication is purely a writing convention, and polysyllabic words may be divided either phonologically, morphologically, visually, or typographically.

To make matters worse—that is, to continue to waste time that could better be devoted to helpful instruction in reading—most reading programs continue to teach additional rules about syllabication. For instance, when children see a single consonant between two vowels (VCV pattern), they are taught to try pronouncing the word giving the first vowel letter its "short" sound and dividing after the consonant following the first vowel; if that doesn't sound like a word, then they are to try the "long" sound for the first vowel and divide before the consonant following the first vowel.

Well, even if you can remember the rule and use it, how would you divide the nonsense word *patum?* There is no way you can decide how to syllabicate that word until you know how it is pronounced. And, if you know how it is pronounced, why do you want to syllabicate it? As pointed out by Glass, the ability to syllabicate comes *after* word identification.

As youngsters meet a number of words ending in a consonant and *le* (*candle, table, turtle*), it can be helpful to call their attention to the final syllable as a pronounceable unit. This *Cle* pattern is a very common syllable, consistently pronounced with the consonant + schwa + /l/. However, here again no attempt should be made to identify the precise point of syllabication; the purpose is merely to identify a part of a word that can be pronounced automatically.

While rules are still taught in many reading programs, the professional literature is replete with articles pointing out the uselessness of such rules. In addition to those mentioned, the reader might examine articles by McFeely or Zuck.

Since syllabication is primarily a writing convention, some might argue that rules should be taught with that in mind. The rules are not reliable enough to use with confidence, therefore the writer is better to use a dictionary for those occasions when breaking a word at the end of a line is essential. For example, even the second rule (VCV pattern), which treats digraphs as single consonants, is inconsistent in words: *mother* and *father* represent the same pattern, yet they are divided differently—*moth-er, fa-ther*.

Affixation

Teaching children to recognize for pronunciation and meaning certain prefixes and suffixes has some limited value at the primary level. Children should be taught for meaning only those prefixes and suffixes that are used frequently and that do have a consistent meaning. If such criteria are accepted, very few prefixes and suffixes, other than the inflectional endings, will be taught at the primary level.

Gibson reported a study of the prefixes and suffixes found in a list of over 2,000 frequently used words. She found only *un-* and *dis-* used frequently enough and with consistent meaning that they should be taught. This list might be expanded at the primary level to include *mis-* and *re-*.

In terms of suffixes, she found only *-less* and *-ful* to be frequently used and consistent in meaning. This is not to say that the more sophisticated affixes and Greek combining forms cannot be useful at upper elementary and middle school levels, where youngsters are getting into technical vocabulary in the content areas.

An interesting point found by Gibson in her study was the existence of about ten times as many instances of anomalous prefixes as there were occurrences of real ones. For example, what happens to a child who has been drilled on the prefix *pre-* as meaning "before" when that youngster comes to the strange word *preach?* Such children will be misled about ten times for every time they are helped.

Usually, the best way to approach the few prefixes and suffixes mentioned as worth teaching is to do so by starting with the words children meet in their reading. Then have them produce other words in their writing that use the affixes introduced in the reading.

SUMMARY

This chapter has presented the dictionary skills and the methods for teaching them at the primary level. As pointed out, most reading and spelling programs include teaching of these skills. However, two aspects of dictionary skill are sadly neglected in both reading and spelling programs: use of a dictionary for pronunciation and use of a dictionary for spelling. The former is poorly done, and the latter is usually not done at all in terms of effective application. A possible reason for the failures here is the point that both must be developed through oral/aural activity. Finally, comments were made about the lack of value of teaching syllable rules, and the limitations in teaching primary children to recognize many prefixes and suffixes for meaning.

References

Gibson, Carol. "Prefixes and Suffixes: An Analysis of the Applicability of Generalizations as Related to a Selected List of Over 2,000 Commonly Used Words." Master's paper, National College, 1972.

Glass, Gerald G. "The Strange World of Syllabication." *Elementary School Journal* 67(1967):403–5.

Hillerich, Robert L. *Spelling: An Element in Written Expression.* Columbus: Charles E. Merrill Publishing Co., 1976.

House, Ralph W. "Do Pupils Learn to Use Diacritical Marks?" *Journal of Educational Research* 37(1944):352–55.

McFeely, Donald C. "Syllabication Usefulness in a Basal and Social Studies Vocabulary." *Reading Teacher* 27(1974):809–14.

Mower, Morris L., and Barney, LeRoy. "Which Are the Most Important Dictionary Skills?" *Elementary English* 45(1968):468–70.

St. John, Dorris. "Difficulties Met by Sixth Graders in the Use of the Dictionary." *Elementary English* 40(1963):30.

Styer, Sandra. "The Comparative Effectiveness of Two Methods of Teaching the Principle of Alphabetizing." *Elementary English* 49(1972):77–82.

Wardhaugh, Ronald. "Syl-lab-i-ca-tion." *Elementary English* 43(1966):785–88.

Zuck, L. V. "Some Questions about the Teaching of Syllabication Rules." *The Reading Teacher* 27(1974):583–88.

9

Using Reading Skills: The Independent Reading Program

A total reading program has two major emphases: the sequential development of essential skills, and the enjoyable application and practice of those skills. A good basal reader, *used with discrimination,* is still about the best vehicle a teacher can use for the basic skill development. However, it must be remembered that this is only half of the job of teaching reading; the other half involves the enjoyable application and practice of these skills in the independent reading program.

The independent reading program refers to those activities conducted with library books or trade books, as opposed to textbooks. *Use* of these trade books includes much more than the allowance of time for the reading of those books in school. Of course, time for the reading is important, too, but unless youngsters have an opportunity to do something with that reading—that is, to *use* the reading they do—half of their pleasure and development is lost. After all, the best teacher of reading is wasting time teaching children *how* to read if he does not, in the process, develop in them *the desire* to read.

Anyone who would question the contribution of the independent reading program to total reading development needs only to look at the research evidence on Individualized Reading that was presented during the early and middle 1960s. At that time a number of educators (Lazar; Veatch; Barbe) said that children cannot be kept locked in a basal reader for their reading program: Children learn at different rates, therefore we need self-pacing; children are interested in different subjects, therefore we need self-selection; children read at different levels, therefore we need a variety of types of materials.

In the process of their enthusiasm, many proponents of this library approach to individualized reading conducted exciting and active reading programs in library books, but they often forgot or neglected to teach the basic skills. In spite of this fact, the research evidence indicates that children in these kinds of programs did at least as well in skill development as those in basal readers (Groff). We need the best of both worlds: the basal reader for the skill development and the trade books for the application and extension of those skills, as well as for the stimulation of enthusiasm and interest in reading. It cannot be emphasized enough that children learn to read by reading.

The World of Children's Books

The world of children's books is relatively new. Of course, one can go back to Bunyan's *Pilgrim's Progress* in 1676 and say that was a book children read. On the other hand, that book—and many of the subsequent books that children read—was not intended for children.

Except for Mother Goose, first published in 1697, and a few fairy tales, it was not until the mid-nineteenth century that children's literature even began, and it began with the fairy tales of Grimm and Anderson and the nonsense of Lear. In fact, children's books of the seventeenth century bear little resemblance to what we call children's literature today. Sloane listed 261 books written for children to read in the seventeenth century. Titles typical of this collection included:

The apprentices warning piece. Being a confession of Peter Moore, formerly servant to Mr. Bidgood, apothecary in Exeter, executed there the last assises, for poysoning his said master. Wherein is observed such lamentable expressions proceeding from him, as may produce a trembling to all who reade or heare thereof, and be a warning to such leud servants who walk the same steps, lest they receive the same punishment. (Edited by Joseph Foster, 1641) (p. 146)

The vanity of childhood and youth; wherein the depraved nature of young people is represented, and means for their reformation proposed: being some sermons preached in Hand-Alley, at the request of several young men. To which is added, a catechism for youth. (Daniel Williams, 1691) (p. 206–7)

Such were all that children had as books to call their own. The general pattern during the seventeenth and eighteenth centuries was a pedantic, moralistic approach, reaching a height in France in the grandiloquence, didacticism, moralism, and floods of tears presented by Berquin (1749–1791), of whom Paul Hazard commented: /He was/ ". . . a man so dreadfully serious, says one of his critics, that no one ever saw him smile during his life—with the result that, after his death, no one ever spoke of him without smiling" (p. 36).

The middle nineteenth century began to offer a few books not written for but read by older children: Cooper's *Deerslayer* and *Last of the Mohicans,* Ewing's *Lob-Lie-by-the-Fire* and *Jackanapes,* and finally Dodge's *Hans Brinker,* as well as Kingsley's *The Water Babies* and Hawthorne's *Wonderbook* and *Tanglewood Tales.*

The first American book for young children was actually Gag's *Millions of Cats,* published in 1928. And, for the very young child just starting to read, the beginning-to-read books did not begin for practical purposes until the publication of *The Cat in the Hat* and its companion books in 1957.

The teacher interested in a full treatment of the history and development of children's literature is referred to Arbuthnot and Sutherland, Huck and Kuhn, Johnson et al., Martignoni, or Meigs et al.

In contrast to the dearth of children's books until this century, today we are swamped, as over 2,000 titles a year are recommended for children. The problem today is not to search out and find books for children, but to sort out and evaluate which are the best.

The Selection of Library Books

The selection of trade books is not the exclusive responsibility of the children's librarian in the school or public library. It is also the classroom teacher's responsibility if that teacher is going to recognize the role of library reading in the total reading program.

First of all, that responsibility includes *knowing* and providing a good selection of outstanding books for children to choose from. There is no point in making up required lists at any level because there is no book that *every* child *must* read. There are, of course, many books so good that it would be appropriate for every child to be exposed to them.

Good literature for children has many of the same qualities as good literature for adults. As stated by Arbuthnot (1966), children's books, like adult books, show "compassionate love and the kind of courage that is another phase of achievement" (p. 16). As the child matures, he shifts from admiring to identifying with characters.

Criteria for Selection

Good literature is well written in terms of style, with content that meets persisting needs for self-understanding or for understanding of the world, or it offers worthwhile escape in humor or in fantasy. Put another way, Smith referred to the elements *universal* and *permanent*—that is, good literature is universal in that it deals with the problems of mankind everywhere; permanent in that it deals with those problems that persist through all history.

Such criteria may sound a little exotic when we are talking about primary children. On the other hand, reduced to application at the primary child's level, there are certainly such books: Hoban's books (for example, *Bedtime for Frances, Baby Sister for Frances,* etc.) deal with problems faced by young children. *Tom and the Two Handles* also by Hoban, is a beginning-to-read book dealing with a persisting problem of young boys, and treats it in an enjoyable manner.

Good books for children have a sound plot. In fact, plot is one of the most appealing elements for children. A good plot is one that unfolds as a natural outgrowth of the personalities, decisions, and situations of the characters; it is not contrived, accidental, or coincidental.

Characterization must ring true. The personalities and/or the "animalities," as Huck calls them, must be real and lifelike. There is no place in children's literature —anymore than in adult literature—for the stereotypes and cardboard characters of the soap opera or Western, where every character is either all good or all bad. Good characterization will have realism in that the reader gets to know the character as a person; it will have consistency in that, knowing the character, one can predict in an unmentioned situation how that character might react; and, in the process of interacting with plot, the character will show growth just as a real person grows through experience.

Again, these are not exotic criteria to be applied only to adult books. Who could confuse some of the mice children should meet? *Anatole* (of *Anatole* by Eve Titus), the self-possessed chief cheese taster in a French cheese factory, could not be confused with *Frederick* (of *Frederick* by Leo Lionni), the dreamer and poet, or with Amos, the subtle braggart in *Ben and Me,* by Robert Lawson.

The content and theme of children's books must be appropriate for them. Usually, the manner in which an author handles the content is more a determinant of appropriateness than is the content itself. An author's theme should be developed through characterization and plot. If authors are so poor they have to tell the reader what the point is, youngsters will not accept them. For example, when Bunyon found that his *Pilgrim's Progress* was being read by children—because they could read it as an adventure story at the literal level—he wrote a book specifically for children called *Divine Emblems*. This latter was rejected by children because of its typical didactic approach.

While we certainly don't want to expose children at the early primary level to books that are objectionable or that are pure trash, there are some books that could be called "stepping stones" to good literature: A youngster must begin somewhere, and the early beginning-to-read books can be classed in that area. While they may not meet all the criteria for good literature, they are interesting, appealing, often humorous, and written at a level that the beginning reader can read.

Tools for Selecting Children's Books

While there is no substitute for personally reading the good books available to your children, it is impossible to rely on personal review for the selection of books. One would have to read about six books every day just to review all the books recommended. Hence, it is important that the classroom teacher become familiar with the tools used by the children's librarian for the selection of books.

Children's Catalog (H. W. Wilson Co., 950 University Avenue, Bronx, New York 10452) is the "bible" of children's books, a comprehensive listing with annotations. Every book listed in this catalog is a book recommended by the American Library Association. The catalog has listings of author, title, and subject headings. For example, the teacher who wants to find more titles about Indians at the primary level can use the subject listing. Some entries are starred (*) or double starred (**) to indicate they are considered most important for first purchase by schools or libraries.

Every elementary school ought to have a copy of *Children's Catalog*. It is revised every five years, and paper supplements are provided during the intervening years.

In addition to this basic catalog, every elementary school should have at least one periodical subscription to help teachers keep up with children's books. The major periodicals are:

School Library Journal (R. R. Bowker Co., 1180 Avenue of the Americas, New York, New York 10036)

The Horn Book (585 Boylston Street, Boston, Massachusetts 02116)

Booklist and Subscription Books Bulletin (50 E. Huron Street, Chicago, Illinois 60611)

Wilson Library Bulletin (H. W. Wilson Co., 950 University Avenue, Bronx, New York 10452)

School Library Journal includes the greatest number of book reviews per issue, and they are usually a paragraph or two in length. It is the precursor of *Children's Catalog* and includes the starred and double-starred notations.

Horn Book doesn't review as many books per issue, but it reviews the books in greater depth. Also, this latter reviews some books in galley proof, so the reader will see reviews before the books are actually available.

A handy catalog for the teacher's personal use is the inexpensive paperback *Best Books for Children* (R. R. Bowker Co., 1180 Avenue of the Americas, New York, New York 10036). This is compiled by the American Library Association also, and it includes about 4,000 book entries, with indications of the recommendations. It is revised annually, and changes about 10 percent with each revision. It includes only recommended books, with one-sentence annotations and indications of approximate grade level.

Scope of Materials

At the primary level, children should be exposed to a variety of kinds of books. This variety should include fantasy, realistic fiction, fact, and poetry.

Mother Goose and nursery rhymes should not be neglected. Some good Mother Goose books are

Brian Wildsmith's Mother Goose, illustrated by Brian Wildsmith. New York: Franklin Watts, 1964.

The Tall Book of Mother Goose, illustrated by Feodor Rojankovsky. New York: Harper & Row, Publishers, 1966.

Mother Goose, illustrated by Tasha Tudor. New York: Henry Z. Walck, 1944.

Real Mother Goose, illustrated by Blanche Wright. Chicago: Rand McNally & Co., 1965.

Through using Mother Goose rhymes, the teacher can expose children to various literary devices. Rhythm can be demonstrated through many selections, such as "To market, to market, to buy a fat pig" or "Tom, Tom, the piper's son."

Rhyme can be demonstrated through almost any of the Mother Goose selections. Alliteration is shown in some selections, such as "Little *boy blue,* come *blow* your horn." Onomatopoeia is demonstrated through "Hark, hark, the dogs do bark."

Imagination is tickled with such items as "If all the world was apple pie, and all the sea was ink." Humor runs through many of the rhymes, including "Jack and Jill" or "Georgey Porgey."

In addition to Mother Goose, every teacher should have a book of poetry to read to children. Arbuthnot's *Time for Poetry* is probably the best collection for the primary level. Another very attractive one is *The Golden Treasury of Poetry,* illustrated by Joan Walsh Anglund.

Folk tales are important for reading to young children, and these may be selected in individual books or in anthologies such as those by Arbuthnot (1971), Johnson, or Huck and Kuhn. Among folk tales, children should be exposed to the cumulative tales, such as "Henney Penney," the talking beast tales ("The Three Little Pigs"), the magic that is in most fairy tales, and some of the simple myths. Even the fables of Aesop can be enjoyed by primary youngsters.

Good book lists are available from a variety of sources. Annually, in the December issue, *School Library Journal* publishes a list of the "Best Books of the Year." Reviews are also available in most elementary professional journals as well as in many newspapers.

While many awards are given for outstanding children's books, the two major awards each year are the Caldecott and Newbery Awards. The former is presented to the child's book that is considered the best illustrated for the year; the latter is awarded to the best book in terms of literary quality. Hence, while there are exceptions, the tendency is for the Caldecott books to be largely primary picture books and for the Newbery books to be directed more to the upper elementary and middle school levels.

While there is no book that every child must read, the Caldecott books and runners-up are important books for children. Table 1 lists those books, which can be used as one source for the selection of books for primary children. The first book in each year is the winner; others are runners-up.

On this list, the illustrator is given prominence because of the nature of the award. Many of the books are retellings, so there is no "author," and the illustrator is indicated. If the illustrator is also the creative author, that name is asterisked, and if there was an author other than the illustrator, that author is given in parentheses.

Table 1. *Randolph Caldecott Award winners and runners-up*

Year	Title	Illustrator	Publisher
1938	*Animals of the Bible*	Dorothy Lathrop	J. B. Lippincott Co.
	Seven Simeons	*Boris Artzybasheff	Viking Press
	Four and Twenty Blackbirds	Robert Lawson	J. B. Lippincott Co.
1939	*Mei Li*	*Thomas Handforth	Doubleday & Co.
	The Forest Pool	*Laura Adams Armer	Longmans Greene
	Wee Gillis	Robert Lawson (Munro Leaf)	Viking Press
	Snow White and the Seven Dwarfs	*Wanda Gag	Coward, McCann & Geoghegan
	Barkis	*Clare Newberry	Harper & Row, Publishers
	Andy and the Lion	*James Daugherty	Viking Press
1940	*Abraham Lincoln*	*Ingri and Edgar d'Aulaire	Doubleday & Co.
	Cock-a-Doodle-Doo	*Bertha and Elmer Hader	Macmillan Co.
	Madeline	*Ludwig Bemelmans	Viking Press
	The Ageless Story	*Lauren Ford	Dodd, Mead & Co.
1941	*They Were Strong and Good*	*Robert Lawson	Viking Press
	April's Kittens	*Clare T. Newberry	Harper & Row, Publishers

Table 1. (Continued)

1942	*Make Way for Ducklings*	*Robert McCloskey	Viking Press
	An American ABC	*Maud and Miska Petersham	Macmillan Co.
	In My Mother's House	Velino Herrera (Ann Nolan Clark)	Viking Press
	Paddle-to-the-Sea	*Holling C. Holling	Houghton Mifflin Co.
	Nothing At All	*Wanda Gag	Coward, McCann & Geoghegan
1943	*The Little House*	*Virginia Lee Burton	Houghton Mifflin Co.
	Dash and Dart	*Mary and Conrad Buff	Viking Press
	Marshmallow	*Clare Newberry	Harper & Row, Publishers
1944	*Many Moons*	Louis Slobodkin (James Thurber)	Harcourt Brace Jovanovich
	Small Rain	Elizabeth Orton Jones	Viking Press
	Pierre Pidgeon	Arnold Bare	Houghton Mifflin Co.
	Good-Luck Horse	Plato Chan	Whittlesey House
	Mighty Hunter	*Bertha and Elmer Hader	Macmillan Co.
	A Child's Good Night Book	Jean Charlot (Margaret Wise Brown)	Scott, Foresman & Co
1945	*Prayer for a Child*	Elizabeth Orton Jones (Rachel Field)	Macmillan Co.
	Mother Goose	*Tasha Tudor	Oxford University Press
	In the Forest	*Marie Hall Ets	Viking Press
	Yonie Wondernose	*Marguerite de Angeli	Doubleday & Co.
	The Christmas Anna Angel	Kate Seredy (Ruth Sawyer)	Viking Press
1946	*The Rooster Crows*	*Maude and Miska Petersham	Macmillan Co.
	Little Lost Lamb	Leonard Weisgard (Margaret Wise Brown)	Doubleday & Co.
	Sing Mother Goose	Marjorie Torrey	E. P. Dutton & Co.
	My Mother is the Most Beautiful Woman in the World	Ruth Gannet (Rebecca Reyner)	Lothrop, Lee & Shepard
	You Can Write Chinese	*Kurt Wiese	Viking Press
1947	*The Little Island*	Leonard Weisgard	Doubleday & Co.
	Raindrop Splash	Leonard Weisgard (Alvin Tresselt)	Doubleday & Co.
	Boats on the River	Jay H. Barnum (Marjorie Flack)	Viking Press

Table 1. (Continued)

Timothy Turtle	Tony Palazzo	Viking Press
Pedro, Angel of Olvera Street	*Leo Politi	Charles Scribner's Sons
Sing in Praise	Marjorie Torrey	E. P. Dutton & Co.
1948 *White Snow, Bright Snow*	Roger Duvoisin (Alvin Tresselt)	Lothrop, Lee & Shepard
Stone Soup	*Marcia Brown	Charles Scribner's Sons
McElligot's Pool	*Dr. Seuss	Random House
Bambino the Clown	*George Schreiber	Viking Press
Roger and the Fox	Hildegard Woodward	Doubleday & Co.
Song of Robin Hood	Virginia Lee Burton (Anne Malcolmson)	Houghton Mifflin Co.
1949 *The Big Snow*	*B. and E. Hader	Macmillan Co.
Blueberries for Sal	*Robert McCloskey	Viking Press
All Around the Town	Helen Stone (Phyllis McGinley)	J. B. Lippincott Co.
Juanita	*Leo Politi	Charles Scribner's Sons
Fish in the Air	*Kurt Wiese	Viking Press
1950 *Song of the Swallows*	*Leo Politi	Charles Scribner's Sons
America's Ethan Allen	Lynd Ward	Houghton Mifflin Co.
The Wild Birthday Cake	Hildegard Woodward	Doubleday & Co.
Happy Day	Marc Simont (Ruth Krauss)	Harper & Row, Publishers
Henry-Fisherman: A Story of the Virgin Islands	*Marcia Brown	Charles Scribner's Sons
Bartholomew and the Oobleck	*Dr. Seuss	Random House
1951 *The Egg Tree*	*Katherine Milhous	Charles Scribner's Sons
Dick Whittington and His Cat	*Marcia Brown	Charles Scribner's Sons
The Two Reds	Nicholas Mordvinoff and William Lipkind	Harcourt Brace Jovanovich
If I Ran the Zoo	*Dr. Seuss	Random House
T-Bone the Baby-Sitter	*Clare Newberry	Harper & Row, Publishers
The Most Wonderful Doll in the World	Helen Stone (Phyllis McGinley)	J. B. Lippincott Co.

Table 1. (Continued)

1952 *Finders Keepers*	Nicholas Mordvinoff and William Lipkind	Harcourt Brace Jovanovich
Mr. T. W. Anthony Woo	*Marie Hall Ets	Viking Press
Skipper John's Cook	*Marcia Brown	Charles Scribner's Sons
All Falling Down	Margaret Graham (Gene Zion)	Harper & Row, Publishers
Bear Party	*William du Bois	Viking Press
Feather Mountain	*Elizabeth Olds	Houghton Mifflin Co.
1953 *The Biggest Bear*	*Lynd Ward	Houghton Mifflin Co.
Puss in Boots	*Marcia Brown	Charles Scribner's Sons
One Morning in Maine	*Robert McCloskey	Viking Press
Ape in a Cape	*Fritz Eichenberg	Harcourt Brace Jovanovich
The Storm Book	Margaret Graham (Charlotte Zolotow)	Harper & Row, Publishers
Five Little Monkeys	*Juliet Kepes	Houghton Mifflin Co.
1954 *Madeline's Rescue*	*Ludwig Bemelmans	Viking Press
Journey Cake, Ho!	Robert McCloskey (Ruth Sawyer)	Viking Press
When Will the World Be Mine?	Jean Charlot (Miriam Schlein)	Scott, Foresman & Co.
The Steadfast Tin Soldier	Marcia Brown	Charles Scribner's Sons
A Very Special House	Maurice Sendak (Ruth Krauss)	Harper & Row, Publishers
1955 *Cinderella*	Marcia Brown (Perrault)	Harper & Row, Publishers
Book of Nursery and Mother Goose Rhymes	*Marguerite de Angeli	Doubleday & Co.
Wheel on the Chimney	Tibor Gergely (Margaret Wise Brown)	J. B. Lippincott Co.
1956 *Frog Went A Courtin'*	Feodor Rojankovsky	Harcourt Brace Jovanovich
Play with Me	*Marie Hall Ets	Viking Press
Crow Boy	*Taro Yashima	Viking Press
1957 *A Tree Is Nice*	Marc Simont (Janice May Udry)	Harper & Row, Publishers
Mr. Penny's Rase Horse	*Marie Hall Ets	Viking Press
One Is One	*Tasha Tudor	Oxford University Press

Table 1. (Continued)

	Anatole	Paul Galdone (Eve Titus)	Whittlesey
	Gillespie and the Guards	James Daugherty (Benjamin Elkin)	Viking Press
	Lion	*William Pene du Bois	Viking Press
1958	Time of Wonder	*Robert McCloskey	Viking Press
	Fly High, Fly Low	*Don Freeman	Viking Press
	Anatole and the Cat	Paul Galdone (Eve Titus)	Whittlesey
1959	Chanticleer and the Fox	*Barbara Cooney	Thomas Y. Crowell
	The House That Jack Built	*Antonio Frasconi	Thomas Y. Crowell
	What Do You Say, Dear?	Maurice Sendak	Scott, Foresman & Co.
	Umbrella	*Taro Yashima	Viking Press
1960	Nine Day to Christmas	*Marie Hall Ets	Viking Press
	Houses from the Sea	Adrienne Adams (Alice Goudey)	Charles Scribner's Sons
	Moon Jumpers	Maurice Sendak (Janice May Udry)	Harper & Row, Publishers
1961	Baboushka and the Three Kings	Nicolas Sidjakov (Ruth Robbins)	Parnassus Press
	Inch by Inch	*Leo Lionni	Oblensky Books
1962	Once a Mouse	*Marcia Brown	Charles Scribner's Sons
	Fox Went Out on a Chilly Night	*Peter Spier	Doubleday & Co.
	Little Bear's Visit	Maurice Sendak (Else Minarik)	Harper & Row, Publishers
	The Day We Saw the Sun Come Up	Adrienne Adams (Alice Goudey)	Charles Scribner's Sons
1963	The Snowy Day	*Ezra Jack Keats	Viking Press
	The Sun Is a Golden Earring	Bernarda Bryson (Natalia Belting)	Holt, Rinehart & Winston
	Mr. Rabbit and the Lovely Present	Maurice Sendak (Charlotte Zolotow)	Harper & Row, Publishers
1964	Where the Wild Things Are	*Maurice Sendak	Harper & Row, Publishers
	Swimmy	*Leon Lionni	Pantheon Books
	All in the Morning Early	Evaline Ness (Sorche Nic Leodhas)	Holt, Rinehart & Winston
	Mother Goose Nursery Rhymes	*Philip Reed	Atheneum Publishers

Table 1. (Continued)

1965	*May I Bring a Friend?*	Beni Montresor (Beatrice de Regniers)	Atheneum Publishers
	Rain Makes Applesauce	Marvin Bileck (Julian Scheer)	Holiday House
	The Wave	Blair Lent (Margaret Hodges)	Houghton Mifflin Co.
	A Pocketful of Cricket	Evaline Ness (Rebecca Caudill)	Holt, Rinehart & Winston
1966	*Always Room for One More*	Nonny Hogrogian (Sorche Nic Leodhas)	Holt, Rinehart & Winston
1967	*Sam, Bangs, and Moon-shine*	Evaline Ness	Holt, Rinehart & Winston
	One Wide River to Cross	*Ed Emberley	Prentice-Hall
1968	*Drummer Hoff*	*Ed Emberley	Prentice-Hall
	Frederick	*Leo Lionni	Pantheon Books
	Seashore Story	*Taro Yashima	Viking Press
	The Emperor and the Kite	*Jane Yolen	World Publishing Co.
1969	*The Fool of the World and the Flying Ship*	Uri Shulevitz (Arthur Ransome)	Farrar, Straus & Giroux, Inc.
	Why the Sun and the Moon Are in the Sky	*Blair Lent	Houghton Mifflin Co.
1970	*Sylvester and the Magic Pebbles*	*William Steig	Simon & Schuster
	Goggles	*Ezra Keats	Macmillan Co.
	Alexander and the Wind-Up Mouse	*Leo Lionni	Pantheon Books
	Pop Corn and Ma Good-ness	Robert Parker (Edna Preston)	Viking Press
	Thy Friend, Obadiah	*Brinton Turkle	Viking Press
	The Judge	Margot Zemach (Harve Zemach)	Farrar, Straus & Giroux, Inc.
1971	*A Story A Story*	*Gail Haley	Atheneum Publishers
	The Angry Moon	Blair Lent (William Sleator)	Little, Brown & Co.
	Frog and Toad Are Friends	*Arnold Lobel	Harper & Row, Publishers
	In the Night Kitchen	*Maurice Sendak	Harper & Row, Publishers
1972	*One Fine Day*	*Nonny Hogrogian	Macmillan Co.
	If All the Seas Were One Sea	*Janina Domanska	Macmillan Co.

Table 1. (Continued)

	Hildilid's Night	Arnold Lobel (Cheli Ryan)	Macmillan Co.
	Moja Means One	*Muriel Feelings	Dial Press
1973	*The Funny Little Woman*	*Blair Lent	E. P. Dutton & Co.
	When Clay Sings	Tom Bahti (Byrd Taylor)	Charles Scribner's Sons
	Hosie's Alphabet	*Leonard Baskin	Viking Press
	Snow White and the Seven Dwarfs	*Nancy Burkert	Farrar, Straus & Giroux, Inc.
	Ananse, The Spider	*Gerald McDermott	Holt, Rinehart & Winston
1974	*Duffy and the Devil*	Margo Zemach (Harve Zemach)	Farrar, Straus & Giroux, Inc.
	Three Jovial Huntsmen	*Susan Jeffers	Bradbury Press
	Cathedral: The Story of Its Construction	*David Macaulay	Houghton Mifflin Co.
1975	*Why Mosquitoes Buzz in People's Ears*	Leo and Diane Dillon (Verna Aardema)	Dial Press
	Strega Nona	*Tomie de Paola	Prentice-Hall
	The Desert Is Theirs	Peter Parnall (Byrd Baylor)	Charles Scribner's Sons

Elements of a Good Independent Reading Program

While the selection of books is important, something must happen with those books as they relate to children. The teacher must be actively involved in seeing that books and children get together. Hence, the first element in a good independent reading program deals with the accessibility of books. Secondly, in making use of library reading, the teacher must help children to become aware of the many books and the contents of the many books around them.

Then too, especially at the primary level, there is a need for a sense of accomplishment among children. Progress in learning to read is not very tangible, and children must see that they are getting somewhere.

Finally, the other elements of the independent reading program have to do with *using* that reading, that is, with performing or sharing in some manner, whether through some artistic activity, through talking, or through writing.

The following sections deal separately with each of these elements of the independent reading program. This is not to imply that the elements are completely discrete; they are all interrelated and contribute to each other. Activities are not organized by age or grade because most of them can be adapted to almost any level.

Insuring Accessibility of Books

In stating that books must be accessible, we mean that books must be *in the class-room* with the children. Most school libraries have moved beyond the "scheduling" of children into the library. We know children must be able to get books at times other than "9:30 on Tuesday" when the class is scheduled. Even so, the "open" or unscheduled library is not enough. The evidence is clear that classroom libraries contribute much more to the use of books than do central libraries (Hillerich, 1966).

Powell, for example, found that children who had classroom libraries checked out twice as many books as did those who had to go to the central library. In contrast, the only evidence found to support the opposite view is a study by Gaver, who compared six schools and found that children checked out more books in the schools with central libraries. The difficulty with that study was that the schools without the central libraries also had less than half as many books and spent less than half as much per child on library books. It is difficult for children to check out books, no matter what the housing, if there aren't many available.

Even with the central library, the classroom teacher should check out twenty-five to thirty books and keep them in the classroom for a period of time until the children are ready for another batch of books. Then the collection can be returned to the central library and another collection brought back into the classroom.

Most public libraries also encourage teachers to take out collections of twenty to thirty books for use in the classroom. Hence, there is little excuse for not having books accessible in the classroom to be picked up and used whenever children have a little time. Every child ought to have a library book at the table or in the desk at all times.

Developing Awareness of Books

The first step in helping make youngsters more aware of good books is to be certain that those books are around all the time. The second step is reading to children, as an essential part of every day's activity. Following are some additional ideas that may be used or adapted to help motivate children to be more aware of the fun of children's books.

1. *"Sell" books* to your youngsters. Every time a new collection of books is brought into the classroom from the central library is a perfect opportunity for the teacher to say a word or two about each book while holding that book up for the group to see. Then pass out the book to any child interested in it.

2. *Specific selling* can be done by pointing out a particular child (making certain all are eventually included) and saying, "Oh, _____, you are always reading horse stories. Why don't you see if this one is any good?"

3. *Children can become reviewers* for the group. When a new collection of books is brought into the classroom, ask each child to take one of the books home to skim through it and see if he thinks it is a good book to keep in the classroom. On the next day, each can give a reaction to the books, and those disapproved may be returned to the central library for replacement.

4. *Book fairs* are good ways to promote children's books. They are exhibits of children's books within the school. Classes are usually scheduled to visit and browse.

5. *Having an author talk* about writing or about that author's books is a certain means of motivating interest in the books.

6. *Storytelling or reading-to* sessions by the school librarian or another capable person are excellent ways of motivating and encouraging the reading of the books discussed.

7. *Chalktalks* by authors or librarians are always fun.

8. *Quiz shows* may be set up with children to develop more awareness of books. These may be patterned after any format of TV show. The child being quizzed is to answer only "yes" or "no" to questions until those doing the quizzing can guess the book or the character that youngster is thinking of.

9. *A Book of the Week or Book of the Month* contest also promotes discussion. Children may compete to "sell" the group their book as the best.

10. *A contest* can be held where children collect the names of all their classmates who have read and who agree that their book is the best for the month.

11. *Pictures may be collected and posted.* These magazine or newspaper pictures should have nothing to do with children's books, but all could be related to some book. Children are to guess what book each picture could be associated with. For example, a picture on the front page of a newspaper of a bull sitting under a tree could very well be the illustration for *The Story of Ferdinand*.

12. *Headlines* also make good attention getters. The teacher should start this activity by putting on the bulletin board (or chalkboard) a headline from which children are to guess the book reference. For example, "Ducks Stop Traffic" would easily be guessed as the headline for *Make Way for Ducklings*. By upper primary levels, children themselves will soon get involved in producing their own headlines for classmates to guess.

13. *"Who Am I?"* envelopes can be placed on the bulletin board. Inside the envelope might be slips of paper, each with a sentence or two giving clues to a book or character. Children are to guess who is referred to. For example, one third grader wrote: "There is a lady next door to me who sings all the time. I can't sleep when she sings. Who am I?" Of course, this is Harry the dog in *Harry and the Lady Next Door*.

14. *"What Am I?"* envelopes can be handled in the same manner.

15. *"Who Am I?"* may also be played as a game with children. The name of a character is pinned on the back of each child. The child doesn't know what name is pinned on and must discover the name by asking questions of other youngsters who may reply only with "yes" or "no."

16. *Twenty Questions* may also be imitated to have children guess characters or book titles.

17. *Information about favorite authors* can be told to children in order to stimulate them to read those books. Good sources for such information include book jackets as well as *The Junior Book of Authors,* edited by Kunitz and Haycraft, and *More Junior Authors,* edited by Fuller.

18. *Sound filmstrips* of the Caldecott Award winners are available from Weston

Woods (Weston, Connecticut 06880) and serve as good motivation for reading those books.

19. *A Library corner* ought to be part of every classroom. Favorite books or timely books will be rotated. A bulletin board display can be arranged to increase motivation.

20. *Rebus titles* can be put on the bulletin board for children to guess the books they represent. Eventually children will begin making their own rebus titles for others to guess. For example:

(*Caps for Sale*)

(*Crow Boy*)

21. *Acting out the behavior* of familiar characters is another way to keep children aware of characters. Have a child perform the actions of a character while others try to guess who that child is supposed to be. For example, after having heard some of the fairy tales, youngsters may perform actions such as sweeping (Cinderella) or skipping (Red Riding Hood).

22. *A trip to the public library* is another way to acquaint children with the wider world of books.

23. *Charades* is another means for children to act out book titles or characters and to have others guess what they are referring to.

24. *A "Name the Character" game* may be played in which a leader begins by naming a character from a book. The next person must name a second book character whose name begins with the last letter of the name of the first-mentioned character, and so on.

25. *Oral reading* of portions of a book by a child can also increase awareness and motivation. For example, children may read the most exciting part, the most interesting part, or the funniest part.

26. *Match the character* may be played with the total group. Write the names of book characters on numbered slips. Also write the names of the books that go with the characters on separate unnumbered slips, and make several copies of each of the title slips. Give each child several of each kind of slip. The child who has character number one will call out the name and the first child to hold up the correct title slip gets the character slip. The one with the most character slips wins the game.

27. *Who would you like to be?* Another way to acquaint children with books and characters is to have a youngster tell what character he or she would most like to be and why.

28. *A class chart of favorite books* should be posted in the room and constantly added to as children decide on another book they like as a favorite. Incidentally, research evidence suggests that the most important recommendation to young children is a recommendation from peers or the teacher.

29. *Have a book parade* where each child has chart paper on his front and back to represent a favorite book.

Providing a Sense of Accomplishment

Since it is important that children see they are making progress when they start to read, there is certainly justification, especially at the elementary level, for extrinsic kinds of records and motivation. The only point is, these records should be noncompetitive. There is no excuse for making charts where children get stars for books read. Under such conditions, the child who is a good reader gets many stars easily, while the poor reader, who needs the encouragement, gives up and withdraws from the competition entirely. All records ought to be noncompetitive unless only equals are competing.

Following are some examples of motivating activities that can lead to a sense of accomplishment.

1. *Bookworms* are often used as group records of accomplishment. In this case, a circular "head" is made for a bookworm and every time anyone reads a book the name of that book is put on another segment (circular piece of construction paper) and mounted on the wall. These bookworms sometimes grow around the four walls of a room twice.

2. *Leaves on a tree* can also be used on a bulletin board for the same kind of record.

3. A *"bookthing"* is a most unusual kind of record. Some children, on their own at second-grade level, decided they did not want a bookworm or any of the conventional records for books read. Instead, they decided on a "bookthing." This was nothing more than a shapeless mass of all kinds of paper, hanging on the wall. Every time a child read a book, another hunk of paper was added to the "bookthing."

4. A *collection of "books"* is another way youngsters can record their progress. Prepare empty paper matchbook covers by pasting a plain white paper over the outside of the cover. Every time a child reads a book, the title of the book is printed on the spine of a matchbook, and the child adds this "book" to his collection.

5. *Personal charts* or personal file cards may also be kept by children as a record of books read.

6. A *bulletin board train* is sometimes interesting to children. All of them want to get on board. Each car of the train has the name of a popular book. Every time a child reads one of the books, that child's name tag goes on the car that has the book title read. Of course, more cars can continually be added to the train.

7. *Other bulletin board kinds of records* for the group include "fishing." Any time someone reads a book, the title of the book is put on a construction paper fish, and that fish is added to the pond on the board. The same principle may be used with a squirrel packing away nuts (book titles) for the winter.

Sharing through Creative Activities

While language activities, talking and writing, are much more valuable, there certainly is a place also for the construction and art types of sharing.

1. *Book jackets* may be designed to illustrate a favorite book.

2. *Book posters* may be made to illustrate a book, and these make interesting bulletin board or hall displays.

3. *A map of a favorite character's travels* may be of interest to some children at upper primary levels.

4. *Dioramas* may be made depicting favorite scenes from books.

5. *Shadow boxes or "peep shows"* may be made from shoe boxes as another means of sharing about books.

6. *Bookmarks* can be made to illustrate a favorite part of a story or a favorite character.

7. *Wanted posters* are often appealing. In this case, the child will make a wanted poster about one of the characters from the story and under it will write why that character is wanted.

8. *Life-size characters* can be drawn on mural paper and may be used to decorate the halls in a school.

9. *Comic strips* can show the sequence of events in a book and can be shared with classmates.

10. *A TV show or movie* can also be made from a box. Cut out one side to form the "screen." The movie or strip can be wound around broom handles and run through the screen.

11. *Mobiles* can be made of characters or objects from books.

12. *Felt-board demonstrations* may be used by some children to tell others about a book they have read.

13. *Children may dress up* as favorite book characters to put on a pageant or to talk about books they have enjoyed.

14. *Clay characters* may be formed to represent characters from different books.

15. *Pantomimes* are also appealing. The rest of the group can try to guess what book is being pantomimed.

16. *A mural* may be created on the bulletin board on which children add cut-out characters as they complete a book. Then the one who adds a character may tell classmates how that particular character fits into the mural.

17. *Sectioned bulletin boards* may be set up for children to complete: "favorite animals," "favorite make-believe people," "favorite things."

18. *Dolls* may be dressed as book characters and put on display.

Sharing through Talking

Children should be encouraged to talk about books and characters. In doing this, they not only increase their own enjoyment of the books, but also motivate others to read the books. In the process, they increase their language development.

1. *Conferences with the teacher* about books read is an essential part of the library reading program. The importance of the conference was demonstrated through studies of Individualized Reading. This conference should not be a quiz session: It is not an effort by the teacher to find out if the child read all the words or even all the sentences or chapters. Rather, it is a mutual sharing about the book.

2. *A trial for a character* or characters in a book is one way to get the group to

react and talk about that character. The trial is held to hear arguments: Is the character innocent or guilty of the charges placed?

3. *Reviews by upper primary children* may be presented to younger pupils. Such activities are especially helpful for the slower reader, who can read beginning-to-read books without a stigma. Children will also find, even through junior high, that those simple books can also be fun to read.

4. *Comparisons of characters* can be enjoyable. For example, children might like to compare boys they have read about, girls they enjoyed, or even some of the fish they like.

5. *Interviews* may be held with a book character to guess who the character is. In this case, the character answers questions only with "yes" or "no."

6. *Tape recordings* may be made by children of their reactions to a book. Some teachers find it motivating to keep the tape recorder and the taped reaction on a table with the book, so others can look at the book and hear what a classmate said about it.

7. *Puppet shows* may be used to dramatize. Puppets can be made from a piece of clay on the end of a pencil, a handkerchief over the hand, or a paper sack.

8. *The overhead projectors* may also be used for dramatizations. In this case, give children clear transparency plastic on which they may draw the characters and backdrops. Then the characters may be cut out and taped on a cotton swab stick. When the story is dramatized with the projector, children see full-size characters in action.

9. *Telling part of a story* and having the group suggest the ending is another way to share. After the group has suggested possible endings, the reporter may or may not want to share how the book actually did end.

10. *"How to" books* may be shared with a demonstration of one of the activities explained in the book.

11. *Pretending they are a character,* youngsters may tell what they would do in a given situation if they were the character under discussion.

12. *The funniest part, the most exciting part, or the most unusual part* of a book may be told to the class.

13. *Youngsters may be the book.* They may dress up in a box, with appropriate illustrations, to pretend they are the book. Then they may talk for the book to say what that book might say for itself.

14. *Dressing up as a character,* the child may tell that character's story to the group.

15. *Crystal-ball gazing* can be fun. In this case, the reporter will sit before a crystal ball and begin giving clues such as "I see a boy hunting a bear . . . . He finds a bear cub . . . . The bear is growing bigger and bigger." Children should be able to guess the gazer is thinking about *The Biggest Bear.*

16. *A man-on-the-street interview* may be held along the lines of the TV show. A big packing box with a side cut out can serve as the TV. Two children may stand inside; one can conduct the interview while the other can answer about the book, character, or about favorite books and characters.

17. *Conversations* may be held between characters and authors. One child is a character and one is the author. What might the character have to say to the author? Conversations may also take place between characters from two different books.

18. *The character I liked/disliked most* is always a good topic for youngsters to share with the group.

19. *The same thing happened to me!* In this case, the children may tell of something that happened to them that reminds them of a character or situation in a book they've read.

20. *"Homework"* may consist of having the child read an easy book at home to a preschooler and then sharing the reaction with the group.

21. *Broadcasts of reviews or summaries* of books may be presented by children over the school intercom.

22. *Reading to kindergartners* is another way for older primary youngsters to get practice and enjoyment from the reading of easy books.

23. *Small group reports* are usually better than total class reports. The class can be broken up into four to six small groups. Within each small group, the children will share informally about books they have read and enjoyed.

24. *A buddy system,* where two children of about equal ability and interest are paired, enables those youngsters to read together, taking turns in reading to each other.

Sharing through Writing

Thus far, no mention has been made of the official "book report," and no mention should be made except to say that formal book reports are probably the best way teachers have invented to discourage children from reading library books. Yet, children can have an enjoyable time writing about books they have read, and—in some cases—approximate the kind of experience they would be doing in the distasteful book report.

1. *A file* may be compiled for class use. In this case, the children may report on index cards the author and title of a book they have read, as well as whether or not they recommend the book and why. This file can then be used by others in the group who might want to check on a particular book.

2. *A cumulative folder* may be kept on favorite books. Each child can add his comment about that book for others in the group to read.

3. *A class book* of favorite books may be compiled. In this case, each child is allowed to write a brief summary and reaction to a favorite book. These are compiled into the class book, with one page from each child. At any time during the year, a child may change the original page, but none will be expected or allowed to have more than one page in the book.

4. *New endings* for favorite books or new adventures for favorite characters may be written.

5. *Headlines* may be written by children and posted on the bulletin board as suggested in activity 12 for "Developing Awareness of Books."

6. *Riddles* may be posted with answers on the back. For example, "I'm an elephant who is faithful 100 percent. Who am I?" Other children should be able to recall Horton of *Horton Hatches the Egg.*

7. *On-the-spot reporting* is an interesting writing activity for upper primary children. They will write a little news item about a book as if they were reporters who were there at the time the events actually occurred.

8. *Letters between characters* offer new opportunities for writing. In this case, the children might write what they think Paul Bunyon would say to Pecos Bill, what Anatole might have to say to Frederick, or even what Swimmy might say to Frog or Toad (*Frog and Toad Are Friends*).

9. *Letters to authors* are good ways for children to express their thoughts about favorite books. While children should not expect individual replies, if the collection of letters is sent as a class project through a publisher, most often a reply will be received by the group.

10. *Radio or TV commercials* may be written by children to "sell" favorite books.

11. *New characters* may be created by better pupils and may be added to a story situation they have read.

12. *A language log* should be kept by all children as soon as they are able to do any degree of writing. This log is a record for any unusual words, descriptions, phrases, and so on that they may want to share with others at some time.

13. *Bulletin board displays* of the "findings" from language logs can help in motivation.

14. *Letters,* recommending a favorite book, may be written to friends.

15. *Bulletin board captions* can be established by the teacher: "suspense," "laughter," "action," and so on. Appropriate paragraphs from favorite books can be added under the proper headings.

16. *Parodies* may be written of poems and fairy tales: "Goldie Bear and the Three Locks."

17. *Poems* can be written in response to those listened to. For example, hearing *Hailstones and Halibut Bones* by Mary O'Neill may lead to writing other poems about color.

18. *Character booklets* may be compiled by some children. They may want to collect favorite types of characters: "Great Girls," "Clever Cats," "Dynamic Dogs," or even "Mighty Mice."

19. *A category game* may be played by the group. Provide each child with a paper divided into columns as indicated below. Whoever can write in the most items wins.

This game can be modified and become a little more difficult by using a word vertically as indicated at the left. Then any entry in the row must begin with the letter indicated at the left of that row.

	Animal	Person	Poetry	Fairy Tale
L				
A				
K				
E				

20. *A lost or found ad* can be written for a person or thing in a favorite book.

21. *A Who's Who* may be developed by the class, listing favorite characters or authors and something about them.

22. *The library corner* may be enhanced by letting small groups of children select a favorite book and letting each group prepare a few sentences to tell why this is an important book to be added to the library corner.

23. *A diary* may be compiled for a favorite character, itemizing that character's adventures.

SUMMARY

This chapter has presented the rationale and suggestions for conducting the independent reading program. About 50 percent of the time devoted to reading instruction—or to readiness instruction at the kindergarten and preschool levels—should be allotted to the enjoyable application, practice, and extension of skills in this program of library reading.

A successful independent reading program requires that teachers know children's books, keep them accessible to the children, and have a variety of ways children can use the reading they do in order to increase their own enjoyment of a book and to motivate others to further reading.

Suggestions were offered as ways of using library reading in order to create an awareness of books among children, to provide them with a sense of accomplishment, and to increase their motivation and that of others by sharing their reading through creative activities, through talking, and through writing.

Enthusiastically conducted, this is the portion of the reading program that takes children who are learning *how* to read and insures that they will also *want* to read and *will* read.

References

Arbuthnot, May Hill. "Developing Life Values through Reading." *Elementary English* 43(1966):10–16.

———. *Arbuthnot Anthology.* Glenview: Scott, Foresman & Co., 1971.

Arbuthnot, May Hill, and Sutherland, Zena. *The Arbuthnot Anthology of Children's Literature.* Glenview: Scott, Foresman & Co., 1976.

Barbe, Walter B. *Educator's Guide to Personalized Reading Instruction.* New Jersey: Prentice-Hall, 1961.

Gaver, Mary. *Effectiveness of Centralized Library Service in Elementary Schools.* New Brunswick: Rutgers University Press, 1963.

Groff, Patrick. "Comparisons of Individualized Reading (IR) and Ability Grouping (AG) Approaches as to Reading." *Elementary English* 40(1963):258–64, 276.

Hazard, Paul. *Books, Children and Men.* Boston: Horn Book, 1947.

Hillerich, Robert L. "Bringing Together Children and Books: A Decentralized School Library." *National Elementary Principal* 46(1966):32–35.

———. *50 Ways to Raise Bookworms, or Using Independent Reading* (pamphlet). Boston: Houghton Mifflin Co., n.d.

Huck, Charlotte, and Kuhn, Doris. *Children's Literature in the Elementary School.* New York: Holt, Rinehart & Winston, 1968.

Johnson, Edna, et al. *Anthology of Children's Literature.* Boston: Houghton Mifflin Co., 1970.

Lazar, May. "Individualized Reading: A Dynamic Approach." *The Reading Teacher* 11(1957):75–83.

Martignoni, Margaret. *Illustrated Treasury of Children's Literature.* New York: Grosset & Dunlap, 1955.

Meigs, Cornelia, et al. *A Critical History of Children's Literature.* New York: Macmillan Co., 1969.

Powell, William R. "Classroom Libraries: Their Frequency of Use." *Elementary English* 43(1966):395–97.

Sloane, William. *Children's Books in England and America in the Seventeenth Century.* New York: Columbia University, 1955.

Smith, Lillian. *The Unreluctant Years.* New York: Viking Press, 1967.

Veatch, Jeanette. *Individualizing Your Reading Program.* New York: G. P. Putnam's Sons, 1959.

10

Individual Differences: Recognizing and Adjusting to Them

This chapter reviews some of the major points about individual differences and how we can accommodate them. The most important point is that while we give lip service to the existence of individual differences, in practice we sometimes act as if they don't exist. For example, to say of a child "He is a second grader" is no more descriptive than to say "He is a male." The latter says nothing about the individual except his physiological makeup; it doesn't even indicate the length of his hair. Likewise, saying "He is a second grader" indicates nothing more than that the child is roughly seven to eight years old.

Range of Differences

Children vary in their aptitude for learning to read just as all individuals vary in aptitudes for any activity. This difference in aptitude is more than merely a difference in measured IQ. It has to do with some of the points mentioned in connection with language development in Chapter 3, and it has to do with many factors we have not yet identified or understood. We do, however, know these differences exist, and we should expect and respect them.

When we talk about reading levels, we often talk about reading test scores or averages. It should be recognized, for example, that "second-grade reading level" refers to an average. Whenever we talk about an average, we expect about half of a group to be above and half below that average.

Figure 1 shows the achievement of three children who have participated in one year of instruction in reading. For the sake of the example, we will make the unreal presumption that all entered that first year with zero reading ability. Naturally, children at any level, including the beginning of schooling, have differences in their levels of development.

Having been taught with average good instruction, the average child would be expected to make one year's growth in reading in that year. As shown in Figure 1, child A is an average child and shows such growth. Child B, with the same instruction and working as hard as he could, gained half a year—and half a year was good growth for that child. Meanwhile, child C, with the same kind of instruction but with a good background, good aptitude, and high motivation gained two years in the one year. Hence, at the end of one year of instruction, the group has a range in reading levels of one and a half years.

It can easily be seen that with each year of instruction, the range of this group will increase. A good rule of thumb is that the range of reading achievement in any group of children is equal to that grade level plus at least one year. In other words, a typical third-grade group will exhibit a range in reading levels of at least four years.

For the teacher's comfort, it might be helpful if we could reduce the range by middle grades. However, such a reduction is unlikely. The only way we can keep the range of achievements in any group, in any area, from increasing is to keep that group from learning anything! Even though it might sometimes appear that we try, we cannot keep children from learning.

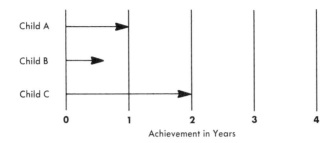

Figure 1. *Reading progress of the average, the poorest, and the best readers in a group after one year of instruction.*

Grouping for Instruction

Of course, there have been attempts to reduce the range of achievements through various interclass grouping plans. We have gone through all kinds—ability grouping, ability-achievement grouping, Joplin Plan, Nongraded, and Open School—but we have yet to find a plan that will contribute as much to the achievement and mental health of children as deliberate "broad range" or heterogeneous grouping (Goldberg et al.).

Most efforts at special interclass grouping are not only a waste of time, but often hide differences that still remain by eliminating a few children who obviously deviate. We fool ourselves if we think we can "homogenize" children. Even by grouping three classes on the basis of their reading scores, we reduce the range only 5 to 10 percent (Wrightstone; Balow and Curtin; Clarke).

Concluding a summary of research on interclass grouping, Hillerich could find no statement to equal that of Shane: "An able teacher, given freedom to work creatively, is more important by far than any mechanical scheme, however ingenious" (p. 427 in Harris).

Let's take a look at *intra*class grouping—the grouping a teacher does with a collection of children. Figure 2 shows a typical third-grade class with a range in reading levels from first grade to beginning fifth grade. Such a range is expected for this age group.

Traditionally, within a classroom we have had three reading groups, as shown in Figure 2, because most teachers know they can handle more than two reading groups, but four get unwieldy. We see no major problem with the reading-group approach as a step toward individualization, with several provisions.

Reading Level   **Skill Needs**

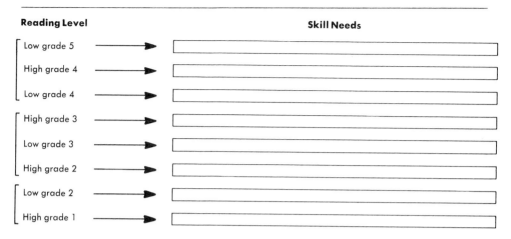

Low grade 5 ⟶

High grade 4 ⟶

Low grade 4 ⟶

High grade 3 ⟶

Low grade 3 ⟶

High grade 2 ⟶

Low grade 2 ⟶

High grade 1 ⟶

Figure 2. *Range of reading levels in a class of eight year olds.*

First, we must be concerned about the reading difficulty of the materials used as a vehicle for teaching. Children grouped in the top reading group in Figure 2, from low grade 4 to low grade 5, must be reading materials no more difficult than low fourth grade; likewise, the average group must have materials no more difficult than high second grade. In other words, if the same materials are to be used by all children in a reading group, those materials must be easy enough for the poorest reader in the group to handle. There is no evidence to suggest that the child reading at fifth-grade level cannot learn from material at low fourth grade, but it is obvious that the child reading at low fourth grade cannot learn from materials *he can't read,* in this case at the fifth-grade level.

Also shown in Figure 2 is the traditional assumption that children at a given reading level need certain skills provided in the teacher's manual at that level. As teachers have moved toward greater individualization, they have become aware that this is not necessarily so. The child reading at low third-grade level may have mastered many of the skills at that level in the manual, may still need some of the skills at low second grade, and may even have mastered some of the skills at fourth grade.

The goal toward which we should be working is, first of all, to separate the idea of "reading level" from "reading skills." We must determine reading level in order to give children appropriate instructional material. Then the job remains to diagnose in terms of skill needs and to provide flexible grouping for the teaching of those skills needed by any collection of individuals. While teacher manuals in basal reading programs are not much help in doing this, most modern reading programs also have management systems to facilitate the task of diagnosing, record keeping, and flexible grouping for skill needs. However, it can't be stated too strongly that the number one priority is to be certain that each child is using instructional materials at his reading level.

Individualization is a matter of insuring this proper placement of children in instructional materials, diagnosing for skill needs, and grouping flexibly to provide instruction in those needs. Individualization does not require that every child be taught separately nor that every child be doing something different at the same time. In fact, in those schools where every child is doing something different at the same time, repeat visits usually indicate that every child is also doing the same thing at different times. This is not individualization; it is pure inefficiency!

Identifying Differences in Reading Levels

We have this responsibility with any group for identifying each child's reading level and for giving each the appropriate reading materials. The identification of this reading level cannot be done with a group test; it must be done with an individual oral reading test. However, this need not be so frightening or so time-consuming as it might sound. There is seldom a reason for testing every child in a classroom to determine the reading level of each. The teacher, with whatever information he has, should have a pretty good idea of the top 40 or 50 percent of the children who are reading at grade level or above and who can read at grade level effectively. There is no reason those children cannot continue in whatever grade level materials are being used for teaching reading. It is academic, in terms of instruction, *how much* above grade level these youngsters are reading. Since children can learn reading skills from material that is easier than it needs to be, but cannot develop reading skills while trying to read material that is too difficult for them, individual tests should be administered only for those children about whom the teacher has a question— those children who may not be able to read at grade level.

The individual oral tests may be an Informal Reading Inventory (IRI), commercially available forms of the equivalent of an IRI, or other oral reading tests. Most basal reading programs have their own placement tests, which are the equivalent of an IRI. If the teacher has no tests available, he can still test whether or not a given book is appropriate for a child by using a selection from the book as an oral reading test in the manner of an IRI. In such a case, the procedure would be to mark off approximately one-hundred words that the child has not read from the book in question. Four literal questions based on the selection should be prepared in advance. These questions merely serve as a check on the child's comprehension of what he reads. The child should be handed the selection and told, "Please read this to me. When you're finished, I'll ask you a few questions about it."

As the child reads, the teacher should have another copy of the selection and should mark the errors the child makes. While the administration of such a test can serve diagnostic purposes for skills as well, our point here is merely to determine reading level. Therefore, the teacher will tally the number of errors the child makes orally in reading the selection. An error is any omission of a word or punctuation, any refusal (a hesitation of more than five seconds, at which point the teacher will provide the word), or saying anything that is not there (mispronunciation, substitution, insertion, reversal).

After the child has read the selection, ask the four questions. Instructional level for reading material is that level at which the reader can read orally with 95 percent word accuracy and 75 percent comprehension (Betts). If the child makes more than five errors in his oral reading of the one-hundred-word selection, or if he misses more than one of the four questions, that material is too difficult for him. Then the teacher must get easier material and try it in the same manner.

Often it is a good idea to administer the oral reading test with a tape recorder, so the errors can be double checked. This is especially true for one without experience in administering oral reading tests. Usually, children are accustomed to tape recorders, so they do not become concerned.

The procedure just suggested for checking the appropriateness of a selection with a child is exactly the procedure followed in an IRI, except that one-hundred-word selections are prepared in advance from each level of a basal reader. When an IRI is used, it is wise to begin the child at a level you can be sure will result in success. The few minutes it takes to administer an extra level or two are well spent, compared with beginning a child at a frustration level and then having to back down to lower levels.

A Word of Caution in Using IRIs

Many comments and reactions have been expressed about IRIs, even to the point of suggesting different criteria for word accuracy (Powell). Pikulski has presented an excellent summary of the research on IRIs. However, regardless of criticism or suggestions, the IRI remains a valuable, practical tool.

With the variability among reading programs today, it is important that an IRI be made from whatever basal reading series is to be used in reading instruction. The accuracy of an IRI rests entirely on its fit with each level of the reading program being used.

Of course, this point has its weaknesses in that very often a poor reader in a class is one who has already been exposed to lower levels of the basal reader. Therefore, that child will not be reading fresh materials in the IRI.

Whatever the material of the test used, it should be kept in mind that if a scoring error is to be made, it should be made in the direction of scoring the test too stringently and thereby possibly placing the child a little lower than necessary. Such an "error" is far better than to be too lenient in administering the test and, as a result, to place the child in reading material that is too difficult.

After gaining some experience in administering an oral reading test, the teacher might like to mark the kinds of errors made by children in oral reading to get some clues for diagnosing skill needs. In this case, the following procedure should serve adequately for identifying the kinds of reading errors made:

1. *Omission* of a word or punctuation—circle the omission.
2. *Hesitation* of two seconds or more—place a check above the word. (This is for information only; and is not counted as an error.)
3. *Refusal*—after five seconds, put a second check above the word and say it.
4. *Repetition*—draw a line over repeated items. (This is for information only, and is not counted as an error.)
5. *Insertion, reversal, substitution, mispronounciation*—write whatever the child says.

Finally, it is unusual for children to fit into our neat little patterns. The criteria referred to for determination of instructional level—95 percent word accuracy and 75 percent comprehension—seldom apply at the same time to a given child. Very often questions will be: "What do I do with the child who has 98 percent word accuracy and 50 percent comprehension?" "What about the child with 90 percent word accuracy and 100 percent comprehension?" While we have been able to find nothing in print to answer these questions, our procedure in working with disabled readers is to work at cross purposes with whatever their past reading program has been.

Take an example of a child who has 98 percent word accuracy and 50 percent comprehension on a given level of an IRI. If that child has been in a standard basal reading program that emphasizes reading for understanding, it seems best to be guided by the word accuracy and assume this was not the frustration level for the child. (Naturally, the teacher would also recognize this as a child who needs considerable work in comprehension.)

On the other hand, given the same performance from a child whose background was an extreme phonics program, the teacher would be guided by the comprehension score and say this was a frustration level because children in such extreme phonics programs tend to be able to say all the words but don't always read with understanding.

Let's take the reverse case, a child who has 90 percent word accuracy and 100 percent comprehension. Such performance is more typical, since disabled readers— and young children as well—have learned to eke out a maximum of information from a minimum of printed clues. In this case, regardless of the reading program the child had, use the word accuracy as an indication that this particular level of the IRI was the frustration level, and drop back to the level at which the child could read with 95 percent accuracy.

Pacing

Once children have been placed properly in materials at their reading level for instructional purposes, theoretically there would never be a reason to retest for placement, so long as each child was paced at his rate in the materials. Some children learn skills faster than others, some are more interested, and some read more. Such children will move to higher levels more rapidly. For those who don't move as rapidly, it is still important that skills instruction and the enjoyable application and practice of those skills in library reading also be part of their program, just as it is part of the program for better readers.

Proper pacing will assure that children do not become misplaced in instructional materials once they have been properly placed through the use of the IRI. To move children too rapidly through instructional materials not only frustrates the children but it "destroys" that material as a possible vehicle for instruction by next year's teacher, who will have the children at a time when that material may have been appropriate.

Naturally, the reverse is also possible: Children may be paced so slowly that they do not grow in reading skills as rapidly as they could and should. This situation, however, is less frustrating and, if library books are available, less likely to inhibit the reading development of the children; they will continue to grow in spite of the snail's pace of the program.

Diagnosing Skill Needs

As pointed out in the discussion of grouping patterns, children differ in their skill development just as they differ in reading levels. While teachers certainly should not get lost—or buried—in bookkeeping hundreds of petty items sometimes referred to as "reading skills," they should be aware of each child's level of development in all the important skills and should be diagnosing specifically for those skills.

For example, Chapter 3 discussed means for diagnosing language skills and needs. When children actually get into reading itself, the first things that were taught were the use of context and consonant letter-sound associations. In listening to a child's oral reading of an IRI, the teacher should be able to determine if that child is or is not using context. Are the word errors the child makes meaningful errors (errors that make sense in the context), or do they more likely approximate the letters of the word in print and completely ignore the context?

Diagnosing for Consonants

Many phonics tests are available commercially for those who would like to use them. However, these phonics tests, if administered as directed, require encoding (spelling), not decoding (reading). Figure 3 is an example of a phonics test for initial consonant sounds, digraphs, clusters, and vowels. It, too, would be a spelling test if administered on a group basis. Typically, on such tests, each child is given an answer sheet such as that shown, but without the answers circled. Then they are told, "Draw a circle around the one that begins like *fish* and *fun*."

Date				Name		
A	Initial Consonants					Pronunciation Guide
1	gam	(fam)	tam	nam		FAMily
2	(rem)	lem	sem	bem		REMedy
3	hol	sol	mol	(col)		COLumn
4	tig	kig	(sig)	hig		SIGnal
5	com	(lom)	rom	wom		LOMbard
6	(biz)	diz	miz	riz		BUsy
7	yaf	waf	(taf)	zaf		TAFfy
8	nug	gug	fug	(kug)		CUp
9	fep	bep	(dep)	tep		DEPth

Figure 3. *Diagnostic phonics test**

*Copyright © 1972 by Robert L. Hillerich. (*Spelling for Writing,* Merrill.)

10	yen	fen	jen	ken	YEN
11	rad	nad	gad	jad	JAm
12	nof	mof	tof	sof	NOt
13	dud	pud	fud	hud	PUDdle
14	vip	bip	gip	pip	GIll
15	lex	nex	bex	wex	WEt
16	bab	hab	lab	pab	HABit
17	vil	ril	nil	wil	VILlage
18	fot	yot	mot	bot	MOTley
19	nom	zom	dom	rom	ZOMbie

B	Initial Consonant Digraphs				Pronunciation Guide
1	thap	knap	shap	whap	SHAck
2	drob	chob	clob	shob	CHOp
3	shek	drek	thek	knek	THEspian
4	drib	shib	knib	whib	WHIp
5	shas	thas	clas	chas	THAt

C	Simple Vowels I				Pronunciation Guide
1	vop	vep	vap	vip	VAPid
2	fip	fup	fop	fep	rIP
3	lem	lim	lum	lom	LOMbard
4	dif	duf	daf	def	DUFfle
5	bom	bem	bim	bam	gEM
6	gef	gaf	gof	guf	GAFF
7	tiz	tuz	toz	tez	TIZzy
8	yit	yat	yut	yot	YUm
9	juck	jock	jeck	jick	JOCKey
10	paf	pif	pof	pef	PEt

D	Simple Vowels II				Pronunciation Guide
1	baipe	beip	beap	boap	pEP
2	zaid	zead	zawd	zaed	tAWDry
3	baup	boop	baip	bewp	pAUPer
4	jowk	jiek	jaik	jook	lOOK
5	sut	sewt	suet	seit	pUT

E	Complex Vowels				Pronunciation Guide
1	voy	vay	vuy	voay	hAY
2	koat	keut	koit	keat	mEAT
3	lai	lea	lau	lue	dUE
4	za	ze	zo	zu	ZEbra
5	vay	voy	vey	viy	VOYage
6	daf	dif	dafe	dufe	sAFE

Figure 3. (Continued)

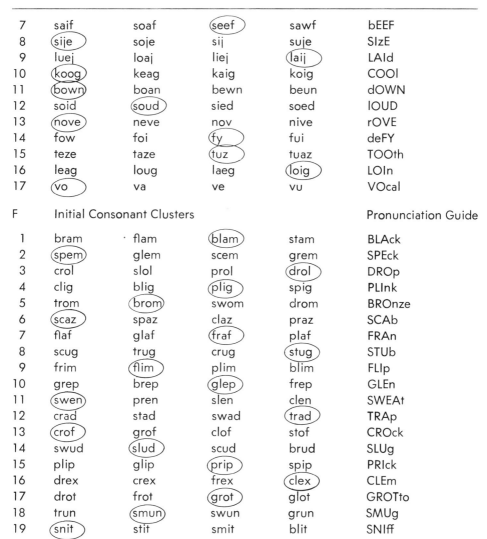

					Pronunciation Guide
7	saif	soaf	(seef)	sawf	bEEF
8	(sije)	soje	sij	suje	SIzE
9	luej	loaj	liej	(laij)	LAId
10	(koog)	keag	kaig	koig	COOl
11	(bown)	boan	bewn	beun	dOWN
12	soid	(soud)	sied	soed	lOUD
13	(nove)	neve	nov	nive	rOVE
14	fow	foi	(fy)	fui	deFY
15	teze	taze	(tuz)	tuaz	TOOth
16	leag	loug	laeg	(loig)	LOIn
17	(vo)	va	ve	vu	VOcal

F	Initial Consonant Clusters				Pronunciation Guide
1	bram	· flam	(blam)	stam	BLAck
2	(spem)	glem	scem	grem	SPEck
3	crol	slol	prol	(drol)	DROp
4	clig	blig	(plig)	spig	PLInk
5	trom	(brom)	swom	drom	BROnze
6	(scaz)	spaz	claz	praz	SCAb
7	flaf	glaf	(fraf)	plaf	FRAn
8	scug	trug	crug	(stug)	STUb
9	frim	(flim)	plim	blim	FLIp
10	grep	brep	(glep)	frep	GLEn
11	(swen)	pren	slen	clen	SWEAt
12	crad	stad	swad	(trad)	TRAp
13	(crof)	grof	clof	stof	CROck
14	swud	(slud)	scud	brud	SLUg
15	plip	glip	(prip)	spip	PRIck
16	drex	crex	frex	(clex)	CLEm
17	drot	frot	(grot)	glot	GROTto
18	trun	(smun)	swun	grun	SMUg
19	(snit)	stit	smit	blit	SNIff

Figure 3. (Continued)

This is an encoding (spelling) activity because the child hears the sound at the beginning of *fish* and *fun* and must find a word that begins with the letter most often representing that sound. Not only is this spelling, but it is multiple-choice spelling, an even easier task. In decoding (reading), one operates in the reverse fashion: The reader sees a letter and—out of the whole world of sound—must decide what sound that letter represents. This is a much more difficult task than multiple-choice spelling.

The test in Figure 3—or any commercial phonics test—can be used as a reading test if it is administered individually. To administer the test for reading, the administrator will sit down with the child to be tested, show the answer sheet, and tell the child, "I'm going to read all the words in each row except the one with the circle around it. Then you read that one."

The administrator will read "gam, tam, nam" and point to *fam.* If the child says "fam," obviously that child has established the sound association for the consonant *f.* Again, not every child should be tested; test only those children about whom there is a question in terms of their consonant sound associations.

Vowel understandings may also be diagnosed, not to determine what rules to teach, but to identify those children who can profit from more experience in exploring the possible representations of vowel sounds.

Diagnosing for Higher Level Skills

Diagnosing for dictionary or comprehension skills can just as well be a criterion-referenced kind of testing that the teacher does. There is no group test that will give the teacher a clear diagnostic picture of the child's comprehension skills (Farr, 1969).

Testing dictionary skills can be done, for example, in many different ways, such as asking the child to alphabetize a group of five or six words, use a dictionary to pronounce a strange word, or take a strange word in context and use a dictionary to determine its meaning.

If the teacher wants to know, for example, whether a child can identify the topic of a paragraph, the best way to find out is to give that child a paragraph *at the appropriate reading level* and ask what title he would give that paragraph. (If the child has had experience with the term *topic,* he can merely be asked to give the topic of the paragraph.)

If a teacher wants to know whether a child can draw conclusions, that teacher should provide a selection *at the appropriate reading level* and ask a question that requires drawing conclusions. Chapter 7 deals with the kinds of questions that should be asked for the various comprehension skills.

Care must be taken to sample a given skill several times with a child, to be certain the correct answer wasn't given by chance to a single sampling question for that skill. This limited sampling of each skill is apparently one of the weaknesses of group tests.

A second major weakness of group tests that can be avoided on a personal basis has to do with follow-up. Care must be taken to question children about *why* they answered as they did. For example, consider the process if you want to ask a child to draw a conclusion after reading the following selection:

> The boy ambled down the street. He gazed in a store
> window. Tarrying by store after store, he shuffled home.

To find out if the child can draw simple conclusions, an obvious question might be, "Was the character in a hurry?" If the child responds as expected and this is tried with several other selections with appropriate responses, that child apparently can draw conclusions at his reading level.

On the other hand, if the child said the character was in a hurry, we would have to ask the basis for this conclusion. That child may have associated *ambled* with *rambled, gazed* with *glanced,* and *shuffled* with another word having to do with hurrying. In other words, there are times when a more basic skill can trip the youngster up and make it appear that he is lacking in some comprehension skill. In this case it was word identification and vocabulary development that were lacking, not conclusion-drawing ability.

Teaching Children from Different Language Backgrounds

As pointed out in Chapter 3, no one can be expected to learn to read a language until he speaks and understands that language. This point applies just as much to non-English-speaking children learning to read in English as it does to English-speaking children learning to read in their own language.

According to research, the best way to start non-English-speaking children to read is to have them begin reading in their native language. Modiano reported a study done in Mexico involving twenty-six schools. Thirteen of the schools taught children to read initially in their tribal tongue before teaching them to read in the national language; the other thirteen began teaching reading in the national language. By the end of the second year in school, those who had begun reading in their tribal tongue first read better in the national language than did those who began to read in the national language. The effectiveness of beginning reading in the native tongue was also reported in Puerto Rico (International Institute of Teachers Colleges).

Arnold, in a study of 287 Mexican-American children in the primary grades, compared the effects of oral-aural English, oral-aural Spanish, and no oral-aural training. He found that those with no oral-aural training showed a significant loss over the summer, while those with the oral-aural Spanish even showed a gain in reading in English.

One explanation for the carry-over from learning to read in a native language to learning to read in a second language seems partially explained by Koler's findings. He reported that with a bilingual individual, two exposures to each of two words—one in the native language and one in the second language—was as effective for remembering the word as were four exposures to the same word in either of the languages. For example, the bilingual Spanish-English-speaking person, exposed to *fountain* twice and *fuente* twice, is as likely to remember either as he would be if exposed to *fountain* four times or to *fuente* four times. The reader appears to store meanings for words rather than the visual images of the words.

Experience in reading in the native language seems to provide some understanding of what reading is all about, and it also begins the process of storing meanings for words in print.

In a study designed to teach Spanish-speaking children to read in their native language first and then to make the transition to reading in English, these children were to be compared with Spanish-speaking children who began their reading instruction directly in English (Hillerich, 1972). Both groups received a strong oral-aural English program, beginning prior to entry to first grade.

Evidence at the end of first grade indicated that children who began reading in Spanish were reading their native language and English at a level only two months below those who began in English. By the end of second grade, the former were significantly higher in reading comprehension than those who had begun reading in English.

A second study, with tighter research controls, was started in the second year. Here the bilingual group made significantly greater gains in reading by the end of first grade. These children, by the end of second grade, not only scored higher in reading achievement, but were also higher on the *Science Research Associates (SRA) Achievement Test* in English mechanics and English grammar as compared with children who began reading in English initially.

Kaufman demonstrated that this transfer in learning from Spanish to English even took place at the junior high level.

In many schools it is not practical to teach children to read in their native language. Not only are there insufficient numbers of a given language group, but there usually are not bilingual teachers available to do the teaching. In that situation, the point still remains that a child cannot learn to read in a language he does not speak and understand. Hence, such children must be provided with a strong oral English program (Cooper; Horn). The oral English program must be one that develops the patterns of spoken English; it cannot merely be a vocabulary or labelling process.

Excellent guides are available from a number of publishers to carry on such a program. Two good ones are:

Understanding English by Louise Lancaster. Houghton Mifflin Co.

English Around the World by William Marquardt, Jean Miller, and Eleanor Hosman. Scott, Foresman & Co.

Children must also get a great deal of experience in talking and listening in English. Since the classroom teacher with one or two non-English-speaking children doesn't have this kind of time, the program can still be conducted, with a minimum of instruction on the use of the manuals, by older children or parent volunteers.

Finally, any teacher working with children from other language backgrounds needs some understanding of the child's cultural heritage (Zintz) and must be aware of points of conflict in the child's native language and English. English idioms are always a problem, regardless of the previous language. There is no way to interpret an idiom, even if children thoroughly understand the meaning of every word used, unless they *know* the idiom. How else can anyone understand "Mother hit the ceiling," "He stuck his nose where it shouldn't have been," or "Don't stick your neck out"?

Children from a more inflected language, such as Spanish, will have difficulty with English word order as well: "Casa rosa" becomes "red house." Furthermore, the teacher must decide priorities—which is the first instructional task, speech correction or reading instruction? The Spanish-American, who did not have /sh/ in his native language, will tend to refer to *ship* as "chip." Eventually /sh/ and /ch/ will become confused and people will be said to sit in a "shair." Such pronunciations normally do not interfere with understanding and therefore should *not* be considered reading problems or even reading "errors."

While some would disagree, we would not attempt, in a school setting, to "correct" the speech patterns of such young children. To do so is to criticize them and their heritage. It is also a good way to get these children to stop talking. It is better to provide a standard English model and to encourage the young children to communicate. Then, by middle grades or later, sessions can be established to examine "the *ways* of speaking." By this time, the student is capable of understanding the abstract nature of language, can compare on a more impersonal basis, and is socially aware enough to make judgments about the use of standard English when it is appropriate.

Teaching Children from Black Dialect

While some have gone in that direction, the principles discussed in connection with children from a different language background do not necessarily apply in the case of children who speak black dialect. In fact, Rystrom demonstrated in a study of four first-grade classrooms that trying to teach English as a second language to children from black dialect did nothing but confuse them: it had a negative effect on their learning to read. The points of overlap in standard English and black dialect are so prevalent that black dialect cannot be considered a different language.

Any discussion of black dialect probably should begin with a clarification of "dialect," since it is surprising how many people have a negative connotation for the term. Everyone speaks a dialect; in fact, everyone also has an idiolect or personal variation of that dialect. Like it or not, we are all linguistically different. This uniqueness of individual speech is even identifiable in the cooing of infants.

Part of this confusion about dialect undoubtedly relates to early efforts to explain black dialect in terms of its discrepancies from standard English. It should be made clear from the start that black dialect is not an inferior or cheap imitation of standard English. Black dialect apparently originated as a West African pidgin English, that is, as a *lingua franca* by means of which the adults from a variety of African tribes could communicate among themselves.

From this origin, black dialect has its own rules, which are similar to other pidgins; it is not a distortion of another language. As with most pidgins, it has a tendency to eliminate redundancy: why use the *s* to mark a plural if it is already marked with *two,* as in "two pencil"?

According to Dillard, a clear history of the elements of black dialect is difficult to assemble because of the confusion of sources. The slaves in this country had different social levels: house servants and mechanics spoke one level of black dialect; field workers spoke plantation Creole; and the newly arrived, the West African pidgin English.

As stated in connection with the previous section, any teacher who hopes to teach children from a different language—or in this case, from a different dialect—must understand that language or dialect. Black English differs from standard English both in terms of phonology (pronunciation) and in terms of syntax (the way words are organized in sentences). Some of the major differences in phonology are shown in Figure 4.

1. r-lessness (/r/ is dropped or replaced with /ə/)

Black Dialect	New England Dialect
(Drop /r/, except in initial position)	(Drop /r/ before consonant or in final position)
tore = toe	tore = toe
guard = god	guard = god
nor = gnaw	nor = gnaw
four times = foe time	four times = foe times
four o'clock = foe o'clock	four o'clock = four o'clock
Carol = Cal	

2. l-lessness (moved to a /w/ glide or disappears)

toll = toe	help = hep
tool = too	fault = fought
all = awe	haul = haw

3. Reduction of clusters, especially after stressed vowels (s̲t̲, f̲t̲, n̲t̲, n̲d̲, l̲d̲, z̲d̲, m̲d̲)

past/passed = pass
rift = riff
meant/mend = men
wind = wine
hold = hole

4. Weakening of final consonant (/t/ and /d/ mostly; sometimes /g/ and /k/)
(Note effect on pronunciation of past marker!)

boot = boo
past/passed = pass
seed/seat = see
road/rowed = row

5. Vowel shifts

/i/ = /e/ before nasals:	pin = pen; beer = bear
/ē/ = /ā/ before /l/:	peel = pail
/u̇/ = /ō/ before /r/:	poor = poe
/ȯi/ = /ȯ/:	oil = awe
/th/ = /f/:	Ruth = roof

Figure 4. *Some elements of black dialect phonology.*

Figure 5 shows some of the differences in syntax. Sources for Figures 4 and 5 are Baratz and Shuy, DeStefano, Dillard, and Laffey and Shuy.

Again the teacher is reminded of priorities. The Black child who does not pronounce the past marker in his normal speech should not be considered as making an error if he does not pronounce it in his reading. The question, as far as reading is concerned, is: Did he notice the past marker, i.e., did he comprehend its meaning? Besides, there are many instances in the normal speech of SE speakers where final

Characteristic	Standard English	Black Dialect
Plural	fifty cents, three toys	fifty cent, three toy
Possessive	Tom's bike, his book	Tom bike, he book
Verb: Third person singular	He works here.	He work here.
Verb: agreement	She has a bicycle.	She have a bicycle.
Verb: 0 (zero) copula	He is working (now). He is working (every day).	He working (now). He be working (every day).
Verb: "is" as question marker	Are they sick? They are sick.	Is they sick? They sick.
Verb: Past tense	Yesterday he worked.	Yesterday he work.
Future	I'll go home.	Ima go home.
Verb: Negative	She isn't going. She didn't go. I don't have any.	She don't go. She ain't go. I don't got none.
Preposition	He is over at the store. He works at Public Park.	He over to the store. He work Public Park.
Pronoun: Substitution	We have to go.	Us got to go.
Nongender	That girl is tall.	That girl he tall.
0 relative	He has a friend who plays games.	He have a friend play games.
or substitution of what		He have a friend what play games.
repeat subject	John went to town.	John he go to town.
"If" construction	I asked if he did it.	I ask did he do it.
Deletion of unaccented	except, you're/we're	'cept, you/we
Substitution	Here are two birds.	Higo two bird.

Figure 5. *Some elements of black dialect syntax.*

consonants—not to mention *-ing*—are not enunciated: "Carrot top" loses a /t/, "latter" and "ladder" are often distinguished only by context, and so on.

In teaching children who speak black dialect, what kinds of materials should be used? Should those materials be written in black dialect spelling and syntax? Most people would be opposed to this kind of approach. Since black dialect has no written form, standard spelling can just as well represent its pronunciation as it does standard English pronunciation. Besides, *right* is no closer to standard English /rīt/ than it is to black dialect /rat/!

Accepting that we should use standard spelling, the question still remains, should children in the initial stages of reading learn from materials in black dialect syntax or in standard English syntax? The minute one begins to think in terms of publishing dialect materials of any kind, the question, as raised by Goodman and Sims, is "Whose dialect for beginning readers?"

There is a great deal of doubt whether there is any need for special dialect materials for children who speak black dialect. Cohen and Kornfeld, working with "disadvantaged" black children, found that only 11 percent of the vocabularly in four standard basal readers was unfamiliar. They concluded from their study that the children's reading problem was not a matter of syntactic deficiencies, a matter of vocabulary deficiencies, or a problem of dialect.

Levy reported a similar study with first-grade black children. She found no support for the assumption that the "disadvantaged" black child was nonverbal or had no linguistic concepts. She also found no support for the assertion that these children are too deficient in linguistic abilities to learn to decode words and to understand written material.

Goodman has now taken a similar position in regard to his view of dialect (Goodman and Buck). He now feels that the disadvantage of any low-status dialect is one imposed by teachers and schools.

Our experience with both suburban and central city black children would support that view. Such children, while they do have some differences in syntax and in pronouncing their expressive language, exhibit no differences so great that they should interfere with comprehension or communication in standard English. There is no reason they cannot learn to read, providing we accept their dialect and provide instruction in reading. Consider DeStefano's report: A *few* characteristics of black dialect in a black child's speech get that child placed as a black dialect speaker, while almost as many of those same characteristics in the speech of a white child do not!

We should go one step further in the initial stages of reading instruction and encourage acceptance of black dialect syntax as well as pronunciation in reading. Suppose the child is to read the sentence: *She is working.* If that child reads "She be working," compliment the child for excellent reading in that the child comprehended and read the way he would talk. On the other hand, if the context of the sentence indicated that she just happened to be working today but didn't normally work, ask the child to read it again to be sure he understood. The child should have read "She working," not "She be working." In other words, the child should be corrected because he did not comprehend—he made a mistake in comprehension as indicated by his own dialect.

If we truly want children to read for understanding, we should be concerned that they internalize what they read and read it as they would say it. Then these children truly comprehend. Certainly, the initial stages of learning to read would be no place to be concerned about correcting a child's pronunciation patterns—his phonology. To some, such a statement might imply an intent to "keep black children in a subservient economic role," to keep them from gaining the economic advantages of learning standard English. Again, considering priorities, admittedly it is an economic disadvantage not to be able to speak standard English, but it is an even greater economic disadvantage not to be able to read!

Let's put first things first. After the child has learned to read, somewhere at middle or upper grades, he should become acquainted with the levels of usage—the various ways of saying things. This is not a reading task; it is an oral activity. The individual will then have options and will be able to use standard English or black dialect, depending on the appropriate situation. The evidence is clear that during the adolescence or teen-age period is the best time to teach standard English to speakers of a different dialect. It is then that the social pressures make it worthwhile to consider the standard dialect as an option (Labov; Plumer; Johnson).

Specific Versus Built-In Adjustment to Individual Differences

As previously mentioned, learning to read is a task complex enough without our making it even more difficult. In the area of specific skills, the wise teacher will make certain that what he is teaching and what he is giving children additional practice in are truly skills that contribute to reading improvement. Unfortunately, the teacher manuals of basal reading series have grown and grown as each publisher has tried to include everything everyone else has plus a few new items. Hence, they include many activities called "skills practice" that are nothing more than busywork, with no evidence to support them as contributing to increased skill in reading.

The wise teacher will evaluate and sort out the activities that deal with true reading skills, be certain the children get these, and will discard activities labelled "skills" that are nothing more than busywork. The latter, while not harmful in and of themselves, are indirectly harmful in that they take time that could be better spent in actual reading.

This book has provided suggestions for diagnosing and teaching the specific skills essential for learning to read. In dealing with these, the teacher should take a diagnostic approach to determine what skills the children have and which they need, then group flexibly in order to teach the skills to children who need them. Meanwhile, those who don't need the particular skills will be involved in other profitable activities.

Since the skills are specific and involve the teacher directly with only part of a class, management techniques must be brought into play. Children not involved with the teacher may be doing some of the independent practice exercises they need, creative writing activities, reading or sharing library books, or even independent work in other academic areas.

Fortunately, there are a good number of important activities in the area of reading that have their own built-in adjustments to individual differences. For example, the suggestions for developing an understanding of vowels (Chapter 6)—the exploration method—involve activities in which all children can participate at their level in the same project. Likewise, all children should be actively engaged in reading and sharing activities with library reading. Furthermore, since learning to read is part of total language development, there are many writing activities that also have their own built-in individualization and which contribute to further mastery of recognition vocabulary and skill in reading.

SUMMARY

This chapter has presented a discussion of the range of differences to be found among children in a typical class and has suggested that the best method of handling this range is to adapt instruction rather than to try to force children into a preconceived mold. This adaptation of instruction requires the identification of the reading level of each child who reads below grade level in order to select appropriate materials to serve as the vehicles for instruction; it also requires identification of the skill needs of each child in order to determine what skills must be taught.

Attempts to implement individualization as one-to-one instruction in the classroom were discouraged as token and inefficient. Flexible grouping in terms of needs has been suggested, along with a number of skill-development activities that have their own built-in adaptation to individualization.

The brief discussion of linguistically different children made the essential point that one cannot learn to read a language that one does not speak and understand. This point, however, cannot be applied to the black dialect speaker, who does speak and understand English. While research is less clear here, our view and that of several leaders in the field is that the major problem the black dialect speaker has in learning to read lies not in that speaker nor in the dialect, but in the view of teachers toward the dialect. The basic prerequisites are there and, with positive acceptance of the child's speech along with instruction in the reading skills, success in reading will follow.

Finally, while some skills can be isolated and specifically diagnosed and taught, mature reading ability is also a result of practice, and that practice will occur only if it is enjoyable. Let's recognize that most children would learn to read in spite of us; with good teachers, all children learn to read to some extent; it is our job to help all children to develop skill and to realize that reading is an information and enjoyment-getting process. It can be—and should be—fun. If we do this, and if we have a pleasant time with them in the process of their learning to read, we will develop children who can read, who want to read, and who do read.

References

Arnold, Richard D. "Retention in Reading of Disadvantaged Children." In *Reading and Realism,* edited by J. Allen Figurel, pp. 748–54. Newark: International Reading Association, 1969.

Balow, Bruce, and Curtin, J. "Ability Grouping of Bright Pupils." *Elementary School Journal* 66(1966):321–26.

Baratz, Joan, and Shuy, Roger, eds. *Teaching Black Children to Read.* Washington: Center for Applied Linguistics, 1969.

Betts, Emmett. *Foundations of Reading Instruction.* New York: American Book Company, 1946.

Clarke, S. C. T. "The Effect of Grouping on Variability in Achievement at Grade III Level." *Alberta Journal of Educational Research* 3(1958):162–71.

Cohen, S. Allen, and Kornfeld, Gita S. "Oral Vocabulary and Beginning Reading in Disadvantaged Black Children." *The Reading Teacher* 24(1970):33–38.

Cooper, James. "Effects of Different Amounts of First Grade Oral English Instruction." *Journal of Educational Research* 58(1964):123–27.

DeStefano, Johanna. *Language, Society, and Education: A Profile of Black English.* Worthington: Charles A. Jones Publishing, 1973.

Dillard, J. L. *Black English.* New York: Random House, 1972.

Farr, Roger. *Reading: What Can Be Measured?* Newark: International Reading Association, 1969.

Goldberg, Miriam L.; Passow, A. Harry; and Justman, Joseph. *The Effects of Ability Grouping.* New York: Teachers College Press, 1966.

Goodman, Kenneth, and Buck, Catherine. "Dialect Barriers to Reading Comprehension Revisited." *The Reading Teacher* 27(1973):6–12.

Goodman, Yetta M., and Sims, Rudine. "Whose Dialect for Beginning Readers?" *Elementary English* 28(1974):837–41.

Hillerich, Robert L. "Beginning Reading for Spanish Speaking Children." *The Instructor* 81(1972):19–22.

———. "A Brief Summary of Research on Interclass Grouping at the Elementary School Level." *Illinois School Research* 4(1968):21–25.

Horn, Thomas. "Three Methods of Developing Reading Readiness in Spanish-Speaking Children in First Grade." *The Reading Teacher* 20(1966):38–42.

International Institute of Teachers Colleges. *A Survey of the Public Educational System of Puerto Rico.* New York: Teachers College Press, 1966.

Johnson, Kenneth. "When Should Standard English Be Taught to Speakers of Nonstandard Negro Dialect?" *Language Learning* 20(1970):19–30.

Kaufman, Maurice. "Will Instruction in Reading Spanish Affect Ability in Reading English?" *Journal of Reading* 11(1968):521–27.

Kolers, Paul A. "Bilingualism and Information Processing." *Scientific American* 218 (1968):78–85.

Labov, William. "The Logic of Non-Standard English." In *Language and Poverty,* edited by Frederick Williams. Chicago: Markham Publishers, 1970.

Laffey, James, and Shuy, Roger. *Language Differences: Do They Interfere?* Newark: International Reading Association, 1973.

Levy, Beatrice K. "Is the Oral Language of Inner City Children Adequate for Beginning Reading Instruction?" *Research in the Teaching of English* 7(1973):51–60.

Modiano, Nancy. *A Comparative Study of Two Approaches to the Teaching of Reading in the National Language.* Cooperative Research Project No. S-237, U. S. Department of Health, Education, and Welfare. New York: New York University, 1966.

Pikulski, John. "A Critical Review: Informal Reading Inventories." *The Reading Teacher* 28(1974):141–51.

Plummer, Davenport. "A Summary of Environmentalist Views of Some Educational Implications." In *Language and Poverty,* edited by Frederick Williams. Chicago: Markham Publishers, 1970.

Powell, William. "Reappraising the Criteria for Interpreting Informal Inventories." In *Reading Diagnosis and Evaluation,* pp. 101–9. Newark: International Reading Association, 1970.

Rystrom, Richard. "Dialect Training and Reading: A Further Look." *Reading Research Quarterly* 5(1970):581–99.

Shane, Harold. "Elementary Education—Organization and Administration." In *Encyclopedia of Educational Research,* edited by Chester W. Harris, pp. 421–30. New York: Macmillan Company, 1960.

Wrightstone, J. Wayne. *What Research Says to the Teacher: Class Organization for Instruction.* Washington: National Education Association, 1957.

Zintz, Miles V. *The Reading Process,* Chapter 16. Dubuque: William C. Brown, 1975.

Name Index

Ackerman, Margaret, 123
Almy, Millie, 27
Anderson, Dorothy, 20
Anglund, Joan, 171
Arbuthnot, May, 168, 169, 171
Arnold, Richard, 201
Aukerman, Robert, 6

Bailey, Mildred, 99
Ball, Samuel, 26
Balow, Bruce, 192
Baratz, Joan, 204
Barbe, Walter, 167
Barney, LeRoy, 160–61
Barnhart, Richard, 28
Barrett, Thomas, 56, 136
Bateman, Barbara, 11
Benenson, Thea, 11
Betts, Emmett, 194
Blakely, W. Paul, 27
Bliesmer, Emory, 7
Bloom, Benjamin, 135
Bodzewski, Ludwig, 156
Bogatz, Gerry, 26
Bond, Guy, 5, 10, 45
Bredin, Dorothy, 123
Brzeinski, Joseph, 28
Buck, Catherine, 206
Burmeister, Lou, 100, 136
Burrows, Alvina, 100

Cahen, Leonard, 102
Carpenter, Ethelouise, 19
Carroll, John, 85
Chall, Jeanne, 7
Chen, Martin, 29
Christensen, Clifford, 147
Clarke, S. C. T., 192
Clymer, Theodore, 14, 99, 100
Cohen. S. Alan, 47, 206
Cohn, Marvin, 58
Cooper, James, 202
Corsini, David, 22
Curtin, J., 192

Dale, Edgar, 84, 133
deHirsch, Katrina, 45–46
DeStefano, Johanna, 204, 206
Dewey, Godfrey, 101, 102–3, (112–16), 117–21
Dillard, J. L., 203, 204
Dolch, Edward, 85
Dunn, Barbara, 26
Durkin, Dolores, 20, 27, 30

Durrell, Donald, 25, 46, 56, 81
Dykstra, Robert, 10

Eames, Thomas, 20–21
Emmans, Robert, 100
Emmer, Sara, 26
English, Marvin, 156

Farr, Roger, 200
Fay, Leo, 7
Fitzgerald, James, 102
Flom, Merton, 21
Flower, Richard, 47
Francis, W. Nelson, 85
Fries, Charles, 9
Fry, Edward, 26, 44, 100
Fuld, Paula, 100

Gagne, Robert, 124
Gates, Arthur, 20
Gaver, Mary, 179
Gibson, Carol, 164
Glass, Gerald, 163
Godbold, John, 134
Goldberg, Miriam, 192
Goodman, Kenneth, 83, 206
Goodman, Yetta, 206
Gorelick, Molly, 90
Groff, Patrick, 58, 101, 167
Guszak, Frank, 134

Halsey, William, 156
Hammill, Donald, 47
Hanna, Paul, 101, 102–3, (108–11), 117–21
Hardy, Madeline, 121
Harnischfeger, Annegret, 26
Harris, Albert, 5, 136
Hazard, Paul, 168
Heilman, Arthur, 27, 136
Hillerich, Robert, 14, 25, 27, 29, 45, 47, 48, 49, 56, 57, 66, 71, 83, 84, 85–87, 88, 102–3, (104–7), 117–21, 122–23, 156, 157, 158, 179, 192, 197–99, 201
Hislop, Margaret, 123
Horn, Ernest, 71, 85, 101, 102
Horn, Thomas, 202
House, Ralph, 161
Huck, Charlotte, 143, 144, 168, 169, 171
Hunt, Kellogg, 21, 48
Ibeling, Fred, 121
International Institute of Teachers Colleges, 201
Iversen, Iver, 25, 56–57
Ives, Josephine, 134

211

Jacob, Nina, 156
Jansky, Jeanette, 45–46
Jenkins, Joseph, 57
Jensen, Norma, 47
Johnson, Edna, 168, 171
Johnson, Kenneth, 207
Johnson, Ronald, 25, 56

Kamatos, Theodore, 156
Karlin, Robert, 46
Kaufman, Maurice, 202
Kelly, Marjorie, 29
Kimmel, Thomas, 144
King, Ethel, 47, 123
King, Martha, 143, 144
Kingston, Albert, 25
Knafle, June, 8
Kolers, Paul, 201
Kornfeld, Gita, 206
Kucera, Henry, 85
Kuhn, Doris, 168, 171

Labov, Williams, 207
Laffey, James, 24
Laubach, Frank, 66
Lazar, May, 167
Levin, Harry, 90, 123
Levy, Beatrice, 206
Lightfoot, Morton, 7
Loban, Walter, 21–22, 50
Loomer, Walter, 28
Lourie, Zyra, 100
Lowell, Robert, 25
Lyttek, Elaine, 8

McCullough, Constance, 136
McDaniel, Ernest, 86
McFeeley, Donald, 163
McHugh, Walter, 25, 56
McNeil, David, 21
Martignoni, Margaret, 168
Marchbanks, Gabrielle, 90
Meigs, Cornelia, 168
Menyuk, Paula, 21, 22
Modiano, Nancy, 201
Moe, Alden, 86
Moore, Walter, 101
Morgan, Elmer, 7
Morphett, Mabel, 20
Morris, Christopher, 156
Morris, William, 156
Morrison, Coleman, 25, 26
Mower, Morris, 160–61
Muehl, Siegmar, 57
Murray, Corallie, 8

Nicholson, Alice, 56, 58

O'Donnell, Roy, 21
Oftedal, Laura, 156
Olson, Arthur, 25, 56

Pikulski, John, 195
Ploghoft, Milton, 27
Plumer, Davenport, 207
Powell, William, 179, 195

Reed, David, 102
Rinsland, Henry, 85
Roberts, A. Hood, 102
Rystrom, Richard, 203

St. John, Doris, 160
Samuels, S. Jay, 57
Schoephoerster, Hugh, 28
Schram, Wilbur, 21
Shadle, Erma, 27
Shane, Harold, 192
Shaw, Jules, 21
Sheldon, William, 27
Shuy, Roger, 204
Silberberg, Margaret, 25, 56–57
Silberberg, Norman, 25, 56–57
Sims, Rudine, 206
Sipay, Edward, 136
Sloane, William, 168
Smith, Frank, 5
Smith, Lillian, 169
Smith, Nila, 8
Spache, George, 5
Sparks, Paul, 7
Stein, Aletha, 22
Stordahl, Kalmer, 147
Strickland, Ruth, 21
Styer, Sandra, 157
Sutherland, Zena, 168
Sutton, Marjorie, 29

Templin, Mildred, 21, 50
Tinker, Miles, 5, 45, 136

Veatch, Jeanette, 167
Venezky, Richard, 124

Wardhaugh, Ronald, 7, 8, 163
Washburne, Carleton, 20
Watson, J., 123
Waugh, Ruth, 11
Weeks, Ernest, 27
Wepman, Joseph, 47
Wiegand, Virginia, 124
Wiley, David, 26
Williams, Joanna, 58, 90, 123
Wise, James, 28
Wolf, Lois, 29–30
Wolf, Willavene, 143, 144
Wrightstone, Wayne, 192
Wylie, Richard, 81

Yardborough, Betty, 7
Young, Francis, 21

Zintz, Miles, 136
Zuck, L. V., 163

Subject Index

Page numbers in parentheses indicate material in tables or figures.

Accent, 161–62
Adverb referents, 139
Affixes, 160, 164
  prefixes, 160, 164
  suffixes, 160, 164
Alliteration, developing appreciation for, 145–46, 171
Alphabetical order, 157–58, (157–58)
Analytic phonics. *See* Meaning emphasis.
Anomalous prefixes, 164
Application of skills, importance of, 88–89, 90, 152, 167
Auditory acuity, 48
Auditory discrimination, 24–25, 38–39, 47–48
  activities for developing, 38–39
  in diagnosis, 47–48
  testing for, 38
  traditional concerns with, 24–25
Auditory emphasis, 11, 122, 124–25
  importance of, 11
  with vowel sounds, 122, 124–25

Basal reader, 9, 77, 167, 207
  as first book material, 77
  as meaning emphasis, 9
  and busywork, 207
  and trade books, 167
Beginning Dictionary, 156
Beginning reading, philosophies of, 5–11
Beginning sounds, 24–25, 61–65
  activities to clarify, 62–65
  as prereading skill, 61–65
  discrimination of, 24–25
  distinguished from spelling, 62
  related to letter form discrimination, 61
  teaching task clarified, 61–62
Beginning-to-Read books, 91–92
Bender Motor Gestalt Test, 46
Best Books for Children, 171
Black dialect, 203–7, (204, 205)
  compared to standard English, 203–7
    (phonology, 204; syntax 205)
  in learning to read, 206–7
  lack of redundancy in, 203
  origins of, 203
Blending, 7, 81
  problems with, 7
  technique, 81
Blends, consonant. *See* Clusters.
Bloom's taxonomy, 135, (135)

Booklist and Subscription Books Bulletin, 170

Caldecott books, 91, 92, (172–78)
  defined, 172
  for reading to children, 91, 92
  listed (172–78)
Cause/effect relationships, 140, 141
  inferential, 141
  literal, 140
Character traits, identification of, 142
Checked vowel sound, defined, 97
Children's books. *See* Trade books.
Children's Catalog, 170
Chronological age, 30, 45
  correlated with reading, 30
  as factor in early identification, 45
Class management. *See* Individual differences.
Clusters, consonant, 80–81
Comparisons, making of, 140
Complex vowel sounds, defined, 97–98, (98)
Compound words, 162
Comprehension, 14–15, 39–40, 48, 92, 122–24, 200–201
  beginnings of, 14–15
  diagnosing for, 200–201
  effect of vowel rules on, 122, 123–24
  levels of, 133
  listening, 39–40, 48, 92
  related to thinking, 15
Comprehension skills, 39–40, 48, 92, 133–45, (135)
  critical reading, 143–45
  development of, 137–45
  inferential, 140–43
  at listening level, 39–40, 48, 92
  literal, 137–40
  outlined, 136–37
  precede reading, 133
  questioning techniques in, 134–36, (135)
Configuration, 11–13, 90
Connotation, understanding of, 144
Consonant clusters, 80–81
Consonant digraphs, 66, 82–83, (66)
Consonant letter and sound association, 65–69, 79–83, (66)
  for consonant clusters, 80–81
  consonant substitution for, 79
  in final position, 80
  in initial position, 65–69 (66)

Consonant letter and sound association (*cont.*)
  isolation of sound, 6, 62
  see-hear-associate method for, 79–80
  with variant consonant spellings, 82–83
Consonants, in reading process, 11–13
Content reading. *See* Study skills.
Context, use of, 11–13, 43–44
  oral, 43–44
  in reading process, 11–13
Cooperative Research Program in First Grade Reading Instruction, 10
Correlation, defined, 44–45
Criteria for selecting trade books, 169–70
Criterion referenced testing, 49
Critical reading, 133, 143–45
  defined, 133
  determining author's competence, 145
  determining author's purpose, 145
  determining slant/bias, 144-45
  distinguishing fact from opinion, 143–44
  distinguishing reality from fantasy, 143
Cross references in dictionary, 159

Decoding emphasis programs, 5–7
Decoding skills, 55 ff
Diacritical marks, interpretation of, 160–61
Diagnosing reading level, 194–96
Diagnosing skill needs, 47–49, 197–201, (197–99)
  in comprehension, 200–201
  in dictionary, 200
  in language, 47–49
  in phonics, 197–200 (197–99)
  in study skills, 200–201
Diagnostic approach to early identification, 25–26, 44–50, (50)
  contrasted to prediction, 25–26, 44–47
  effectiveness of, 49–50, (50)
  factors in, 47–49
  techniques, 47–49
Diagnostic phonics test, 197–200 (197–99)
Dialect, defined, 203
Dictionaries, 102–3, 156
  differences in, 102–3
  suggested, 156
Dictionary readiness. *See* Picture dictionaries.
Dictionary skills, 155–62, (157–58)
  locational skills for, 156, 157–59, (157–58)
  for meaning, 156, 159–60
  outline of, 156–57
  in picture dictionaries, 155–56
  for pronunciation, 156–57, 160–62
  for spelling, 155, 156, 160
Digraphs, consonant, 66, 82–83
Disability in reading, factors associated with, 45–47
Discovery approach, 125
Dolch Basic Sight Vocabulary, 85, 86
  compared to Starter Words, (86)
  datedness of, 85
Drawing conclusions, 140–41

Early identification, 44–50, (50)
  diagnostic approach to, 47–49
  effectiveness of, 49–50, (50)
  factors in, 45–49
  prevention vs. prediction of failure, 44–47
  typical concerns, 44–47

Emotional problems, as factor in early identification, 45
Empathy in trade book reading, 145
English Around the World, 202
Evaluation. *See* Diagnosing . . .
Experience, as factor in readiness, 22–23
Experience charts, 70
"Exploration Method" for vowels, 124–25

Figurative language, interpretation of, 142–43
Following directions, 43, 48, 147–48
  oral, 43, 48
  in reading, 147–48

Genres, developing awareness of, 146
Ginn Beginning Dictionary, 156
Glided vowel sound, defined, 97
Golden Treasury of Poetry, 171
Grapheme-phoneme correspondence. *See* Letter-sound association.
Graphs and tables, reading of, 150–51, (150–51)
Grouping, 30, 192–201, 207, (192, 193)
  flexible, 207
  heterogeneous, 192
  interclass, 192, (192)
  in kindergarten, 30
  by level, 193–96, (193)
  by skills, 197–201
  traditional, 192–93, (193)
Guide words, 158, (158)

High frequency words, 70–72. *See also* Starter Words.
Homographs, 138, 159
Homophones, 138, 159–60
Horn Book, 170–71

Idioms, 143, 202
  interpretation of, 143
  problems for linguistically different, 202
Immature speech and auditory discrimination, 39
Independent reading. *See* Trade books.
Independent reading program, elements in, 179–87
  accessibility of books, 179
  awareness of books, 179–82
  sense of accomplishment, 182
  sharing through creation, 182–83
  sharing through talking, 183–85
  sharing through writing, 185–87
Individual differences, 191–207, (192, 193, 197–99, 204–205)

Individual differences (*cont.*)
and Black dialect, 203–207, (204, 205)
built-in adjustment to, 125, 207
grouping for, 192–201 (193)
and linguistically different children, 201–3
pacing for, 196–97
range of, 191, (193)
in rate of growth, 191. *See also* Diagnosing reading level, Diagnosing skill needs.
Individualization vs. inefficiency, 194
Individualized Reading, 167
Inferential comprehension, 133, 140–43
defined, 133, 140
drawing conclusions, 140–41
identifying cause/effect relationships, 141
identifying character traits, 142
identifying main idea, 141
interpreting figurative language, 142–43
making judgments, 142
predicting outcomes, 142
recalling sequence, 141
Inflected forms in dictionary, 159
Inflected endings, 83
Informal reading inventory, 194–96
cautions for, 195–96
procedures for, 194–96
Initial consonant letter and sound association, 65–69, (66)
activities for, 65–69, (66)
as prereading skill, 65–69
teaching task clarified, 65–66
Initial reading materials, 77–78
Introducing new words, 78–79
Isolation of consonant sounds, 6, 62

Judgments, making of, 142

Key pictures, use of, 66, (66), 124
for consonants, 66, (66)
for vowels, 124
Kindergarten, skills instruction in, 26–30
Kinesthetic methods, 60–61, (60), 71–72
with letter form discrimination, 60–61
with word recognition, 71–72

Language development, 19–25, 41–43
methods for, 41–43
phonology in, 22, 24–25
syntax in, 19, 21–22
verbal stimulation in, 22
vocabulary in, 19, 21, 42
Language skills for reading, 37–44, 48
auditory discrimination, 38–39
following oral directions, 43
listening comprehension, 39–40
oral language development, 41–43, 48
outline of, 37
recalling sequence, 40–41
use of oral context, 43–44
vocabularly, 42–43
Laterality, as a factor in early identification, 45

Left to right orientation, 69–70
Letter form discrimination, 56–61, (60)
activities for, 59–61, (60)
contrasted to letter naming, 56–57
sequence for instruction, 57–59
teaching task defined, 57
Letter names, knowledge of, 46. *See also* Letter form discrimination.
Letter sound association, 65–69, (66), 80–83, 98–100, 118, 121–25
for consonant clusters, 80–81
for final consonants, 80
for initial consonants, 65–69, (66)
for variant consonant spellings, 82–83
for vowels, 98–100, 118, 121–25
Library books. *See* Trade books, Independent reading program.
Linguistic reading programs, 7–9
Linguistically different children, 86, 201–7, (204, 205)
Black dialect, 203–7, (204, 205)
native language first, 201–2
necessity of oral English, 201
non-English speakers, 201–3
and word recognition, 86
Listening comprehension, 39–40, 48, 92
activities for, 39–40
as factor in diagnosis, 48
foundation for reading, 92
Literal comprehension, 133–40, (135)
as comprehending, 135–36
defined, 133
identifying main idea, 139
making comparisons, 140
recalling detail, 139
recalling sequence, 139–40
seeing cause/effect relationships, 140
sentence meaning, 138–39
word meaning, 138
Literary appreciation, 145–46, 171
alliteration, 145–46, 171
empathy, 145
genres, 146
humor, 146
onomatopoeia, 146, 171
repetition, 146
rhyme, 171
rhythm, 145, 171
"Little words in big words," 90, 162
Locating information, 146–47
Logic in critical reading, 145
"Long" vowels, 97

Main idea, 139, 141
inferred, 141
literal, 139
Management, class. *See* Individual differences.
Math, reading in, 148–50
Meaning, dictionary use for, 156, 159–60
Meaning emphasis programs, 5–9
Mental age in readiness, 19, 20
Metaphor, interpretation of, 142–43

"Mind set," 123
Minimal pairs, defined, 97
Minimal terminal unit (T-unit), 48
Modalities, 11
Morphophonemic alteration, 124
Mother Goose books, 171
Motivating trade book reading, 179–87
Motivation in readiness, 23
My First Dictionary, 156

Neurological problems in early identification, 45
New Iowa Spelling Scale, 101
Newbery Award, defined, 172
Norm referenced testing, 49

Onomatopoeia, developing awareness of, 146, 171
Oral context, use of, 43–44, 48, 55–56
  activities for, 43–44, 56
  as factor in diagnosis, 48
  as prereading skill, 55–56
  testing for, 43–44, 56
Oral context and consonant sound association, use of, 69, 71
Oral directions, ability to follow, 43, 48
Oral language development, 41–43, 48. *See also* Language development.
  activities for, 41–43
  as factor in diagnosis, 48
Oral reading, 90–91
Outlining, foundation for, 151

Personification, interpretation of, 143
Phoneme, defined, 97
Phonics, 5–7, 13–14. *See also* Letter-sound association.
  philosophy, 5–7
  role in reading instruction, 13–14
Phonograms, 8, (81–82)
Picture dictionaries, 92, 155–56
  for dictionary readiness, 92, 155–56
  for spelling reference, 155
  types suggested, 156
Pidgin, defined, 203
Placement tests. *See* Diagnosing reading level.
Practice materials, evaluation of, 88–90
Predicting outcomes, 41–42, 142
Prediction of reading success/failure. *See* Early identification.
Prefixes, 160, 164
Prereading skills, 55–72, (60, 66)
  beginning sounds, 61–65
  consonant letter and sound association, 65–69, (66)
  high frequency words, 70–72
  left to right orientation, 69–70
  letter form discrimination, 56–61, (60)
  oral context and consonant sound association, 69, 71
  overview, 55

Prevention of reading failure. *See* Early identification.
Printed language, differs from speech, 5, 22, 39
Pronoun referents, 139
Pronunciation, dictionary use for, 156–57, 160–62
Purposes for reading, setting of, 138, 147–48. *See also* Study skills.

Questioning techniques, 134, 145. *See also* specific comprehension skills.
  concerns with, 134
  for literary appreciation, 145

Rand McNally Picturebook Dictionary, 156
Readiness, 19–26, 44–47
  auditory discrimination in, 23–24
  defined, 19, 25
  diagnosis vs. prediction, 25–26, 44–47
  experience in, 22–23
  language development in, 19, 21–22
  mental age in, 19, 20
  motivation in, 23
  social development in, 23
  traditional concerns in, 19–25
  visual discrimination in, 23–24
  visual maturity in, 19, 20–21
Readiness tests, 25–26, 45–46
  in early identification, 45–46
  effectiveness of, 25–26
Reading, 5–13
  auditory vs. visual emphasis, 11
  decoding emphasis, 5, 9
  defined, 5
  linguistic approach, 7–9
  meaning emphasis, 5, 9
  patterns in, 8
  process of, 11–13
  redundancy in, 5
Reading achievement, effect of time on, 26
Reading groups. *See* Grouping.
Reading levels, 191–96, (192, 193)
  different from skills, 193
  identification of, 194–96
  range of, 191–92, (192, 193)
Reading process, 11–13
Reading vs. spelling contrasted, 98–99, 197, 199
Reading to children, 39–40, 91–92
Rebus sentences, 71–72
Recalling sequence, 40–41, 48, 139–41
  activities for, 40–41
  as factor in diagnosis, 48
  as inferential comprehension, 141
  as literal comprehension, 139–40
  as listening comprehension, 40–41
Recognition vocabulary, 70–72, 83–87, (87)
  context vs. isolation, 83
  defined, 70–71
  development of, 71–72, 83–87, (87)
  frequency of exposure, 86

Recognition vocabulary (*cont.*)
  limited size, 71, 84
  rebus sentences for, 71–72
  words for initial development, 71, (87)
Redundancy, in Black dialect, 203
  in standard English, 5
Referents, pronoun and adverb, 139
"Regularity" in English orthography, (104–116), 120–21
Relationship words, as factor in diagnosis, 48
Rhyme, developing appreciation of, 171
Rhyming words, 82. *See also* Phonograms.
Rhythm, developing appreciation of, 145, 171

School Library Journal, 170, 172
Schwa sound, 101–3, 117
  frequency of use, 101, 117
  handling of, 101, 102–3
See-hear-associate method, 79–80
Sequencing. *See* Recalling sequence.
Sesame Street, evaluation of, 26
Sharing about books, 182–87
"Short" vowels, 97
Sight vocabulary. *See* Recognition vocabulary.
"Silent" letters, 83, 103
Similes, interpretation of, 142–43
Simple vowel sounds, defined, 97–98, (98)
Skills instruction in kindergarten, 26–30
  effectiveness of, 26–29
  with prekindergartners, 29–30
  workbook vs. nonworkbook approach with, 28–29
Skills summaries, 37, 50, 55, 77, 133, 136–37, 146, 156–57
  comprehension skills, 133, 136–37
  decoding skills, 55, 77
  dictionary skills, 156–57
  language skills, 37
  study skills, 146
  typical grade one entry skills, 77
  typical kindergarten entry skills, 37, 50
Social development as a factor in readiness, 23
Socio-economic status as a factor in early identification, 45
Spanish background children, 201–3
Spelling, dictionary use for, 155, 156, 160
Spelling vs. reading contrasted, 98–99, 197, 199
Stanford study, 101–3, (108–11)
Starter Words, 84–87, (87)
  compared to Dolch Basic Sight Vocabulary, 85–86
  development of, 84–85
  listed, (87)
  norms with primary children, 86–87, (87)
Statistical significance clarified, 46
Stress, in pronunciation, 161–62
Structural analysis, 83, 160–64
  affixation, 160, 164
  compound words, 162

Structural analysis (*cont.*)
  identification of number of syllables, 162–63
  inflected endings, 83
  rules: Cle—163, VCCV—163, VCV—163–64
Study skills, 146–51
  foundation for outlining, 151
  locating information, 146–47
  outline of, 146
  problems in content reading, 147
  reading to follow directions, 147–48, (149)
  reading graphs and tables, 150–51, (150, 151)
  reading in math, 148–50
Suffixes, 160, 164
Syllable rules, problems with, 162–64. *See also* Structural analysis.
Syntax in oral language, 21–22
Synthetic phonics. *See* decoding emphasis.

Tables and graphs, reading of, 150–51, (150, 151)
Teacher judgment as a factor in early identification, 46
Thorndike-Barnhart Beginning Dictionary, 156
Time for Poetry, 171
Trade books, 167–71, 178–87
  and basal readers, 167
  brief history of, 167–68
  criteria for, 168–70
  quantity published, 168
  scope of content in, 171
  suggestions for use of, 178–87
  tools for selecting, 170–71
T-unit, defined, 48
  as factor in diagnosis of language, 48

Understanding English, 202

Visual acuity, as factor in diagnosis, 48
Visual discrimination, 22–24, 46. *See also* Letter form discrimination.
  gross, 23–24
  as word matching, 46.
Visual maturity as a factor in readiness, 19, 20–21
Visual-motor skill, as a factor in early identification, 46–47
Vocabulary, oral, 21–22, 41–43, 48
  activities to develop, 21–22, 41–43
  as a factor in diagnosis, 48
Vocabulary, reading, 71–72. *See also* Recognition vocabulary.
Vowel sounds, 97–125, (98, 104–116, 117, 119, 120, 126–28)
  defined, 97–98, (98)
  dialect differences in, 102–3
  differences in classification of, 102–3
  effectiveness of generalizations with children, 121–24

Vowel sounds (*cont.*)
  "exploration" method for, 124–25
  frequencies, (117)
  generalizations examined, 98, 99–100, 118
  representations of, (120, 126–28)
  symbol-sound correspondences, 101–21, (104–116, 117, 119, 120, 126–28)
Vowels, 97–128, (98, 104–16, 117, 119, 120, 126–28)
  defined, 97, (98)
  frequency of occurrence, (104–116, 117, 119)
  in reading process, 11–13
  representations, (120, 126–28)
Webster's New Elementary Dictionary, 156
Wepman Auditory Discrimination Test, 47

Wilson Library Bulletin, 170
Word frequency counts, 85–87
Word identification, contrasted with word recognition, 70–71
Word introduction, 78–79, 90
  purpose for, 79, 90; techniques contrasted, 78–79
Word recognition. *See* Recognition vocabulary.
Writing as an aid to reading skill, 71–72, 84, 142–46, 185–87
  in appreciation literary language, 145–46
  in identifying slant and bias, 144
  in interpreting figurative language, 142–43
  in sharing about books, 185–87
  in word recognition, 71–72, 84